BEATING THE BUSHES

BEATING THE BUSHES

Frank Dolson

ICARUS PRESS
South Bend, Indiana
1982

BEATING THE BUSHES

Copyright © 1982 by Frank Dolson

1   2   3   4   5   6   7   87   86   85   84   83   82

Icarus Press, Inc.
Post Office Box 1225
South Bend, Indiana 46624

Library of Congress Cataloging in Publication Data

Dolson, Frank.
    Beating the Bushes

    Includes index.
    1. Baseball clubs—United States.   I. Title.
GV875.A1D64   1982   796.357'64'0973   82-15464
ISBN 0-89651-055-7

796.35764409 73

To all those minor league baseball players
whose dream didn't come true—

Contents

1. Introduction   1
2. The Can't-Miss Kid (*Pat Bayless*)   9
3. Nobody Said It Was Perfect (*fields and parks*) 26
4. Perfect Pitcher, Imperfect World (*Jim Bunning*) 36
5. Laugh, Clown, Laugh (*Max Patkin*) 84
6. When Being Black Isn't Beautiful (*racism in the minors*) 99
7. Baseball and Booze (*alcoholism in the minors*) 108
8. Remembering Where They Came From (*nostalgia for the bushes*) 124
9. They Even Drove the Buses (*managers*) 150
10. The Winter Game (*winter baseball*) 164
11. The Dream Ends, The Nightmare Begins (*failing in the minors*) 182
12. The Professionals (*minor league mis-management*) 192
13. The Axman Cometh (*making the team or getting cut*) 196
14. Look for the Union Label (*the Players Association*) 203
15. The Hardest Job of All (*umpires*) 218
16. Follow the Bouncing Check (*owners*) 227
17. Climbing the Glass Mountain (*from minors to majors and back*) 235
18. A Look Back . . . and a Look Ahead 245
19. Epilogue 252
Index 270

1

INTRODUCTION

Baseball. There's no game like it. No game that grabs you and sticks with you the way baseball does. It seems crazy, but a baseball fan—I mean a real baseball fan—can remember details of games played 10, 20, 30 years ago. The memories of a towering Mickey Mantle home run, a leaping Willie Mays catch, a stinging Ted Williams line drive seem to grow more vivid, more beautiful with the passage of time. So, too, do the voices, and the descriptions, of the great baseball announcers of the past. Close your eyes, concentrate, listen closely and you can still hear Red Barber's voice rise as Cookie Lavagetto's pinch double with two out in the bottom of the ninth turns a 2–1, no hit victory for Bill Bevens and the New York Yankees into a 3–2 win for the Brooklyn Dodgers. Lavagetto's big hit came 35 years ago in a ball park—Ebbets Field—that no longer exists, yet Barber's voice still echoes in my head. "Here comes the tying run . . . and here comes the winning run." The drama of that moment remains as fresh today, in 1982, as it did then, in 1947—as fresh as the memory of Bobby Thomson's ninth-inning, pennant-winning home run at the Polo Grounds in the New York Giants-Brooklyn Dodgers playoff of 1951. Is there a Giants fan past 40 who can't remember where he was on that unforgettable afternoon? Is there anyone who heard Russ Hodges' call on the radio who can't remember the words of the late, great Giants announcer: "There's a long drive to left field. It's going to be, I believe. The Giants win the pennant! The Giants win the pennant! The Giants win the pennant! I don't believe it. I don't believe it. I do not believe it. . . ."

There's a magic in baseball, a quality that makes even a game that we didn't see, but only heard on the radio, an enduring experience. Maybe it's the one-on-one aspect of the game, the pitcher vs. the batter, a series of individual confrontations waged within a team concept. Maybe it's the fact that in baseball it's all out in the open for anybody to see—even somebody sitting in the last row of the bleachers or the top row of the upper deck. Baseball managers may not all be the brightest guys to come down the pike, but when's the last time you heard one shrug off a defeat by saying, "I won't know what happened until I see the films"? Maybe it's the daily flow of a pennant race, something that becomes a part of our lives in early April and remains a part of our lives for half a year. Maybe it's the nature of this unique game, the timelessness of it. Of all the major team sports, only in baseball is there no clock to fight. A baseball team trying to protect a three-run lead in the ninth inning can't fall on the ball to kill the final seconds, can't go into a "four-corners" stall to keep the ball away from the opposition. In baseball, the trailing team can make time stand still by getting hits and walks and runs.

Baseball is a game that can be played in the mind, as well as on the field. It is a game of anticipation, a game that moves along very slowly at times, then erupts in a sudden surge of action, then slows down again, giving us time to savor what we have seen, and to think about what we are going to see.

This, then, is a book about baseball, a very special game. But not all baseball is what we see on our television screens or in those fancy, new parks with their electronic scoreboards and bright green carpets of artificial grass. And not all professional baseball is played by men with guaranteed, million-dollar-plus contracts who make commercials for deodorants or soft drinks in their spare time.

The game's the same in the minor leagues. It's 90 feet from home to first, 60 feet, six inches from the pitching rubber to home plate. Three strikes and you're out, four balls and you're on. There are three outs per half inning, nine innings per game (except for those seven-inning games in minor league double headers, but let's not quibble).

The minor leagues have fascinated me almost as long as baseball has. And, if anything, that fascination has grown in recent years, even as the gap between the minors and the majors—in terms of salaries and benefits—has grown.

In the big leagues, the game of baseball has evolved into the business of baseball. Elsewhere, though, in that slowly dying bit of Americana we call minor league baseball, the game is still the thing. The great majority of players, in the low minors at least, haven't had a chance to grow rich, or cynical, or lazy. They put up with a life that is often hard and cruel because they honestly love the game, and because they are little boys at heart with little-boy dreams.

For all the hardships, all the heartaches, all the hard-luck stories, when you ask the young men who have experienced life in the minor leagues to reflect on those years, most of them talk about the fun they had and the friends they made. Can it be "fun" riding on a bus for six or eight or 10 hours, then rushing out to a dimly lit ball park to play a twi-night double header? Can it be "fun" living on $500 or $600 a month as a fledgling pro? Can it be"fun" dressing in cramped, poorly equipped clubhouses? Well, maybe when it was happening it wasn't all that much fun. But the fact remains that many of those who didn't make it to the big leagues, as well as those who did, have a tendency to remember the good times, the good friends, the funny experiences.

Having spent several weeks each year bouncing around the minor leagues—from A ball to Triple A, from Eugene, Ore., to Tidewater, Va.—I can understand why. Things happen in the minors that would be unthinkable in the majors. Nutty things. Amusing things.

There was that first trip to Raleigh-Durham in the Class A Carolina League to see a budding, young slugger named Greg Luzinski play. It was late afternoon when the plane landed. Walter Brock, the general manager of the Raleigh-Durham team, was at the gate to meet me. "Take your time," he advised me after introducing himself. "There's no rush. Tonight's game has been postponed because of rain."

"Gee," I said, "that's too bad. I was really looking forward to seeing Luzinski play."

"Don't worry," Brock said soothingly, "you'll see plenty of him. We rescheduled the game as part of a triple header tomorrow night."

And in case three games weren't enough to lure the natives through the turnstiles, GM Brock had a trick golf-shooting exhibition set up between games two and three. It sounded jazzy—just a wonderful, fun-filled eight or nine hours sitting on hard slabs of wood at the ball park. Somebody up there loved us, though. It came down in buckets the next day and all three games, not to mention the trick golf-shooting exhibition, were washed out. Better yet, the Raleigh-Durham club was scheduled to start a road trip the following day, thus wiping out any plans the GM might have had of scheduling a quadruple header on that date.

Only in the minor leagues can things like that happen. That's the fun of it all, the charm of it, the frustration of it. As far as the public is concerned, professional baseball players are the guys they see on their television screens. They make hundreds of thousands of dollars a year. They drive fancy cars. They live in magnificent homes. It doesn't matter all that much if they hit .240 or .360; their multi-year contracts are guaranteed. The minor leagues?

"A lot of people don't even call it the pros," discovered Mark Davis, a young lefthander who is one of the top prospects in the Phillies organization. "My friends would say, 'When are you going to make it to the pros?' I'd say, 'Look, I am a pro. I'm in the minor leagues of professional baseball.' I'd tell them, 'I play for the Spartanburg [S.C.] Phillies.' They'd go, 'Who?'

" 'The Spartanburg Phillies.'

" 'The Phillies are in Philadelphia.'

" 'I know. I play in the minor leagues for them.'

" 'Oh. When are you going to get to the pros?'

" 'I'm already in the pros.'

" 'You are? I thought you said you played for Spartanburg.' "

That's life in the minor leagues. You beat your brains out, dress in crummy locker rooms, take long bus rides, squint at sharp-breaking sliders through the semi-darkness, somehow manage to have a decent year, and then your friends ask you, "Hey, when are you going to turn pro?"

"My wife," said Mark Davis, "when she first came out to the ball park in Reading [Pa.] she thought the Reading Phillies were little kids—you know, Little Leaguers. It was funny."

It's enough to make you cry, if you weren't laughing instead. "They think you're playing semi-pro ball," said Joe Kerrigan, a relief pitcher who knows what it is to ride minor league buses as well as big league jets. "That's a standard line you hear in the minor leagues. People don't believe you get paid for it."

And, in most cases, they don't get paid very much for it—certainly not enough to approach the lifestyle the American public has come to associate with professional baseball players. And they play most of their games under far less than optimum conditions.

"Rocky Mount [N.C.]," Joe Kerrigan said, "is like playing on the dark side of the moon. The lights weren't very high. If you hit a ball above the lights you lost it temporarily."

"John Poff [who played briefly in Philadelphia and Milwaukee] hit a pop up one night in West Haven [Conn.]," pitcher Warren Brusstar recalled. "It was late in the game. Two men were on base. Poff hit one straight up. The catcher comes running out, the third baseman comes running in. They're standing there, looking at each other. Plunk. The ball landed right on the third base line. Two runs scored. We [the Reading Phillies] won the ball game. That was a terrible place to play, one of the worst."

There are a lot of terrible places to play in the minor leagues. And some nice places. There are parks with bad lights and parks with good lights. There are parks with lousy clubhouses and parks with nice clubhouses, and occasionally parks with no clubhouses. But the parks are only part of the story. It's getting there that's half the battle.

Even in Triple A, traveling can be an adventure.

"We're leaving Springfield [Ill.] one day," Warren Brusstar said. "They took us from the motel to the airport in a school bus. The back three-four seats weren't there; that's where they put the luggage. There's not enough room for guys to sit. They're on top of bags, in the aisles, everywhere. We get to the airport and they throw the bags out. Everybody's trying to get his bag, and then this little guy comes running up. He's shouting, 'I tried to call you at the hotel. I tried to call you at the hotel. Your flight's been canceled.' "

"We took a train one time," said Joe Kerrigan. "Rochester to Toledo. Supposed to leave at two in the morning. The train shows up at 4:30 in the morning. It's an eight-hour trip, and it's Labor Day weekend. We've got no sleeping berths. They just loaded us into the club car, and we all get to sleep. Six o'clock, they wake us up. 'What are you guys doing in here? Get the hell out. We've got to clean this up.' The train is packed. We've got no place to sit. Mike Wallace [a lefthanded pitcher with big league experience] and I threatened to get off at Erie and get a rental car. Finally, they put us in the back of the train. I'm not kidding, it had to be a meat locker. I mean, it was like 61, 62 degrees. We had to stay there for the last six hours of the trip."

Only in the minor leagues. "If you could just catalog the stories that are told in the back of a bus during a road trip, when guys get a few beers in them, that would be a Pulitzer Prize," Joe Kerrigan said. "You could write novels and novels and novels. . . ."

You could write about Joe Charboneau, the toast of Cleveland and the scourge of the American League in 1980 who wound up living in a minor league clubhouse in the summer of ' 81. Joe's only complaint: Charleston [W. Va.] manager Frank Lucchesi kept coming in early in the afternoon and waking him up. Don't laugh. Sleeping in minor league clubhouses isn't all that unusual. Joe Kerrigan slept in one in Rochester in 1980. "It was better than some of the apartments I stayed in," he said. "You've got TV and a stereo and a refrigerator in there. And you can't beat the rent."

Or you could write about John Felske, who managed the Class AA Thetford Mines team for Milwaukee in 1975. "We were in

Reading one night," Felske said. "We were going to Pittsfield after the game. The bus driver [a French Canadian] didn't speak any English. So I showed him on the map how I wanted him to go."

Felske leaned back in his seat and dozed off, confident that everything was under control. "When I woke up," he said, "we were in downtown New York City."

Like I said, only in the minor leagues. But don't get the idea that baseball has a monopoly on such crazy happenings. For example, there was the time I went to Johnstown, Pa., to cover a Philadelphia-Johnston Eastern Hockey League game. A staunch Philly rooter—we'll call him Harry because that was his name—went along for the ride. When we got to the arena he asked me if he could join me in the press box. I said sure. So up we went.

Naturally, the people in the press box assumed my friend, Harry, was another Philly sportswriter. Near the end of the first period a man walked over from the Johnstown radio booth and invited the two of us to drop by for a between-periods interview. Harry had never been interviewed on the radio before. He delivered milk for a large dairy in Philadelphia, so his overall media exposure up to that point had been minimal. He seemed thrilled at the prospect of making his radio debut.

The period ended and off to the radio booth we went. The local announcer knew I worked for *The Philadelphia Inquirer*. He assumed Harry worked for one of the other Philly papers publishing at the time, either *The Bulletin* or the *Daily News*. After all, why else would he be sitting with me in the press box?

The interview was a beaut. Harry handled himself like an old pro. He had strong opinions and he wasn't afraid to express them. Finally, the interview about at an end, the announcer thanked us for our expertise and, almost as an afterthought, asked Harry which Philadelphia paper he wrote for. "I don't write for any paper," Harry replied. "Uh, well what do you do?" the announcer pressed on bravely. "I'm a milkman," Harry told him. End of interview.

I bring that up because the incident was not unlike one that occurred prior to a Pacific Coast League baseball game in Spokane, Wash., several years later. The Phillies' Eugene farm club was playing Spokane and a local announcer saw me talking to the players and the managers, asked somebody where I was from, was told Philadelphia, and immediately assumed I was a big league scout in town to check out some hot prospects.

He walked over, shook hands and asked me if I'd be a guest on his pre-game show. I told him I'd be delighted. Before I knew it, it was show time.

From the opening question I knew I was in trouble. The guy kept asking me for opinions on Spokane ball players, practically none of whom I had ever seen before. Was the catcher a potential major leaguer? Did the second baseman do a good enough job turning the double play? Did ace relief pitcher so-and-so have a chance? As I recall, my answers were (in order), "I don't know," "I'm not sure," and, "Would you mind repeating that question?"

As I spouted out my words of wisdom I had the uncomfortable feeling that the announcer was growing increasingly unfriendly. "Well," he finally snapped, "why don't you know anything about those players? If you're a scout, it's your business to know."

"But I'm not a scout," I informed him over the air.

"You're not?" he said, unable to keep the shock of that discovery out of his voice. "What are you?"

"I'm a sportswriter," I replied.

From the look on his face I suspect he would have been more impressed if I had said, "I'm a milkman."

Let's face it. Things like that just don't happen in the big leagues. That's the beauty of the minors. The unexpected is routine. The ridiculous is ordinary, the absurd a matter of course.

I'm not saying it's all good. To the contrary, much of it is very, very bad. And some of it is downright disgusting. Fine, young prospects graduate from college to the "pros" and are shocked to discover that the playing conditions, the living conditions, the traveling conditions are vastly inferior to what they'd grown accustomed to as amateurs. And yet, with it all, most of the ball players I've met along the way—both the ones who went on to make it in the big leagues and those who didn't—talked about those difficult times with more fondness than bitterness.

That doesn't surprise me, at all. There's something exhilarating about traveling through the minors, watching tomorrow's TV stars and 7-Up salesmen develop. What can be more satisfying than discovering a Greg Luzinski when, as a teenaged, baby bull, he was leaving a trail of tape-measure home runs through the Carolina League and the Eastern League and the Pacific Coast League? Or watching a raw—very raw—talent named Mike Schmidt struggling to make contact with the ball in Reading and Eugene, yet showing flashes of the awesome power and ability that would serve him so well down the road in the big leagues?

Some of the names in this book will be instantly recognized by anyone who follows baseball. I'm talking about the Schmidts, the Luzinskis, the Larry Bowas, the John Stearns, the Ed Farmers, the Dane Iorgs, the Dick Ruthvens, the Alan Bannisters, the Willie

Stargells, and many others who won the struggle and made it to the big leagues.

What their minor league experiences meant to them, how they look back on them today is part of what this book is about, but only part.

This book is also about a lot of guys who didn't make it in the big leagues. They played with the Schmidts, the Luzinskis, the Bowas and the rest in the bush leagues, but they never quite reached the jet set. They're the pros who had to explain to their friends what they did for a living. They're the players who settled for $12.50 a day meal money (and less), not the $40 the big leaguers get today.

This book is about young men who flashed briefly across the big league skies—the Wayne Simpsons, the Dave Downs, the Mike Rogodzinskis—and then faded out of sight. And it's about young men who never quite got there, at all. Many of those who didn't have gone on to become successes in other fields. A few of them haven't. Most of them think of their experiences in pro baseball as happy ones. A few of them don't.

You meet all sorts of people in the minor leagues, a cross-section of America (and Latin America), really. Their stories are at times happy, at times inspiring, at times disappointing, at times tragic.

They had one thing in common. They played a game called baseball and, even those whose careers ended in the minor leagues, played it uncommonly well. I hope after you read these pages and meet these men you'll have some of the feeling for the minor leagues, and for the men who play and manage and coach and umpire and drive buses there, that I have.

2

THE CAN'T-MISS KID

It was nothing important, just an exhibition game in the late '60s between the Phillies and the Braves at West Palm Beach, Fla. The batter was Henry Aaron, who surely doesn't remember. The pitcher was Pat Bayless, who may never forget.

Earlier in the game Aaron had smashed a ball off the left field wall against the young righthanded pitcher. This time the count went to three balls, two strikes. The kid threw a fast ball, the future Hall of Famer swung . . . and missed. Pat Bayless, the kid, had struck out Henry Aaron, the superstar.

It was a meaningless episode for Aaron, an electrifying moment for Bayless, one he would relive many times in the years that followed as he battled to fulfill his great promise and make it to the big leagues, where he could face Henry Aaron again—in a game that counted.

The first thing you noticed about Pay Bayless was his smile. It was a beautiful, warm smile. It would light up a room. One look at it and you understood why they dubbled him "Mr. Personality" in his high school yearbook. The next thing you noticed was his fast ball. And his control. And his determination to make the big leagues.

Pat grew up in Livermore, Calif., about an hour's drive from San Francisco. He was number two of three sons born to Joan and Lowell Bayless, but as an athlete he was number one.

"One time when they were in high school," Joan Bayless said, "there was a track meet and Jeff [Pat's younger brother] did very well in it. Next day in the newspaper article they put 'Pat Bayless' instead of Jeff Bayless."

That's how good Pat was. His name was on everybody's lips. In Livermore, the people just knew that someday Pat Bayless would make it big in athletics.

9

He played football as a kid—a lanky, 6-ft., 2-in. halfback with surprising speed. That career ended in a hurry, though. "Everybody told him, 'Don't play football, Pat, because if you get hurt you won't be able to play baseball,' " Joan Bayless said.

Sound advice. Pat was a freshman at Livermore High School when he got seriously injured in a scrimmage against the junior varsity team. "I was running" he remembered. "I got tackled by two guys; they must've weighed about 250 apiece. One hit me from this side, one from that side. I was probably 160 pounds then at most."

"I was delirious," Pat said years later, "and my best friend helped carry me off the field. He told me I kept saying, 'Will I be able to play baseball? Will I be able to play baseball?' " Baseball was Pat Bayless' game, his love, his passion.

The blow he sustained on that play shattered his leg. "The doctor told us the only way anybody could break a leg like that was to jump off a bridge and land feet first," Pat's mother said.

His football career was over; he was in a body cast for seven months. But to Pat Bayless only one career really mattered. He wanted to be a baseball player. One look at him on the mound in those early years and you knew he was special. He had all the tools plus a single-mindedness of purpose, a devotion to the game that was rare in a kid his age.

Eddie Bockman, who scouted the area for the Phillies, saw him and liked him. Pat reminded people in those days of a young Jim Bunning, the way he came hurtling off the mound after each pitch. Bockman signed him out of high school for a $1,200 bonus. Pat was thrilled.

"He went out and bought a suit for me, a pair of shoes for his dad," Joan Bayless said. And he bought an overcoat for himself. He was ready to face the world.

How good was Pat Bayless? So good that the Phillies sent him to the tough California League in his first pro season. So good that Paul Owens, the Phillies' farm director at the time, said recently, "I thought he was the best-looking kid we had in camp."

They all thought so. Frank Lucchesi was a minor league manager in the Phillies' farm system then. "He told me [in spring training], 'You'll win 12 ball games in Bakersfield,' " Pat recalled. "I said, 'I dunno.' He said, 'You'll win 12 games there. You'll see.' I remember I told him, 'I'll sure try.' "

Twelve wins that first year would have been great, but Bayless surpassed all expectations. He won 18 games, including a no-hitter and a one-hitter, and lost eight, completing 15 of the 29 games he started and giving up only 179 hits in 219 innings. Pat's strikeout-walk ratio, considered a key factor by most baseball scouts, was an eye-opener. All the 19-year-old kid did that first pro season was strike out 217 batters while walking 82.

"There's a kid," said Larry Bowa, "who had the world by the tail."

Bowa was in his second year of pro ball when Bayless joined the Phillies organization. A scrawny, gung-ho shortstop, he matched Bayless in enthusiasm for the game, if not in God-given talent. There were many people in those days who doubted if Bowa would ever make it to the big leagues. When it came to Bayless, there were very few doubters.

They were both Californians whose lives revolved around baseball. It was only natural that they became friends and, eventually, roommates. "We were real close," Bowa recalled. "I used to stop off at Pat's house and stay there on the way to [spring training in] Florida."

Joan Bayless will never forget how it was when the two of them—the lanky power pitcher from Livermore and the scrawny shortstop from Sacramento—got together in those days. Larry was a bundle of nerves. He couldn't wait to leave, couldn't wait to get to Florida. And Pat was just about as bad. "We were keyed up," Bowa said, smiling at the memory of those rah-rah, baseball-crazy kids so eager to get to the major leagues.

"We roomed together in Florida," Bowa recalled, "and in the Instructional League, too. We called Pat 'Sugar' because everything was so sweet. Talk about an arm!"

Bayless and Bowa began climbing up the ladder together. Reading (Eastern League) in '68 . . . Eugene (Pacific Coast League) in '69. And then they parted company, going in opposite directions. But that's getting ahead of the story.

Those first couple of years—in Bakersfield and Reading—were everything that Bayless had imagined they would be. "I thought it was the greatest life a guy could have," he said.

To know Pat was to instantly like him. He was so outgoing, so determined. And that smile of his just made you feel warm all over.

Pat's first general manager in pro ball was a man named Bob King. "He wrote us a letter after Pat left Bakersfield," Joan Bayless said. "He told us, 'If I ever have a son I'd want him to be exactly like Pat.'"

Pat's mother vividly remembers his first game as a pro for the Bakersfield Bears. Joan and Lowell Bayless were there. "It was in Stockton," she said. "It had been raining, but it stopped when we got there. There were probably about 50 people in the stands. Pat won.

After the game, we walked down to the field and kids were coming up to him, asking for his autograph. Pat looked at us and said, 'This is the life.' "

But there were problems, too. Larry Bowa was only too aware of the struggle Bayless was waging to make it to the top. After all, Bowa was struggling, too.

"Pat always acted like he was cool," Larry said, "but down deep there was that doubt. I remember a couple of games he pitched— really good games, like he might've won, 3–2 or 2–1—and when they were over he was down. I said, 'Damn, what's wrong with you?' He said, 'Man, I can't give up that many runs.' "

There are those who feel Pat's father was, in part, responsible for that. A one-time minor league baseball player himself, Lowell Bayless was Pat's biggest booster and, apparently, severest critic. "The kid was almost afraid of his father," Paul Owens said. "You could tell. He wasn't a bad man; don't get me wrong. But I think he pushed him too much."

"Pat would throw a two-hitter," said Larry Bowa, "and his dad would tell him, 'God, you could've thrown a one-hitter.' There was a lot of pressure on him. I'd tell him, 'Don't be so hard on yourself.' Imagine *me* telling anybody that. That's unbelievable."

If Pat's father pushed him—well, he isn't the first father to do that and he won't be the last. Looking back on it recently, Pat insisted, "He never pushed me. I pushed myself." And Joan Bayless concurred, saying, "Lowell never pushed him. He knew Pat loved the game and he might say after he came home something about, 'You should've done this, Pat,' or 'You should've done that,' but he didn't push him."

The truth is, there's enormous pressure on a kid—any kid—trying to beat the odds and make it to the big leagues. Some can handle it. Some can't.

There was very little indication that Bayless couldn't handle it during his second pro season. Pat picked up in Reading where he had left off in Bakersfield. He won 12 and lost eight in the Double A Eastern League and allowed only 139 hits in 179 innings, striking out 130 and walking 71. His earned run average—a good 3.04 at Bakersfield—was a brilliant 1.76 at Reading.

Denny Doyle, Larry Bowa's double play partner in the minors who made it to the big leagues with the Phillies, Angels and Red Sox, said, "Pat Bayless did it all. He threw hard, really hard. He had a good breaking ball, a good off speed pitch. He was one of those guys who impressed you in the low minors. You watched him and you said, 'No way he can miss. It's just a matter of time.'"

Bayless and Bowa lived in an apartment on the top of a hill. "I look back on it now," Bayless' old roomie said, "and I wouldn't go near that place. I mean, it was just a small thing. But at the time we thought it was a castle. I'll tell you what, I wouldn't want to go back and ride the buses, but it *was* a lot of fun."

Those were crazy, carefree times. Even the blunders were good for a few laughs. Bowa recalled the night Reading had the bases loaded with Bayless coming to bat. Manager Frank Lucchesi called him over for a brief conference. "I may try a squeeze," Lucchesi told his star pitcher. "Look for the sign."

Bowa was on deck. "Here, try this heavy bat," Larry said to his buddy. "All you have to do is stick it out."

Pat walked up there ready to lay down the greatest squeeze bunt in the history of the Eastern League. His manager had forewarned him. His best pal on the team had given him a bat with a barrel so big it was practically made to order for the situation. So what happened? Let Bowa tell it:

"Pat takes the bat. The skip [Lucchesi] flashes the squeeze sign. Pat swings—and doubles over the left fielder's head."

OK, so everybody makes mistakes. For most of those first two years, though, even Pat Bayless' mistakes had a way of coming out all right. But there were some serious problems developing.

"I know his back was really hurting him," Bowa said. "He was always complaining about his back, his back. I said. 'Don't pitch. Tell them.' 'No, no,' he'd say, 'I can't do that. I can't miss any starts. I've got a chance to get to the big leagues.' So he kept pitching and pitching, and it hurt more and more. Then, when it was too late, he told somebody his back hurt."

Why would a kid endure so much pain? Why would he refuse to skip a turn? Bowa understood the answer to that. He, too, played hurt. He, too, had his whole life wrapped around getting to the big leagues. "Pat wanted it maybe even more than I did," Larry said. "He was obsessed with it, really obsessed with it."

Frank Lucchesi managed Bayless at Reading in '68 and in Eugene in '69. "He was all baseball," Frank remembered. "He wanted to make it. But his makeup was that he was kind of a high-strung kid. I don't mean that in a negative way, though. What I mean, he wanted to do so good that he would put himself under pressure. He was always a good competitor. If he did get hurt he didn't want anybody to know about it. 'I want to go out and pitch,' he'd say. 'Is it my turn tomorrow?' He might have 101 fever, but he'd go out and pitch. He was that type of kid, just a good kid on the club."

The "good kid on the club" started running into setbacks, though. He won his first five Triple A decisions in Eugene in '69, but he seemed tired. He'd lost something off his fast ball. And pretty soon he began losing games, too.

Maybe the Phillies deserve some of the blame for that. Bayless, after all, was still a kid. Yet, as so often happens with especially promising kid pitchers, they tried to rush him along, had him pitch winter ball in the Dominican Republic after going through a full summer of pitching in the minors. When he returned from the Dominican and began spring training in '69, Bayless complained about feeling tired and overworked. Later events indicated that he knew what he was talking about.

"If I wouldn't have pitched all year I would've been in the big leagues in '69," he said recently. "I would've gone to spring training and blown 'em away just like I did the first two years. But I was so damn weak from playing in Reading, then Florida [the instructional league], and then the Dominican, and then a week off and back to spring training."

Whatever his reasons, his record at Eugene in '69 dropped off sharply to 6–8 with a 4.44 earned run average. For the first time in his pro career Pat gave up more than one hit per inning (155 in 142 innings) and his strikeout-walk ratio was a mediocre 67–54. As a result, when Larry Bowa went to Philadelphia to start his big league career in 1970, Pat Bayless was an hour and 20 minute drive away—in Double A Reading.

It was a tough year, nothing at all like his first season. Pat Bayless won eight games and lost 11. His earned run average zoomed to 4.02, more than twice what it had been two years before. Pat had reached the crossroads. He desperately needed a big year in 1971 to reestablish himself as a top prospect. To his credit he did everything in his power to make that big year a reality.

The Pat Bayless who came to spring training early in 1971 seemed ready to put it all together and live up to his earlier promise. He was in excellent shape when he arrived in Clearwater, Fla., the Phillies' spring training base, and he worked harder than anybody else in camp. This was a young man totally dedicated to doing what was necessary to achieve his goal.

The brass was impressed. It was impossible not to be impressed. So it was that the Phillies named Pat Bayless winner of the Bob Carpenter Award at the end of spring training, an award presented annually to the Phillies minor league player who "has been outstanding in attitude, hustle, desire and advancement potential." Even now, the Bob Carpenter plaque is mounted near the entrance to the locker room at the Phillies' minor league complex, where it serves as an inspiration to the young men who report to spring training.

Each year the winner's name is engraved on a small, gold-colored plate. One such engraving says, "Pat Bayless, Pitcher 1971."

Four months after receiving the award, Pat Bayless was given his unconditional release. The shock, the disappointment changed—even ruined—his life.

The first shock, however, came shortly after Bayless received the Carpenter Award. He assumed, of course, that he was on the way up again, that as the standout pitcher of the minor league camp he would be assigned to a spot on the Phillies' Triple A team in Eugene. Instead, the Phillies sent him back to Double A Reading. It was a blow. One day, he was on top of the world, reading and rereading the letter that accompanied the winning of the spring training award. Next day, he was depressed and confused. The Phillies had built him up, then knocked him down. He felt they had deceived him. "I asked [after getting the Carpenter Award], 'Am I going to Triple A?' " Pat said. "They told me, 'Yeah, you're going.' "

But he didn't go. And he was sick about it. In retrospect, it all could have been—*should* have been—handled so much better.

Bayless' confusion that year was apparent off the field, as well. There was an unfortunate, short-lived marriage. There was a brief period when he jumped the Reading team. There were charges leveled against the manager of the team, whom Bayless claimed had made advances to his wife in the clubhouse at Reading, charges that Bayless later told farm director Owens were incorrect.

"He had accused our manager [Nolan Campbell] among others—and I say 'among others' meaning fellow teammates and others—with either making advances or having some type of relations with his wife," Owens recalled years later in a deposition. "And of course when I got wind of it I talked to my people, who denied it . . . So in order to straighten the thing out I called him, the manager and a couple other people that were supposedly being accused into my office. After laying the thing out I just said, 'I want to find out who's telling the truth here.' Pat Bayless then backed down and denied all of the accusations . . . and as I best remember told me that he had done some checking and that he was sorry about it and apologized to everyone in the room."

One good thing came out of that stormy year. Pat met Mike Schmidt, then a young college grad just starting out in the pros. Pat and Mike were road roomies in '71 at Reading. "I was his first roommate," Bayless said. "He had a Corvette in Reading and he let me drive it all the time. We'd go out on shopping sprees together. . . ."

Pat liked gaudy clothes. "I had green shoes to match green slacks and a green sweater," he recalled. Those shopping sprees with Mike Schmidt were the highlight of an otherwise miserable season.

"He used to really dress well," Mike said. "Whether he latched on to me in Reading or I latched on to him, I don't know. I guess he was my perception of what a pro baseball player should be like at the time. He sure looked like a good pitcher to me.

"I remember I had a Corvette and he always wanted to use it. I think he liked my car more than me. But we roomed together on the road and I think he even met my parents when they came into town and went out to dinner with us one time. He was one of my best friends on the team at that time."

One night in Pawtucket, R.I., the two friends—the slugging third baseman from Ohio and the struggling pitcher from California—had a late-night, post-game snack in a little diner across the street from their hotel. "We sat at the counter," Schmidt said, "and we waited to get waited on, and we waited . . . A couple of thugs came in and sat down and they waited on them and Bayless said something, and it looked like we were going to have an all-out brawl in this diner. Eventually we walked out and exchanged a few words, and then those guys went back in the diner and we went back to the hotel."

Their dinner plans destroyed, they prepared to call it a night. "We were laying in bed," Schmidt said, "and he whips this gun out. I had no idea he had a gun. It scared the shit out of me. He had a bag of bullets—like a sanitary sock full of bullets—and he sat there and started loading this thing. He was acting like he was going back down there and shoot up the place. I remember him saying, 'I'm go-ing over and kill those guys.' I started begging him not to do it, and I finally talked him out of it."

That was Mike Schmidt's first clue that his roommate might be having mental problems.

Eventually, the Phillies sent Pat to Eugene. By now, though, he had severe back problems and arm problems. And somewhere along the line he had become involved with drugs.

"I was hooked on 'Speed' in baseball," Bayless said. "I used it off and on for a while."

If so, he wasn't the only one. "Speed" or "Greenies" were fairly common in baseball clubhouses. "They wouldn't just hand them out," Pat said, "but ball players had their own prescriptions for them. They don't know what they're messing with. . . ."

Bayless found out—the hard way. The "Greenies"—another name for amphetamines or pep pills—were only part of it. Pat claimed he was given pain killers in Reading to enable him to pitch and, in fact, in a memo dated November 9, 1971, Dr. Patrick Mazza wrote, at Bayless' request: "To whom it may concern, This is to certify that I attended Pat Bayless when he played for the Reading Phillies. On one occasion I injected a tender nodule in the left sacroiliac region with 10 cc. Decadron with Xylocaine. There was complete remission of symptoms at the time." Apparently the dosage was actually only 1 cc., not 10, but Dr. Mazza's secretary signed his name to the note without realizing the mistake.

At any rate, the end of Pat Bayless' baseball career came in Eugene, Ore., in August of '71.

Paul Owens related the story of Bayless' release in a deposition taken at the law offices of John I. (Jack) McMahon in King of Prussia, Pa., on November 7, 1978, as follows:

Q. Well, what happened out in Eugene that eventually led to his release?

A. "Well, he went out there and he just—he told the manager (Andy Seminick) he was real pleased. He said that he felt that this is where he should have been all year and subsequently he went out and just pitched very badly . . . After about three weeks or so, as I best remember, the manager just could do nothing else but call me and say, 'He just can't pitch here. He's not doing the job.' I said, 'Well, it just so happens I'm going to be coming out. Why don't you wait and we'll decide that. That will give me a chance to see for myself.'

"I went out and I saw him pitch a couple of times in the 10 days I was there . . . and he just showed no ability towards ever becoming a major leaue pitcher. He was just being eaten up. . . ."

Q. Were you there when he was released?

A. "I released him myself. I called him in and talked to him."

Q. Do you recall the essence of the conversation and his reaction?

A. "No. He didn't seem overly surprised. . . . Releasing someone is probably the hardest thing to do in baseball. I released hundreds over the years. . . . Many of them accept it, almost knowing that the handwriting was on the wall. Some break down and cry. They do a lot of different things."

Q. Do you recall whether or not he made any complaints about any injury to his body?

A. "No. I think—and I can almost remember it specifically—he said, 'Well, I think you're making a mistake. I think you've held me back.' I said. 'You've been given every opportunity in my opinion.' I said, 'You have a right to think anything you want.' He said, 'I'll come back and haunt you because I'm going to make the big leagues,' I said, 'Fine. When you do I'll be the first one to congratulate you.' "

A short time later, Paul Owens outlined the reasons for Pat's release in a letter written to Pat's father. Owens concluded, "A release is not the end of the world in our game, and perhaps it will be a blessing in disguise for Pat. It may wake him up while he is still young enough to profit by this release."

Owens was wrong. In a very real sense, Pat Bayless' world ended on that August day in 1971.

"He was so bad when he came home that he didn't come directly to our house," said Joan Bayless. "Pat went over to my youngest son's house and Jeff kept him there for a day or two until he came off of some of the drugs. Then he brought him over to our house and Pat passed out right on the living room floor with the pain he was in. Lowell took him to a neurosurgeon and they did a milogram and they put him right in the hospital and the day after they operated on him. Just so simple, you know. Just so simple. Pat said they [the Phillies] didn't even X-ray him. Well, Mazza did X-ray him. Pat doesn't remember.

"Pat brought the X-rays home with him, and do you know the X-rays were mixed up. They were the X-rays of a pregnant woman's back and the letter they sent to the Phillies said, 'No sign of any back problem.' The letter was with the X-ray and it was referring to a girl named—I think it was Pat Boyles or something like that. They could have done a milogram in Philadelphia; they could have operated and he would have been out of baseball maybe a quarter of a season. The whole thing was just a big, big mess."

The Pat Bayless who went off to play professional baseball in Bakersfield, Calif., in 1967 was not the Pat Bayless who returned from Eugene, Ore., in 1971. What happened to him in those four years—and especially what has happened to him since—constitute one of the great tragedies in baseball. The back operation he underwent a month after his release cost his family approximately $5,000. But the real tragedy is what happened in Pat Bayless' head. He grew increasingly violent in the years immediately following his departure from pro baseball, and for five years was in and out of mental institutions. In January of '82 I drove from San Francisco to Livermore to see him for the first time since he left the minor leagues. We had talked on the phone dozens of times in the intervening 10½ years; Pat, although he hasn't worked since his baseball dream was shattered, thinks nothing of placing long-distance calls to all parts of the country. But frankly I was apprehensive as I approached his home town—a city of some 60,000.

Would he be glad to see me? Would he recognize me? Would I recognize him? The questions, and the doubts raced through my head on that drive along Route 580 into the valley. Pat and I had been close during his pitching days, but those days—and that Pat Bayless—were long gone.

My fears were groundless. The 34-year-old man who met me at the gas station on the outskirts of Livermore and led me to his parents' rented house was obviously delighted to see a face from the past. He was much heavier, and his hairline was receding, but the smile—on those rare occasions when he flashed it—was still the same, still big enough to light up a room.

"When you called up yesterday to say you were coming, he was in seventh heaven," Joan Bayless said. "Before you called, he was sitting there, really depressed. Today he's fine."

But if Pat Bayless was fine today that was because he had gotten his shot yesterday. "The shot"—a tranquilizing drug—"is supposed to last a week," Joan Bayless said. "But I don't think it lasts more than three days or maybe four. He got it yesterday at noon, so you're seeing him on a good day."

A good day, but also a heartrending day. "I haven't worked in 10 years," Pat said for openers. "Got to be on medication the rest of my life, a shot in the arm every week . . . I've had so much taken away from me. I'm just rolling with the punches now. That's about all I can do, just try to keep my head up and plug along and remember the good times and remember I was a good pitcher and remember the good people I met.

"That's all I remember about it. I don't remember any particular time—A ball or Double A or Triple A or spring training with the big league team. I don't remember anything. I just remember I played baseball a long time. . . ."

The five years following his release had been a nightmare. Seeing him now, calmly discussing that period of his life, it was hard to imagine what a terror he must have been.

"I was a headache for the first five years out of baseball," he said matter-of-factly. "Always fighting, carrying on. But I haven't been in a fight the last five years. I learned my lesson. I saw the outcome of me getting mad. It was no good."

That's putting it mildly.

"I just started blowing up," he said. "I was mad at everybody. If I'd seen you 10 years ago I wouldn't even have talked to you because

I was mad at everybody regardless of what their name was and what they did for me and what they didn't do for me. . . ."

"Pat's gone through hell," Joan Bayless interjected.

"My whole family's gone through hell," Pat corrected her.

"The first time they took him over to the county hospital, that was bad," his mother said. "He was still really withdrawing [from the drugs]. Lowell and I went over to see him one night, and I don't know what had happened over there, but I guess he really went on a rampage. They had him in—they called it a 'quiet room'—just a room with a cot and he was strapped, and he was just sweating and yelling and screaming."

He wound up in the state hospital at Napa. Once he was there for six months. "Pat and Jeff were in a bar here in Livermore," Joan Bayless said. "Jeff was trying to protect Pat and the police came in and Jeff was trying to hold Pat back from the policemen; he knew that Pat didn't know what he was doing. Well, Pat broke a couple of jaws and that was when Pat went to Napa the first time. . . .

"One time when I was at work—this goes back probably seven, eight years ago—he called me up and told me he was going to commit suicide."

Pat was at his parents' house at the time. The police station was two blocks away. So his mother called the police, and they rushed over. When they arrived, there was Pat, his suitcase packed, ready to be taken away. "I think," said Joan Bayless, "he just wanted to go to the hospital."

"When I first got out of baseball," recalled Pat, "I was throwing boulders at the church. Big rocks. I'd stand on the corner throwing them because I thought God was the one that broke me down, that did this to me. But it wasn't Him. It was the drugs."

"You knew Pat's personality before," Joan Bayless said. "It was just a complete change. Not like the same person. One time he came walking down the street punching trees—like big oak trees—and he punched them so hard that he had to go to the emergency room and have stitches put in his hand."

The kid whose life revolved around baseball won't watch a big league baseball game on television now—not even when his old friends Larry Bowa and Mike Schmidt are playing. "I can't watch them," Pat said, although he remembered trying in 1980 when the Phillies won the World Series and his old roomies were playing a vital part in that success.

"He watched it two minutes and he walked out," his mother recalled.

And on at least one occasion, when the sight of his friends from a bygone day stirred up visions of what might have been, Pat picked up an object—a shoe, something—and hurled it at the TV screen. Joan Bayless can appreciate the terrible frustration he feels.

"The first year that the Phillies were in the playoffs [1976]," she said, "when they started the National Anthem and introduced the ball players and Larry Bowa came up, it just tore my heart out because I thought, 'Pat should be there with him.' "

The old memories can be so painful that Pat, in a fit of rage one day, destroyed the scrapbooks filled with stories of his baseball exploits. "I had five scrapbooks of everything I ever did," he said, "from the time I was eight years old until I was 23 and released."

"About a week before I saw the scrapbooks under the bed," said his mother, "and I knew Pat's depression and I thought I'd better put those books away, and I didn't. I came home one day and he had them cut up into little pieces."

"I ripped 'em up with my bare hands," Pat said.

The Baylesses collected the pieces, stuffed them in a suitcase and turned them over to Jack McMahon, the lawyer who became so interested in Pat Bayless' case that he spent countless hours and approximately $25,000 of his own money in an effort to build a case against the Phillies.

Jack McMahon met Pat Bayless for the first time in 1974, three years after the pitcher had been released by the Phillies. The Bayless case had been referred to McMahon by a San Francisco attorney, Bob Cartwright.

"I went out to see Pat and was very much impressed with the guy," McMahon said. "I thought he was a dynamite person. Great speaking voice. A fantastic smile. A tremendous way of telling what happened. I thought, 'There's got to be something I can do for this guy.' "

McMahon talked to attorney Cartwright. "I told him, 'I think there's more than meets the eye here and I want to check out the drug aspect.' " The Bayless case was reopened.

Jack McMahon plunged into it all the way. He was a successful attorney with more than a passing interest in sports; one of his clients was Billy Cunningham, the coach of the Philadelphia 76ers. Pat Bayless had told him, in that face-to-face interview, that the Phillies gave him drugs to mask the pain in his back so he could pitch.

"It was incredible to me to think that in April [1971] the guy could be on top of the world," McMahon said, "and by August be out of baseball. From a lawyer's standpoint that was such a fantastic striking had to happen to take this guy from the top of the mountain right down to the pits."

So McMahon began an exhaustive investigation. "I went back to San Francisco," he said, "and back to Livermore. I interviewed the chief of police there; he was the one who told the bizarre stories of Pat going down the street and shadow boxing and hitting trees and breaking noses and two instances where he threw police officers through the window of the bowling alley. We interviewed Pat's high school coach, who wanted to blame everything on Mr. Bayless."

Pat's father, of course, saw things differently. "You can sum up his feelings in one sentence," Jack McMahon said: "The boy that he sent away to the Phillies was not the boy they sent back."

McMahon and his investigators interviewed Eddie Bockman, the Phillies scout who originally signed Bayless. Bockman readily attested to the bright future the young Bayless appeared to have. The investigation was nothing short of exhaustive. They tracked down Pat's first wife in a beauty shop in Oregon. They talked to some of his high school teachers, and to his neighbors. By the time they were done they had a pretty good idea of what Pat Bayless was really like in those days before his pro baseball career ended. The findings corroborated their first impressions. Here was a kid with a one-track mind, a kid determined to play major league baseball. "He was just hell bent to be a major leaguer," McMahon said. "Really had the blinders on. Everybody liked him. He was a normal, nice, law-abiding kid. Tremendous personality. No drugs. No drinking. No fights. No nothing."

They even went to Napa State Hospital, where Pat had spent some of his most tragic, post-baseball days. Gaining access to Bayless' records there was a problem. "They kept making us get different authorizations," McMahon said.

The records, when they finally saw them, were "at least three or four feet high."

"The letters were pathetic," said the lawyer, "something like out of *The Snake Pit*. He'd write, 'How do I get out of this place? These people are crazy.' "

It was while they were going through those voluminous records at Napa that the first mention of the drug called butazolidin occurred. "A neurologist-resident in Napa had this little, nondescript note that it should not be ruled out that butazolidin had been given to the patient in massive quantities," McMahon said, "and that butazolidin has been known to cause hallucinations and psychotic problems such as the patient was exhibiting."

McMahon went to the medical books to find out all he could on the anti-inflammatory agent known as butazolidin, or Bute. Under the heading, "Reactions associated with overdosage," he found a list that included: "convulsions, euphoria, psychosis, depression, headaches, hallucinations, giddiness, vertigo, coma, hyperventilations, insomnia." Perhaps, McMahon thought, "massive quantities" of Bute were responsible for Bayless' deteriorating mental condition in the months and years following his release.

A \$4.6-million law suit was filed—\$2.6 million in compensatory damages and another \$2 million in punitive damages; in other words, about what some of the day's big league free agents were getting on the open market.

There was precedent for such cases in sports, although the majority of drug-related charges occur in football, not baseball. One of the most highly publicized involved Dick Butkus, an All-Pro linebacker with the Chicago Bears. McMahon went to Chicago one miserable, cold winter day to see James Dooley, the attorney who represented Butkus' and check out the details.

"The story was a pretty good one," McMahon discovered. Also, it seemed relevant to the Bayless case.

In a nutshell, Butkus thought he was under a multi-year agreement with the Bears, but actually had merely been signed to a series of one-year contracts requiring the player to pass a physical examination prior to each season.

"Butkus had made his deal with Mr. Halas [George Halas, the venerable owner of the Bears] unrepresented," McMahon said. "It was sort of a father-son, uncle-nephew type of thing. Butkus started to deteriorate at the second half of the first year. He finally took himself out of a game and said that he was getting pushed around . . . Prior to that time, every Monday morning Butkus would come in and the team doctor—they [some of the players] called him 'Dr. Needles,' 'Dr. Strangelove,' 'Dr. Pain'—he had a whole bunch of funny [nick]names—would keep shooting him up. On Friday the doctor would come up to the coach and tell who could play and who couldn't."

Butkus, the doctor would announce, could play. And so he did—on a badly injured knee shot full of pain killers.

"What brought the case out into the open," McMahon discovered, "Butkus came back the second year, could not pass the physical and said to Mr. Halas, 'Look, I know I have four years left on my deal. I don't expect you to pay it up front, just pay it out as you go.' And Mr. Halas said, 'You don't have four years left on your contract. If you look at it closely, if you can't pass your physical it's no deal.' "

End of father-son, uncle-nephew relationship. Butkus blew his top, went to a lawyer . . . and wound up collecting $650,000.

There were other cases, as well. "Anywhere there was a drug-related situation I either saw the lawyer in person or contacted him by phone," McMahon said. "It was mostly to get ideas for trial time."

But the statute of limitations prevented the case of Patrick Bruce Bayless vs. the Philadelphia National League Baseball Club from ever going to trial. Jack McMahon fought through a series of appeals and eventually hit a dead end.

In an attempt to hurdle the statute of limitations barrier, McMahon dug up an old case involving another former Phillies minor league player, an outfielder named Gerald Gemignani.

Gemignani signed a pro contract in September, 1958, and the following spring was examined by a doctor working for the team at the minor league complex. It was alleged that the examination uncovered a symptomatic blood condition, but neither the ball club nor the doctor treated Gemignani for it. Nor did they advise the player or his family of its existence, thus precluding early treatment. In July, 1960, Gemignani was given his unconditional release. Three weeks later he was hospitalized with a serious kidney problem. One month after that, the young man died.

Gemignani's father brought a suit against the Phillies in 1967. As in the Bayless case, the statute of limitations presented a major hurdle since, under the law, you have two years from the time of injury or the time you should have been aware of the injury to file suit. The U.S. District Court in the Eastern District of Pennsylvania ruled in Gemignani's favor. The case was settled out of court.

Bayless, on the other hand, has lost the legal battle once and for all—a fact he has had difficulty accepting. Even now he talks about the money he expects to get and how it will help him start a new life. "They ruined my life," he told me that afternoon in Livermore, "and they're going to pay for it, too, before I die. You can bet on it."

"It's really sad," Jack McMahon said. "I'm sure a week doesn't go by that he doesn't call either here [McMahon's law office in King of Prussia, Pa.] or my home. Usually, Pat calls Sunday night around six. It's been going on for years. All my kids know him. They all talk to him. They all say, 'How ya doin'?' "

The answer, of course, is not all that well. Pat, who remarried five years ago, spends most of his time sitting in his parents' home in Livermore, or in his small apartment, or walking the streets, or drinking coffee and talking to the townspeople in Lyon's Restaurant, an all-night, downtown coffee shop. Not long ago a story about Pat Bayless appeared in the local paper. His mother clipped it out and sent it to the Phillies. "I told them," she said, "that I hoped they weren't giving out that award any more because it doesn't mean a thing."

On the day I visited the Baylesses in Livermore, Pat, his mother and I had lunch at Lyon's Restaurant, his favorite hangout. Everybody knew him, and greeted him.

On the way out, a little, white-haired, elderly lady walked up to Bayless, called him by name and asked, "Are you going to play baseball again?"

"No," replied Pat.

"Oh," she replied, "that's too bad."

"It's all right," he told her kindly. "There'll be another Pat Bayless."

He meant, of course, a Pat Bayless who would make it to the big leagues, a Pat Bayless whose baseball dream would come true. Even in a city the size of Livermore that is not so far-fetched.

Time goes on, and new "can't-miss" pitching prospects flash across the baseball horizon. Pat Bayless, Livermore's first great major league hope, didn't make it; now it's lefthander Mark Davis' turn to try. He, too, was signed by Eddie Bockman. He, too, is blessed with great natural ability and a warm, winning personality. He, too, grew up in Livermore.

"We went into Lyon's Restaurant one day," Davis said, "and he [Bayless] was coming out. That's the first time I ever met him."

Eddie Bockman introduced them, and they talked for a while. "He looked like—well, like an ex-ball player," Davis thought.

That's what Pat Bayless is, an ex-ball player.

He is an ex-ball player who, once upon a time, a lifetime ago, threw a 3–and–2 fast ball past Henry Aaron; an ex-ball player whose only tie with the good, old days is the Christmas card he receives each year from Larry and Sheena Bowa.

He is an extreme example of how a baseball dream can turn into a nightmare.

3
NOBODY SAID IT WAS PERFECT

There are places that stick in your mind, places you can't forget—no matter how hard you try. The nice minor league ball parks, the nice minor league hotels all seem to blend together into an indistinguishable mass of so-what memories. If you've seen one Holidasy Inn you've seen them all. Ditto for your average, decent minor league stadium. But not all minor league ball parks are comfy and cozy, bright and pleasant. Some of them, even in this supposedly enlightened era, are so dark that they ought to ask the paying customers to bring candles. And some of them are so small, and dingy, and unprofessional in appearance that it's hard to believe the men who run the big leagues would permit their most highly regarded prospects to play under such conditions.

"I've seen clubs out in dirty uniforms and torn uniforms," Paul Owens, the general manager of the Phillies, was saying recently. "How much would it cost you to dry-clean the uniforms? It sounds like a small thing to do, but hell, you wouldn't expect a kid to go out and spend eight hours in a uniform that stinks, would you?"

On the other hand, those stinking uniforms fit in beautifully with those stinking ball parks and those stinking club houses and, occasionally, the stinking hotels/motels the kids have to live in between trips to the ball park on road trips.

Thetford Mines was one of those minor league towns people never forgot. For a couple of years in the mid-'70s it operated in the Eastern League. Pittsburgh had its Double A team there in 1974, Milwaukee in '75. Some pretty fair ball players called Thetford home in those days. They called it a lot of other things, too.

Willie Randolph played there. And Omar Moreno. And Lenn Sakata. And Jim Gantner. They were all graduates of Thetford Mines. Or maybe it would be more accurate to call them survivors.

Tony Siegle was Milwaukee's farm director when the Brewers found themselves saddled with an Eastern League team in this asbestos mining town in French-speaking Canada, a little more than an hour's drive from Quebec City. "I wrote [to the National Association, the ruling body of minor league baseball] the previous November," Siegle said, "and begged them not to make us go to Thetford Mines. Hank Peters was the head of the Association then, and he ignored my letter. Then when he got up there he saw for himself."

"He came in," said John Felske, who managed the Thetford Mines team for Milwaukee in 1975, "and he looked at the field, and he looked so sad. He said, 'John, I apologize. There should never have been a baseball team in this town.' "

If Hank Peters was sorry, think how Siegle and Felske and the poor guys who had to play professional baseball up there must have felt.

Joe Kerrigan was pitching for Montreal's Quebec City farm club at the time. The club would commute to Thetford, which wasn't bad. And the players would change into their baseball uniforms in the visiting clubhouse, which *was* bad.

"We used to dress in a trailer," Joe recalled. "That was the locker room."

The home players? They had a trailer, too. Many a day they must have wished they could hook it up to a car and get the hell out of town.

"It was an experience," said Felske. "The park was nothing but— well, they just went out and made an area to play. They took sheets that they used for putting up concrete and made a fence out of them. They had a backdrop [for the batters], which was canvas. . . ."

And they hollered, "Play ball." And, by golly, they played. Neither sleet nor snow nor freezing cold could deter Eastern League baseball players from their appointed rounds.

"It must have been an experience for guys coming out of college," Felske said. "They must have thought, 'This is pro ball?' "

To professional baseball's everlasting discredit, it was.

"Tony [Siegle] and I went up there in the winter time to look the place over," Felske said. "We looked at each other like, 'You got to be kidding. There's nothing here but snow.' "

They flew in to Montreal, arriving in the middle of a snow storm, and embarked on the next leg on their daring journey. "I'll never forget it," said Felske. "The guy that picked us up [in Montreal] was a lawyer. He was doing 90 miles an hour and there's all this slop [snow and ice] on the street. I'm saying to myself, 'My God, what's going to happen here?' We went through these little, tiny towns, places with names like Black Lake and. . . ."

And Thetford Mines.

"The people up there are OK," Felske said. "Some of them even spoke English."

But the facilities weren't OK. Not for a professional, Double A baseball league.

"I'll tell you how bad it was," offered Felske, relishing the task. "We took batting practice one day and out in left field was some round, tin house where they stored all the equipment for the city. In right field was a little park for the kids. . . ."

It was a long-ball hitter's paradise. Balls would jump out in all directions—onto the roof of the tin house in left, into the kids' park in right, everywhere.

"I told them, 'You're going to have to put somebody out there when we take batting practice to get the baseballs,' " Felske said. " 'If you don't, you're not going to be able to afford this.' "

Apparently, something got lost in translation. Felske's pleas were ignored. As predicted, batting practice turned into a daily home-run orgy. "It was nothing for me to put three dozen balls in a bag and halfway through you'd have to get more balls; we'd be out of them. We wound up using new balls for batting practice [a minor league no-no]. And the last three weeks of the season we couldn't take batting practice, at all. We had no baseballs."

Not many fans, either. "If they drew maybe 500 people they had a tremendous night," the former Thetford Mines manager said. "They couldn't support baseball."

And the fact that the miners went out on strike didn't help matters. "They had a rule, if the town went on strike nobody had to pay any bills," Felske said. "They also had this thing called 'Caribou Week'. Everybody rode a horse. You couldn't ride a car. No cars in town, just horses. If you didn't have a horse, you walked."

You'd be surprised how few minor league baseball players own horses.

Joe Kerrigan remembered going there one night in late August and finding the stands—wooden planks behind first and third—had been removed. "We asked the home players what had happened," Joe said, "and they told us they had to use the stands for firewood."

That, Felske insisted, was not quite true. "They took some of the bleachers out for a softball game," he said.

Either way, nobody ever mistook the "stadium" at Thetford Mines for Yankee Stadium. There were days, however, when it bore a fleeting resemblance to the North Pole.

"We pulled in on opening day," said Felske, "and it was snowing. There's nine feet of snow sitting around the ball park."

Did they play?

"Oh yeah," Felske replied. "We played every time it was humanly possible to play. There was nothing else we could do."

And yet, in a strange sort of way, it was fun for some of the kids on their way up, all part of the wonderful, new adventure called professional baseball. "In the low minor leagues," said Jack Bastable, a catcher who came close to making it to the big leagues with the Phillies, "you didn't know how bad things really were. You were naive, and that naivety bred contentment. You were still living in some fantasy land of what baseball is all about."

Even when that fantasy land clashed with the stark reality of playing baseball games in Thetford Mines, or Sacramento, where a 97-pound weakling could pop a ball over the nearby left field fence, or West Haven, Conn., where the visiting clubhouse made you long for a return to the trailer at Thetford Mines.

Eddie Molush, now a Philadelphia high school teacher and baseball coach, was pitching in the Phillies farm system during the Thetford Mines era of Eastern League baseball. Minor league baseball—simply the thrill of being a part of it and the struggle to go higher—was mostly enjoyment for him. "I even liked the bus trips to Canada," he said. "I must have been nuts. I liked the whole ride."

What he liked most, probably, were the stories he stored up in his head—incredible tales well calculated to keep his high school students and players in stitches.

"One time," said Molush, "we were supposed to play in Thetford Mines, but the field there was nowhere near ready, so we went to another town. I remember, we were driving all over the East Canadian wilderness. Nobody knew where we were. And when we got where we were going the wind was blowing and there were snow squalls. Wellman [Bob Wellman, the manager of the Reading Phillies then and a scout for the New York Mets now] just told us to sit tight."

Wellman went out to look things over. He could hardly believe his eyes. "He said the pitching mound was a piece of wood nailed to the mud," Molush reported. "The lights didn't work. There was a big hole over by third base. . . ."

It was, as they say in golf, an unplayable lie.

If that was bad, Thetford Mines wasn't much better. "You had to rush to get back to the hotel [after the game]," Jack Bastable remembered. "If you weren't one of the first two or three guys to take a shower there you got cold water."

You will not find that Thetford Mines hotel in your Automobile Club guide book. "The carpeting on the floor was a little bit thicker than scotch tape," Molush said.

"And it was all over the walls, too," added Bastable. "The rooms looked like the inside of a van. It was nasty, dirty."

It was the Double A Eastern League, circa 1974–75. "I had Randy Lerch on a trip to Thetford Mines," Phil Johnson, the Reading Phillies' bus driver, was reminiscing one day. "He told me, 'I hope this is the last time I see this godforsaken place.' I bought some post cards when we were there the next year and when Randy [now a Milwaukee Brewer, then a Philadelphia Phillie] won his first big league game I sent a card to him. 'Keep up the good work,' I wrote, 'so you don't have to come back.' I saw Randy in Philly. He said, 'I got your card and I kept it. That's incentive to stay where I am, to keep out of Double A.' "

Still, the Eddie Molushes, the Jack Bastables, the Joe Kerrigans enjoy talking about those days, enjoy reliving the crazy things that happened. "It's a hassle, I guess, to have places where the showers don't work and the fans are ignorant of what's going on and the temperature's lousy," acknowledged Molush. But to most of the kids harboring big league dreams, the hassle, the inconveniences, all the things that add up to baseball in the minors—particularly the low minors—aren't intolerable. Quigley Stadium in West Haven, Conn., came close, though.

Quigley was another Eastern League stop; still is, for that matter. It's a little better now than it was in the '70s, but calling Quigley a stadium is like calling a mud puddle an ocean. Time and again, Eastern League veterans, asked to name the worst place they ever played in, unhesitatingly—and with feeling—named Quigley. I don't know who Quigley is, but the guy should get a good lawyer and sue the person or persons who named that ball park after him.

My first trip to Quigley Stadium, back in the days when West Haven was a Yankee farm club, inspired me to jot down several pages of notes on the place, some of which I'll attempt to reconstruct now.

The first thing I remember was the voice on the loudspeaker. "Ladies and gentlemen," it inquired, "would you all rise for the playing of the National Anthem?"

And so they did. All 177 of them. Grateful for a chance *not* to sit on those old, splintered wooden benches for a minute or so, they stood and faced the tattered American flag waving in foul territory behind third base and applauded politely when the scratchy record ng had ended.

Game-time was at hand. With the utmost care, all 177 of them sat down again, knowing that one sudden move could be curtains for their clothing. Those were big-league splinters in that minor league ball park—at least until the wooden slats were replaced a few, short years ago.

Quigley Stadium, as anyone who is toying with the idea of going there should know, is one of those parks where the most dangerous position is spectator and the most exciting play is a foul pop that clears the rickety, weather-beaten stands. You can see the fans tensing as the ball vanishes into the night. There are cars parked out there, all of them inviting targets.

Anxiously, on the night in question, the loyal 177 waited to hear the telltale sound of baseball smashing against metal—or, worse yet, against glass. No wonder the billboard in the right field corner advertised an outfit called A & P Motors, which specialized in "general repairs."

But if this was a tough park for spectators, it was no bargain for players, either. The startling thing about Quigley Stadium is that it's only two steps from the big leagues and only an hour and a half by car from Yankee Stadium.

The visiting clubhouse was so bad that the young men who played for the Phillies' No. 2 farm club in those days dressed at the motel. To dress at Quigley would have been ridiculous. There were holes in the ceiling of the clubhouse and water leaked—no, poured—through whenever the stands were hosed down. As a result, there were puddles on the clubhouse floor. "What are they doing, growing potatoes here?" wondered infielder John Vukovich as he looked around.

Actually, there wasn't much to see. An electric water heater stood in a corner near the door. Facing the door were four shower heads and two toilets, one of which worked. There were no lockers, only hooks on the wall. No self-respecting college would have these facilities; yet these weren't college kids using them. These were pros.

OK, you say, that's Double A. Nothing like that has to be endured in Triple A.

Wanna bet?

"Did you ever go to Iowa?" lefthander Mark Davis asked me when the subject of bad minor league ball parks came up. "Is that the worst? Do you know how depressing it is to go to a ball park like that? You hope to God the pitching rotation works out so you don't pitch there. I hated that place. The lights were bad (presumably an advantage for the pitchers), but I'd rather pitch against the best team in the league in the best park with the best lights than pitch there."

Copies of that unsolicited testimonial for Sec Taylor Stadium in Des Moines, Iowa, are available to members of the Des Moines Chamber of Commerce upon request. Please enclose a stamped, self-addressed envelope and $75 to cover the cost of having your letter checked for explosives.

The visiting clubhouse at Sec Taylor Stadium was ideal—for a team of midgets. To make matters worse there was a steel girder then angled down to within four feet of the floor. Scrawled on it were the names of players who had smacked their heads against it, with the dates and perhaps a drop or two of their blood.

On a day he was scheduled to pitch there for the Oklahoma City 89ers, Randy Lerch stood up—and gave himself an awful crack.

"How's that feel?" inquired trainer Ted Zipeto, rushing to the side of the stunned lefthander.

"It feels hard," Lerch told him.

At least most of the hotels and motels in Triple A are decent. Most, not all.

"In Toledo," said Joe Kerrigan, "they've got a place called the Executive Inn. It's a box. I mean, it looks like a box. There's no lobby, just a little window where you go up and pay your bill, and that's it. Like a drive-in window [at a bank]. We got in there and we got into our rooms. I turned my lights off. I stretched out in bed and I looked up at the ceiling and I could see a light coming from the next room. There was a space between the walls. I got up in the morning—guys don't believe this; it got to be a running joke about the place—but I got up and I could hear the guy in the next room shuffling his morning newspaper."

Joe Kerrigan, it should be pointed out, is no run-of-the-mill critic. In 1981, he and pitcher Bill Bonham, another player with considerable major league experience, roomed together on road trips with Cincinnati's Triple A club in Indianapolis. To give themselves something to do, and to provide a much-needed service for their teammates, they rated hotels, motels, restaurants in each American Association town. "We put out our own book of lists," Joe said. "We had places to eat, places not to eat. We gave 'em stars. And we listed the best hotels to live in. That was our hobby. We hung the list up on the bulletin board in the locker room."

Kerrigan and Bonham should have been with the Toledo Mud Hens in 1974 on a particularly memorable excursion to Rhode

Island. They'd have been seeing stars instead of handing them out.

Normally the Mud Hens—God, isn't that an awful name?—stayed at a Howard Johnson's Motor Lodge along the highway, a few miles from the ball park, but this time their general manager, a man named Charley Senger, gave orders to switch. So the Mud Hens, then an International League team affiliated with the Phillies, landed at the Biltmore Hotel in beautiful downtown Providence, R.I.

From the first glance you could tell that the Biltmore had been rather special in its day, one of those old-time, elegant hotels. The lobby was huge with a very high, ornate ceiling and a chandelier hanging down from it. It was the chandelier that provided the first clue that the Biltmore wasn't all that it was cracked up to be. As big as that chandelier was, and as impressive looking, it had only two—count 'em, two—light bulbs in it.

Other clues followed in rapid-fire order as the Mud Hens prepared to move in. All the restaurants in the place were closed. So was the newsstand. The good news was that the lobby had a cigarette machine, a soft drink machine and a coffee dispenser. The bad news was that they were all out of order. Come to think of it, that was one good thing about the Biltmore; it was hard to spend money there.

George Culver, a veteran pitcher with considerable big league experience, and Ed Farmer, who would go on to achieve big league fame and fortune with the Chicago White Sox and Philadelphia Phillies, were members of that Toledo team. They took one, long look at the stately, old Biltmore and moved out, choosing to pay their own way at Howard Johnson's. Lee Elia, the present-day Chicago Cubs' manager who was coaching for the Mud Hens then, should have moved, too. But he didn't.

Elia, arriving dog-tired with the rest of the group at 5:30 in the morning, picked up his key at the desk and went up to his room. At least, he assumed it was his room. Lee opened the door and found that it led to a foyer, and another door. Opening that, he found himself in a small hallway that led to yet another door. Ah, finally he had arrived.

The weary traveler opened the third door, turned on the lights and saw two twin beds. Like the clubhouse in Des Moines, they were perfect—for midgets. "No way," mumbled Lee, and he retraced his steps to the desk.

"Got a room with a double bed?" he asked the clerk.

The guy smiled reassuringly. "No problem," he said, and he gave the Mud Hens' coach another key.

Encouraged, Lee went up to his new room, unlocked the door,

poked his head inside and—sure enough, there was a nice, big double bed, as promised. Only one trouble. There weren't any sheets on it, just a bare mattress.

Back downstairs went Elia, a little miffed by this time, and explained his latest setback to the helpful clerk.

"No problem," the guy told him, and produced yet another key, this one for a room on the 16th floor.

Elia headed for it. Early signs were all favorable. The key fit in the lock. The key turned. The door opened. And there it was, a treat to his long-suffering eyes: a big, double bed with sheets, blankets, a pillow, everything a tired man could want. "I thought, 'Finally, a good room,' " Lee said.

The poor fella should have known better. He opened up the bathroom door, turned on the lights, and recoiled in horror. The walls were covered with red roaches.

Elia didn't want to get a reputation as a hard-to-please guest, but he decided to give it one more try.

"I go back down," he said, "and I tell him what I saw, and he says, 'Yeah, a lot of rooms on the 16th floor have roaches. I'll give you a room on the 12th.' "

By that time Elia would have settled for a room on the roof. He was coming off one of those all-night bus trips; he was exhausted.

Up to the 12th floor he went, still lugging his suitcase. Again, first appearances were good. There was a double bed with sheets, blankets, pillows, and the pillows were even covered with pillow cases; the place practically reeked of class.

"Everything looked good," Lee reported. "The TV even worked. So I got undressed to take a shower. I put out my clean clothes on the bed, and I got in the shower, and I turned it on."

Nothing happened. Apparently the reason they didn't have any roaches on the 12th floor was that they also didn't have any water there.

Mike Rogodzinski, an outfielder on that Toledo team, wasn't too crazy about the Biltmore, either. "I called down the next night," he said. "I asked what floor the Coke machine was on. 'There's only one,' the guy told me. 'It's in the lobby, but it doesn't work.' "

Rogodzinski, his throat parched, his mouth watering for a Coke, digested that information for a second or two, then said, "Can you send a bellboy out for some Cokes?"

"I'm sorry, sir," replied the ever-helpful clerk. "He's off tonight."

Somebody—it might have been me—asked George Culver why he moved out of the Biltmore.

"I was afraid the elevator was going to fall," the pitcher answered. "You notice I said elevator—singular. Only one was working when we got there, and when I tried to go up to the room they gave me, the elevator went past my floor twice. I'm telling you, it's haywire."

No, it was the Biltmore Hotel in Providence, just before they closed it down for repairs. All part of the minor league experience.

Crazy things can happen in new hotels, too, as Ted Zipeto found out in Sherbrooke, Quebec, when he was trainer for the Reading Phillies. He'd had a few at the bar before calling it a night. Now he awoke, in the wee hours of the morning, and stumbled out of bed. "I got up to go to the bathroom," he explained.

Easier said than done. "I'd never been in the damn room before that night," he said.

Still, there was no need to turn on the light. Hell, he probably couldn't have found the light switch, anyway. So he felt around for the bathroom door. Thinking he'd found it, Zipeto yanked the door open and—whoops! Wrong door. He was in the closet.

Nothing to do but keep trying. Again, he searched for a doorknob. Again, he found one. This was it. This *had* to be it.

The bleary-eyed trainer opened the door, entered what he thought was the bathroom, and closed the door behind him. Only then—moments after hearing the click—did he realize his terrible mistake. He was in the hallway, not the bathroom. He'd locked himself out of his room and he wasn't wearing a stitch of clothes. And somebody was coming. Frantically, Zipeto pounded on the door of a nearby room occupied by a Reading coach. The man opened the door a crack, observed the naked trainer standing there—"You can imagine what I thought," he joked—and, spotting the genuine terror in Zipeto's eyes, let him in.

All of which proves, travel long enough with a minor league baseball team and there's no telling what you're liable to see.

4

PERFECT PITCHER, IMPERFECT WORLD

Jim Bunning is a politician now, a Kentucky State senator with the dream of making it to the United States Senate. And he's the vice-president of a brokerage firm in Cincinnati. And he's an agent for some two dozen baseball players. The man likes to work.

Nothing came easy for Bunning. He had to sweat to get to the big leagues, and yet after he got there he achieved extraordinary success. He became the second pitcher in the history of the game—Cy Young was the first—to win 100 games in each major league. At the time of his retirement at the end of the 1971 season he ranked second only to Walter Johnson in career strikeouts with 2,855. He pitched no-hitters in each league, something only Cy Young had done before him, and the second of Bunning's no-hitters was an historic perfect game for the Phillies against the Mets at Shea Stadium in 1964.

In the late '50s and throughout the '60s Jim Bunning was one of the premier pitchers in the big leagues. When his playing days were over, he could have done any number of things—gone full-time into the brokerage business perhaps, or taken a crack at radio-TV. The opportunities for solid, good-paying jobs were numerous. Unlike many ball players, Bunning wasn't dependent on the game to make a living. The fact was, to make really good money he had to get out of baseball. Instead, this rather remarkable person, this man who won 224 big league games in 17 seasons and won his first major election campaign as a Republican in a Democratic area, chose to return to the minor league to learn how to become a manager.

Bunning began managing in Reading in the Double A Eastern League. From there he went to Eugene in the Triple A Pacific Coast

League, and to Toledo in the Triple A International League, and finally to Oklahoma City in the Triple A American Association. He managed the way he played, asking no favors and giving none. Jim Bunning called things the way he saw them; in his pitching days if a writer asked him a stupid question Jim was apt to stare coldly at the fidgeting culprit and tell him just how stupid the question was. He never played up to the press—or anybody, for that matter—a fact that may help to explain why he hasn't come close to being elected to baseball's Hall of Fame.

Few big league stars would be willing to return to the minor leagues—least of all a Double A bush league—to learn the ins and outs of managing. Bunning, a father of nine with opportunities in other fields, *was* willing, however. He was one of the rare ones who attempted to learn the job from the bottom up. In that, he was successful. In the five years he spent managing in the minor leagues, and the two winters he managed in the winter leagues, Jim Bunning learned how to manage. But the reason he did it was to earn a big league managing job, and in that he failed.

That "failure" is worth examining because it tells you a lot about a man who is worth knowing about. And also about the sometimes strange workings of professional baseball.

Bunning's first tour of the minor leagues had come in the early ' 50s. He was only 18 when he broke in with Richmond of the Ohio-Indiana League, only 19 when he took that first, long bus ride—a murderous 525-mile trip from Waterloo, Iowa, to Evansville, Ind., while playing for Davenport in the Three-I League. After that it was Williamsport in the Eastern League, Buffalo in the International League, Little Rock in the American Association, Buffalo again, and then Charleston in the American Association at age 24, his final minor league stop . . . as a player.

It's one thing to do it as a young man with visions of the big leagues dancing in his head. It's another to return to the minor leagues as a 40-year-old ex-big league star. Only a special sort of person can handle a return to the bushes at that stage of his life.

In the spring of his final season as a pitcher for the Phillies Jim Bunning first talked seriously about the possibility of a managing career. "I don't know if I have the patience to be a manager," he said. "I'd like to find out."

Among those who encouraged him to find out was Dallas Green, who worked under Paul Owens in the Phillies' farm system at the time. Green and Bunning were close friends—"about as close as you could get," Jim would say years later—and the fact that Dallas was part of the minor league operation made the job more attractive.

"About the middle of the '71 season I was thinking about what I was going to do because I knew I was going to retire at the end of the season," Bunning said. "In one of my talks with Dallas—he was then assistant farm director—he said, 'Would you like to stay in the game?' I said, 'Doing what?' He said, 'Managing or something. . . .' I said, 'I'll think about it.' Then I went in and talked to Bob Carpenter [the owner of the Phillies] and he wanted me to stay in the organization. He said, 'I think you can do one of two things. You'd make a good broadcaster and I think you'd make a good manager.' So I thought about it a while and I said, 'Yeah, why not? I'll give it a shot.' I figured I could finance myself. I had deferred payments coming from two different ball clubs [the Phillies and Pirates]."

But there seemed to be a snag. "The thing was," Paul Owens hedged at the press conference called to announce Bunning's retirement as an active player, "he was determined not to go below Triple A."

"Would you consider a job in Double A?" Bunning was asked at the press conference.

By way of a reply, Jim talked about life in a Double A league, about the long bus rides and the rotten playing conditions and the bad hotels. And then, a flicker of a smile crossing his face, he said, "In other words, if the right situation in Double A arose, I would probably take it, but I don't want to take it. Now that's the best I can say it."

A short time later Jim Bunning became the manager of the Double A Reading Phillies. His goal: to work his way back up to the big leagues.

"I was going to do it the right way," he said. "I didn't expect to start at the top."

Bunning had played for a lot of managers in his time—good ones and not-so-good ones, tough ones and easy ones, managers like Freddie Hutchinson who could look you straight in the eye and tell you what they thought, and managers like Bucky Harris, "who couldn't face anybody one on one."

Jim had a soft spot in his heart for most of them. Not for Harris, obviously. And not for Chuck Dressen, who never recognized Bunning's value as a starting pitcher when Jim was with the Detroit Tigers. But Bunning had fond memories of Jack Tighe, the first manager who really believed the tall, slender righthander could be a first-rate starter. And for Bill Norman, who used to tell the young Jim Bunning, the one who might fly off the handle at any time, that he had "a million-dollar arm and a nickel head". And for Jimmie Dykes, the old-school, "we'll-get-'em-tomorrow" type manager. And for Bob Scheffing, the friendliest of them all on a personal level. And for Frank Lucchesi, who inherited that awful Phillies' club of the early '70s and frequently asked Bunning's opinion about things.

Jim played, however briefly, for Walter Alston in Los Angeles, but little of Alston rubbed off on him. "To me, he was the quietest manager I ever played for," Bunning said. "You very seldom talked to Walter Alston. He was kind of aloof from his players, more than any manager I ever played for."

One manager stood out in Bunning's mind. Gene Mauch knew how to run a ball game. To Bunning—to most observers—he always seemed to' be one step, maybe two ahead of the guy in the other dugout. Gene's rapport with the fringe players wasn't too hot in those days—"I thought it was absolutely terrible," Bunning said—but Jim, of course, had been no fringe player. He and Mauch got along exceptionally well. There can be little doubt that some of Mauch had rubbed off on Bunning as the former All-Star pitcher returned to Double A.

The First Year (1972): Manager of the Reading Phillies (70–69 in the Eastern League)

Ah, the Eastern League. Unlike some things, it didn't seem to improve with age. They had added Canadian teams in the early '70s and the traveling, bad before, became dreadful. There's nothing like an 11–hour bus ride to the snow country in April or May to make a man wonder if he's in the right business.

"There's such a tremendous gap between the major leagues and the minor leagues," said Lee Elia, who returned to professional baseball as a coach for Bunning in Triple A. "People think about the ball players in the big leagues, about all the money they make, but down there is where the reality of the game is."

It was that reality that Jim Bunning returned to in 1972.

"I wasn't going to let it bother me," he said. "I expected the worst. It *was* the worst—and it didn't bother me one damn bit. I tried to make the best out of what the situation was. I knew that people watching me were going to say, 'That son of a bitch, he's been there [in the majors] for 17 years now; why's he doing this?' I made up my mind I wasn't going to let them know it was bothering me."

But it *was* bothering him. Those bus rides, for instance. They seemed longer by far at age 40 than they had at age 20. "My elbows swelled up and my ankles swelled up," Bunning said.

So many years had passed since he last played in a bus league that he didn't really remember details of how it had been—"except," he said, "the facilities and the conditions we were playing under were worse than I remembered."

His team in those early managerial days wasn't so good, either. There was that spring night at Reading Municipal Stadium when a cold wind whooshed out toward the scoreboard in left center that Greg Luzinski had used as a target area two years before. Heavy rains were forecast. At game time a misty drizzle was already falling. No matter. Manager Bunning wanted to play the game. His players needed work, not rest.

So Jimmy Bronson, the young general manager, opened the gates and 211 fans walked through. "There will be no attendance guessing contest this evening," the public address announcer informed them.

Think of it. Two hundred and eleven. That many kids used to stand outside Connie Mack Stadium hoping for a glimpse of Jim Bunning.

Still, the home games were the least of his problems. The Reading ball park was made of bricks and concrete; it was a nice place to spend an evening, nicer than some Triple A parks. But the road trips. . . .

There are people—Jim Bunning among them—whose backs begin to ache just thinking of those Eastern League road trips.

Besides, how could Bunning sleep on that first bus ride to Three Rivers, Quebec? His Reading Phillies had just thrown away the final game of a home stand by making 10 errors, five of them in the ninth inning.

"It's been a while since I saw a game like that," the shell-shocked manager said. "I might never have."

And then to top it off Jim and his fumble-fingered players had to board that confounded bus. Granted, no team had ever picked a more opportune time to leave town under cover of darkness, but not even that Reading team deserved an April road trip to Canada.

It was a horror show from beginning to end. "They didn't have a blade of grass in Three Rivers," Bunning said upon his return. "Sherbrooke [Quebec] was worse. It's frightening. Actually, the ball park in Sherbrooke is a Little League park. They've got to do something about the playing conditions. . . ."

They did. Two years later they put a team in Thetford Mines, which was even worse.

Bunning had no way of knowing his good fortune at missing Thetford Mines, though. He was furious after that trip to Sherbrooke. The president of the Eastern League would hear from him, he said. "I don't expect Veterans Stadium," he stormed. "All I want is a field that's playable, a place where you can get a shower."

In Three Rivers there was no water. "It was frozen," Jim said.

In Sherbrooke there was cold water, but no hot water. There *was* live entertainment at the hotel, though. Trouble was, Bunning didn't consider hard rock terribly entertaining. "My room was right over the steel guitar," he said, his body still vibrating from the experience.

The ordinary, first-year, minor league manager might have stuck his head under a pillow and suffered through the ordeal. Not Bunning. He yanked his team out of the place. "The players gave me a cheer and a round of applause when we got to the new hotel," he said.

And then they went out and lost a double header, 12–1 and 8–0, making a half dozen errors in the process. In all, Bunning's Reading Phillies committed 41 errors in their first 13 games, enough to make the manager regret the promotional tape he made for a local radio station, in which he talked about the team's improved defense. "There's been a change in the copy," a man from the station said that night.

But if it was hard on Bunning—and it most surely was—the '72 season was no picnic for his players, either. Jim was a stern disciplinarian, a man who could freeze you with a single stare, destroy you with a single word. To many of the players, this big league superstar turned Double A manager was unapproachable. Frankly, he frightened some of them half to death.

"They never had a manager so involved in the game before in their lives," Bunning said. "They never had anybody scream on the bench, '*son of a bitch!*' when a guy screwed up a ball. I wasn't mad at the guy; I was just upset that we screwed it up."

Yeah, but the poor guy who made the bad play didn't always know that. There was Jim Bunning, the idol of his youth, the winner of 224 big league games, shouting, glowering and—perhaps most intimidating of all—dictating into a tape-recorder while the game was in progress.

There were some frightened young ball players on that Reading team. They weren't acccustomed to his approach; in many cases they weren't able to handle it. At that stage of their careers they expected a manager to be a father substitute. Jim Bunning was no father substitute, even if he did have nine children at home.

"My first meeting with the club I told them, 'Hey, I got nine kids of my own,' " Bunning said. " 'I don't want any other ones. I don't need 21 more kids. I'm going to treat you like men until you act like boys and then I'm going to treat you like boys.' It was kind of cold, kind of harsh. 'Oh, what a bastard this guy is [they must have been thinking]. He doesn't want to hear anything about our personal problems. He just wants us to play baseball.' "

It was an approach that didn't work with the modern ball player, Bunning would discover in time, and he gradually—yet significantly—changed that approach in the years that followed.

"I was an overbearing kind of manager," he would admit later. "My idea of managing was to train the kids to be prepared for the major leagues. If you could play for Jim Bunning you could play for anybody. If they went to the big leagues I wanted them to be ready to play. I didn't realize the young people wanted somebody a little closer to them. They didn't want a manager who managed the way they did in the major leagues. I wasn't prepared for the way they felt. I'd coached high school basketball. I'd coached college basketball. But this was professional and I didn't think that approach was needed. I didn't want to get close to the players. That's the big thing I remember about Reading. I was too stand-offish."

The symbol of his detached, hard-line attitude was the tape recorder he used to keep track of things that happened during the games. A player would make a bad play—miss a cutoff man or throw to the wrong base or fail to advance a runner—and there was Manager Bunning, talking into his tape recorder.

"The only thing I wanted to do was make sure I would remember what was happening, what we were doing wrong," he said.

The players didn't see it that way. The tape recorder underlined the impersonal approach and heightened the fear.

"Every time I went to that tape recorder somebody flinched," Bunning said. "After a while I would kind of sneak over to it, but that didn't work either so finally I quit using it because I knew it was affecting them. So I started writing things down instead, the way Mauch used to do."

For Bunning, this was all part of a new learning process. As a player he had been his own man, dependent on no one. As a manager he was totally dependent on the young men who played for him. If he couldn't relate to them, if they couldn't perform for him, he would fail. It was that simple, and that complex.

A man like Jim Bunning doesn't change overnight. In the most basic, most important ways he never really changed that much, at all. He remained a strict disciplinarian by today's standards. He demanded professionalism on and off the field. But as time went on he inevitably drew closer to his players, and they to him.

Among the young men who played for him that first season in Reading were several who would go on to reach the big leagues. Dane Iorg, now a .300–hitting outfielder with the St. Louis Cardinals, played for Bunning that year, although not for long. A pleasant, soft-spoken graduate of Brigham Young, Iorg had much difficulty accepting Bunning's hard-line approach; after 43 at-bats he was sent down to Class A. Jim Essian, a catcher who made it with the White Sox five years later, was there, too. A hard-nosed type, Essian was better equipped to handle the Bunning technique, even if he didn't enjoy it. It took a while, but Essian found ways to inject some fun into a sometimes stormy relationship.

"One time he was having bed check," Essian said, "and I hid behind the door. Bunning looked in, didn't see me and marked me down. Just then I stepped out from behind the door. . . ."

Lucky thing he did, too. When a player broke curfew, Bunning hit him where it hurt—in the wallet. In later years, he—or, more often, a coach—would warn the players that a bed check was imminent by advising them that it would be "a good idea" to be in their rooms at the appointed hour. That first year, though, the warnings weren't always that obvious and fines totaled roughly $300, all of which Bunning sent to the Fred Hutchinson Cancer Fund, a practice he continued during his entire managerial career.

Some players thrived under Bunning and built up lasting relationships. Jim's greatest success in Reading involved two young pitchers, righthanded starter Dave Downs, a big, good-looking, good-natured kid nicknamed "Baby Huey" by his teammates, and Mac Scarce, a lefthanded reliever with a wicked slider and a seemingly unlimited future. Perhaps Bunning's biggest thrill that year was watching Downs—whose kid brother Kelly is now a top prospect in the Phillies farm system—pitch a shutout against the Braves in Atlanta Stadium in his first big league start after being called up. Sadly, that was Downs' last big moment in baseball; his promising career was cut short by a bad arm.

Scarce was downright brilliant. Appearing in 23 games he struck out 54 Eastern League batters in 39 innings and had an earned run average of 0.46. Although Bunning felt he wasn't ready for the big leagues, the Phillies rushed him up there—and found out Jim was right. In the years that followed, as Scarce bounced from league to league, Bunning remained the only manager who could get him to pitch up to his considerable potential.

"When I played for him in '72, so many people didn't like the way he managed," Scarce recalled. "I thought he was great. He wanted everybody to do well; he was a great baseball man."

One player who became a "Jim Bunning man" was Dick Wissel, a lefthanded-hitting, outfielder-first baseman who spent a decade in the minor leagues. Wissel and Bunning first met in Reading when Dick joined the club following a stint in the Mexican League.

Their initial confrontation was memorable. "I'd just come from Mexico," recalled Wissel, who now drives a truck for United Parcel Service in Richmond, Ind. "I got on the bus wearing sandals. Dave Downs was sitting behind me. Jim said, 'Mr. Downs, will you tell Mr. Wissel that we don't wear sandals.' "

The next Bunning-Wissel meeting wasn't much better. "He called me up to the room," Wissel related. "He said, 'Wiss, I've heard about you.' I said, 'What do you mean?' He said, 'I hear you like to drink a little bit. Stay away from my ball players.' 'Wait a minute,' I told him, 'I'm not an alcoholic.' 'From what I heard,' he said, 'you've got a real good chance.' The funny thing was, the next four times he saw me I had a can of beer in my hand."

Somehow, from that rather shaky beginning a genuine understanding—even a warm friendship—arose. One thing about Dick Wissel. He wasn't about to let Bunning browbeat him.

"In Reading one time I was going over to get a bat and Jim said, 'Wissel, will you get a bleeping hit?' " Dick recalled. "I picked up the bat and I handed it to him. 'Here,' I said, 'you think you can do better? You go up there and hit.' "

And then there was the night the harried manager was going through a pack of cigarettes and Wissel walked over to him and said, "Damn, you sure smoke a lot. You must go through two packs during a game. You're like a chimney."

Bunning gave him that long, hard, withering stare. "Managing you," he replied, "is what got me started."

The Second Year (1973): Manager of the Eugene Emeralds (64–79 in the Pacific Coast League

Eugene, Ore., was a long way from Kentucky, where Jim lived, a long way from Detroit and Philadelphia, where Jim spent most of his playing years. Come to think of it, Eugene, Ore., was a long way from most places, but it was a lovely town. Drive a few minutes from downtown Eugene and you were in God's country—green trees, sparkling, blue water, fresh air. It wasn't Eugene's fault that Jim Bunning spent his worst year there. "The total height of my frustration," he called it.

The funny thing was, it began as a year filled with promise. Bunning left spring training with a ball club he considered a solid Triple

A contender. But the parent Phillies, desperate for new blood, kept raiding the Eugene roster. Pretty soon, Bunning's Triple A juggernaut looked more like a Tinker Toy.

"By the end of June we had gone from a good situation to absolute, *absolute* zero," Bunning said, "and my frustrations got greater and greater, and my reports to Philadelphia got more cynical and nasty. I was screaming for help. I sent in one report, 'If anybody cares if we win or lose would you please pick up the telephone.' "

They didn't pick up the telephone. But they did send him a sharp letter or two telling him to stop complaining. Jim was going out of his mind. There he was, in this northwestern paradise, sucking in all this fine, clean air, and smothering to death professionally. In a period of about six weeks the big club stripped him virtually bare, taking away Mike Rogodzinski, a lefthanded-hitting outfielder who was leading the league in runs batted in; veteran righthanded reliever Darrell (Bucky) Brandon, his bullpen "stopper"; Mike Wallace, a lefthander who would put together a fine year with the Yankees before slipping back to the minors, and Dave Wallace, a righthanded reliever from Connecticut with a sharp slider and a sharp mind who learned to get along with Jim Bunning, and enjoy playing for him, before it was fashionable.

"I think a lot of guys were [adversely] affected by him at first," said Dave, now a pitching coach in the Los Angeles Dodgers' minor league system. "Jim was such a perfectionist and he was such a successful player, such a prominent baseball figure that it was hard for them to perform because this 'person' was watching. It was like Mickey Mantle was there. It was just hard for them to believe Jim Bunning was their manager."

Wallace was one of the few who wasn't in awe of Bunning from the start. He didn't see Jim as an unapproachable superstar; he saw him as a human being, a family man who had successfully raised nine kids. "You could see the rapport he had with his children," Dave said, "and the respect he had, and the way he and Mary [Jim's wife] got along. To me that was more 'awesome' than having 17 years in the big leagues."

Mike Rogodzinski was another who saw nothing "scary" about this stern-looking man who had come down from the majors to learn how to be a manager. "I always knew if I had a problem I could sit down and talk to Jim," Rogodzinski said. "I've been in his room at three o'clock in the morning talking to him. The curfew was one, but we'd be talking. That's the kind of guy he was. He's one of the few managers I ever played for, anything he'd ask me to do, I'd do. Andy Seminick [Bunning's predecessor at Eugene] was another . . . Jim was a very independent person, and he let you know it, and I respected him for it. As far as I'm concerned he might be the greatest man I ever met. That's why I always got so upset when people said bad things about him."

Which meant that Rogodzinski must have spent a fair amount of time being upset because it wasn't unusual in those days to hear people bad-mouth Jim Bunning.

One of the young men on that Eugene team who had difficulty relating to Bunning at first was Alan Bannister, an All-American shortstop from Arizona State who had been the Phillies' prize pick in the draft. For Bannister, now an established big leaguer with the Cleveland Indians, it was a rugged introduction to pro ball—going from position to position, facing tough Triple A pitching, playing for a bad ball club and a frustrated, uptight manager.

The transition had to be especially hard for a young man who had played for Bobby Winkles at Arizona State. "Winkles told me, 'Remember one thing. No matter how bad you're going, no matter how bad the team's going, this was designed as a game,' " Bannister said. " 'You should have fun.' "

That was what made it so hard for Alan that first year. Most of the time it wasn't fun.

There were exceptions, of course. Like the night one of the Eugene Emerald outfielders missed the cutoff man, a fundamental mistake that drove Bunning up the wall. Next time it happens, Jim told the troops, it would be an automatic $50 fine.

Grimly resolving not to miss another cutoff man, the Emeralds took the field. "There was a pop fly to short right field," Bannister recalled. "The second baseman, Rich Severson, ran back. The right fielder, Keith Lampard, ran in. The ball dropped between them and rolled to the wall with both of them running after it. . . ."

Lampard got there first in a near photo-finish. He picked up the ball and fired it to the cutoff man, just as Bunning had ordered. Unfortunately, his cutoff man—Severson—was standing barely 10 feet away at the time.

"He threw it so hard he knocked him down," Bannister said.

"Well," said Lampard with understandable satisfaction, "I didn't miss him."

Jim Bunning couldn't hold back. "He almost fell down laughing," Bannister said.

Another thing that brightened Jim's mostly dismal year was the arrival of a new coach, Lee Elia. Brash and outgoing and dedicated, the one-time Cub and White Sox infielder—and present Cub manager—was an ideal buffer between Bunning and the players.

"Jim wanted Ruben Amaro," Elia would recall years later. "They told him, 'You can't have Ruben.' So then he wanted Howie Bedell [who had coached for him part of the previous season at Reading], and they told him, 'You can't have Howie.' Then he wanted Larry Rojas [who took over at Reading when Bedell switched to a rookie league team], and they said, 'You can't have Larry.' So he said, 'Then I don't care who I get,' and he got me."

They were a perfect combination, although it may have taken a while for both of them to realize it.

"I thought maybe he was being a little too tough on the players, a little too disciplined," Elia said. "I didn't understand at first what the end result was going to be. But you work with a guy for a while you understand what his feelings are. 'Do everything the best you can on a day to day basis in the right frame of mind and eventually you're going to develop positive ways, professional ways of doing things.' "

By the end of the long, hard season Elia and Bunning were a team—so much so that Jim made up his mind if he got a big league managing job Lee would be one of his coaches. Ironically, it would be Elia, not Bunning, who made it to the big leagues as a manager.

"If you could play for Bunning," Elia came to realize, "you were definite major league material. If you couldn't play for him [in the minors], how could you expect to play [in the majors] before 60,000 people? No way, that's how. Jim was so honest it was scary. He was a straight forward man, and there are very few of them left in this game."

He was also a stickler for the rules, and those rules included a nightly curfew, generally two and a half hours after the game. Most nights, of course, Bunning didn't check. But if he did check, you had to be there or pay the consequences. And for a minor league ball club, those were pretty stiff consequences: $100 for a first-time offender, $200 for a second-time offender. Nobody was quite sure what would happen to a three-time loser, but the thought was frightening.

Bed checks almost invariably followed games, and the players were usually given a strong warning. "Curfew is 1:30," Elia would announce as the bus returned to the hotel, "and it's a good night to be in." Those words meant that come 1:30 A.M., Jim Bunning, in person, and his coach would be making the rounds, pounding on doors, looking for money to donate to the Fred Hutchinson Cancer Fund.

"The reason I did it personally," Jim said, "was that I resented it when I was in the major leagues and coaches would come around half bombed out of their minds to check me into bed. I made up my mind I was going to do it myself, and I was going to take a coach with me so there'd be no misunderstanding. He'll be there to verify what I say. I know Lee didn't enjoy it. Probably none of the coaches did."

But then, the players weren't too wild about it, either. Especially when the Eugene Emeralds limped into Hawaii for a series that season.

"It was always an unwritten code when you go to Hawaii there's no curfew," Elia said.

With Bunning in charge, codes had to be in writing. His team was playing terrible baseball and the sight of this tropical wonderland wasn't designed to improve the standard of play. Sure enough, the first game was another defeat. "We got off the bus," Jim recalled, "and all we said was, 'Gentlemen, curfew is at 1:30.' "

There was no warning. No "and-this-would-be-a-good-night-to-be-there" from Lee Elia.

"I hadn't told Lee I was going to check," Bunning said. "I knew if I told him he'd have told everybody, 'Get your butts in that room.' "

"It was probably my fault we had the bed check," Elia said later. "Jim said, 'Tonight would probably be a good time to have bed check,' and I said, 'Nah, you'd be wasting your time. Everyone's probably in.' Now if I'd have agreed with him we probably would've finished our coffee and gone to bed. But after I said what I did he said, 'You've got to be kidding me. You don't really think they're in, do you?' "

And so they went back to find out. Deep in his heart, Elia suspected that the Cancer Fund was about to receive a windfall.

"I talked him into starting at the top of the hotel," Lee said. "That way if there was anybody coming in at the last minute, it would give him a chance to get up to his room."

Stories differ slightly on precisely what happened after that. Larry Christenson, a tall, good-looking bachelor with a big league future, remembers being on the sixth floor, debating the advisability of going downstairs to get his laundry. "I had two pairs of pants and a shirt sent out," Christenson said. "Mike Martin [a lefthanded pitcher whose brother, Jerry, made it to the majors] said to me, 'Don't go down. You'll get caught.' "

It should be pointed out at this time, in the interest of accurate reporting, that Christenson's version is open to some serious doubt. To put it another way, those who know Larry best seriously doubt that he was spending his post-curfew hours doing his laundry. Nevertheless, let him continue. . . .

"I go out and ring the elevator," he said. "It's maybe 1:35. The elevator comes, the door opens and there's Bunning and Elia. The funniest thing was Elia. He sees me standing there and he goes like this"—putting his hands to his head. "I don't know if he was laughing or saying, 'Oh my God.' Jim looked at me and he said, 'Mr. Christenson, that'll be $100 for being out after curfew. Pay Mr. Elia later.' There I am barefooted, wearing cutoffs and a tank top shirt at 1:35 in the morning and he thinks I'm going out. I'm saying, 'But Jim, really, I'm going down to get my laundry. . . .' "

Bunning was not impressed. "Why would you go get your laundry with swim trunks and a tank top shirt on?" he would say later. "I mean, I'm not going to call him a liar, but it appeared to me he was lying, and he was also out after curfew. I told him the laundry was going to cost him $103.95. He said, 'That's about right. Three-ninety-five for laundry [and $100 for the Cancer Fund].' "

If you've been paying attention, you noticed the Christenson and Bunning versions don't quite jibe. Larry claimed he was wearing cutoffs. Jim said he was wearing swim trunks. Let's hear Elia's version.

"We got on the elevator and just as the door opened there was Christenson all dressed up in a suit and tie, getting on the elevator to go down. He was dressed up to beat the band. Jim says, 'Where are you going?' He says, 'I'm going down to get my laundry. I just saw a message in my box and my laundry's ready.' Jim says, 'That laundry's going to cost you $100.' "

So there it was, the Great Laundry Caper of 1973. Let the record show that Larry Christenson, wearing either cutoffs, swim trunks or a suit and tie, was the first big loser on that trip to Hawaii. But he wasn't the last. "There were a lot of ball players out that night," Elia said. "We were lucky we didn't catch 20."

They caught enough, though, that the fines totaled a rather impressive $1,200. It was Elia's not-too-pleasant task to collect the money.

I'll never forget Pete Koegel [a six-foot, six-and-a-half-inch-tall catcher-infielder]," Lee said. "It was the second time for Pete, so he had to pay $200. He came out to the ball park with $200 in pennies. He was going to drop them on Jim's desk. I said, 'You can't do it.' He said, 'Why not?' I said, 'Because I'm the guy who's going to have to throw the money in a bag and take it to the bank. So you're not showing him up. You're showing me up. He's always one step ahead of you guys.' "

Deeply disappointed, Koegel returned his 20,000 pennies to the bank and paid by check.

One man beat the rap, though. George Brunet, a rather large

lefthanded pitcher who had lasted 15 years in the big leagues, was playing out the string on that Eugene club. When Elia knocked on Brunet's door that night in Honolulu, there was no answer. Next day, Lee gave him the bad news.

"I said, 'George, it'll cost you 100 bucks for missing curfew.' He said, 'Wait a minute. I was in my room.' I said, 'Don't tell me you were in your room. I can take anything, but don't tell me that. I took the bed check myself and I was pounding on your door.' He said, 'Well, how the hell do I tell Jim Bunning that I was blown away on Margueritas and I was laying on my bed and I was paralyzed and I couldn't get to the door? But I was in my room.' "

Elia listened to Brunet's sad tale with growing compassion. "Well," he told him, "let me see what I can do for you."

Up to Bunning's room went the coach. "I said, 'Jim, the guy was in his room. I think I can vouch for him. He wouldn't lie to me. I've known him for a long time.' 'Dammit,' Jim said, 'you know my feelings about that. . . .' "

Lee knew. A player either answered the knock on his door or paid the price. But Elia wanted to see justice done. He continued to argue Brunet's case. Finally, Bunning told him, "Collect the money and I'll consider [returning] it."

The money was collected. "About two weeks later," recalled Elia, "George came up to me and he said, 'Christ, are you pulling for me or what?' I said, 'Yeah, I'm pulling for you because I believe you.'

"So I kept telling Jim. I said, 'The guy just came over from Mexico. He's not making good money . . .' Jim said, 'All right, take it out of the fund and give it back to him.' "

The battle won, Elia returned the $100 to George Brunet. "Thanks a lot," the pitcher told him. "I'm glad Jim was so understanding."

A nice, warm story, right? Hold it. There's a postscript.

"Now the season's over," said Elia, "and we're leaving. Everybody's saying goodby. Brunet gets in his car and he pulls away and he calls out the window, 'Hey, Lee, I wasn't in my room. Fuck Bunning.' "

In addition to being a stickler for curfews, Bunning had some strong ideas about how his players should dress, particularly on road trips.

"We were staying at the Plaza-International in Tuscon [Ariz.]," pitcher Dave Wallace recalled. "They have a bus that takes us to the park every day. Well, I got on the bus around 4:30 or 5—it was a really hot day in July, like 104 degrees—and I go to the back of the bus and Bob Spence and John Werhaas are talking. One's saying to the other, 'You ask him.' And the other one's saying, 'No, you ask him. You're hitting better than I am.'

"I didn't know what they were talking about so I asked them. 'What's the problem?' I said. 'What do you guys want?'

"Werhaas is like 35 years old and he'd been up in the big leagues. Spence is maybe 30 at the time and he'd been up in the big leagues. Two guys like that and they're trying to get up courage to ask Jim Bunning a question."

Spence explained their dilemma to Wallace. "We were just wondering if we can wear sandals," he said.

"Why don't you ask Jim?" Wallace inquired.

"He's liable to get mad at us," Spence replied

Wallace decided to show Spence and Werhaas the folly of their ways. Taking matters into his own hands, Dave hollered up to the front of the bus, where Bunning was sitting in the righthand seat, as usual: "Hey Jim, can we wear sandals?"

"No," Bunning called back. "You may not."

"OK," Dave yelled. "Thanks a lot, Jim."

"OK, Wally," Bunning said.

"And to think," Dave Wallace said later, "there are still people who consider Jim Bunning unapproachable."

Then there was the bus ride from the old hotel in downtown Spokane, Wash.—the hotel they were remodeling while the team was staying there—to the ball park on the outskirts of town. The chartered bus pulled away from the curb with Bunning in his customary seat. He was wearing a neatly pressed, gray suit. His tie was perfectly knotted. He looked like a businessman going to the office, not a minor league baseball manager going to his next defeat.

The driver glanced over his right shoulder at the man in the front seat, right hand side. Maybe he was somebody important. He *looked* like somebody important.

"You know Maury Wills?" he asked, trying to open a conversation.

"I know of him," Bunning replied coldly.

The man pressed on. "You the Spokane Indians?" he inquired.

"No."

A block passed. Two blocks. Finally, the driver blurted out another question. "Well, who are you?"

"Eugene," Bunning replied, and the conversation ground to an uncomfortable halt, resuming only when the serious-faced man in the gray business suit with the neatly knotted tie shifted his position and a spring dug through the seat of his trousers.

"If they're torn I'll send the company a bill," Jim told the driver. If ever a man looked out of place in the minor leagues. . . .

And yet he was learning how to be a manager, doing it the hard way, which was the only way he knew how.

"All he asks is that you come to the ball park and bust your tail every night," said outfielder Scott Reid, who went on to become a coach for Bunning, and eventually a scout for the Phillies. "I always thought he'd be a good manager. I was right. He's the best manager I ever played for. He's a winner."

But the "winner" was losing, and he took it hard. He wasn't the only one.

Dave Wallace shared Bunning's intensity about the game, and sometimes that led to problems. There was the time in Tuscon when Bunning called him in from the bullpen with the game tied, runners on second and third, two out and a righthanded-hitting outfielder at the plate. "I had him 1-and-2," Wallace said. "I threw a great slider, and he reached out like this and he chinked it over Spence's head at first base for a double. Jim came out to get me. I said, 'Gee, Jim, I don't know how he hit that pitch. It was a good pitch.'

" 'Good pitch my ass,' he said. 'It was a two-run double.'

"I got mad. 'A two-run double!' I said. 'That was a damn good pitch. If I make that pitch again he doesn't hit it.' Can you imagine? We got into a big argument right there on the mound."

Then there was the night in Hawaii when the Emeralds— wonder of wonders—had a 6-1 lead in the ninth behind Joe Moeller, who finally started to weaken. There was a home run, and a double, and the call went out for Dave Wallace to relieve. He got to the mound and Manager Bunning was standing there, rubbing up the ball.

"We need this game," Jim told him.

Wallace nodded and stuck out his gloved hand, expecting the manager to drop the ball into it. Instead, Bunning kept rubbing, and talking.

"Forget the runner on second base," he said. "Concentrate on the batter. . . ."

Dave had heard all he wanted to hear. Three more outs and the game would be history; they could all get out of there.

"I know," he told Bunning. "I *know*. Now give me the damn ball."

Jim looked at him, saw the fire in his eyes, handed him the well-rubbed baseball and tried unsuccessfully to hide a smile as he walked back to the Eugene dugout.

Don't get the idea that the 1973 Eugene Emeralds, as bad as they were, didn't get involved in some truly memorable plays. This was one of Alan Bannister's favorites:

"We were playing at home," he said, "and we got a guy in a rundown between first and second, except all of a sudden there was nobody covering second base. So the left fielder comes racing in and the center fielder and the third baseman, all running to second base, and the runner's coming in and the umpire's rushing over. There's a collision, and the umpire broke his leg, and the runner was safe."

What can you say? Occasionally, even on a Jim Bunning-managed team, there's a breakdown in fundamentals.

On top of everything else, 1973 was the year that Bob Gibson of the St. Louis Cardinals passed Bunning as the second leading strikeout pitcher of all time. "It was the talk of the clubhouse the night it happened," Dave Wallace said, "but nobody said a word to him."

The following night, Wallace kidded Bunning about his drop in the strikeout standings. "Well, Jim," Dave said, "you're No. 3. . . ."

Wallace's teammates were shocked at such irreverence.

"What's wrong?" Dave said, looking around the suddenly quiet room. "He's a human being, isn't he?"

From the looks on some of their faces Dave Wallace got the idea they hadn't considered that possibility before.

The Third Year (1974): Manager of the Toledo Mud Hens (70–74 in the International League)

The season in Eugene had been difficult, but at the least the town was nice and the name "Eugene Emeralds" had a nice ring to it. Which is more than you can say about "Toledo Mud Hens," the team that Jim Bunning managed the next two years.

Actually, the ball park that the Mud Hens called home—and whatever other names they could think of—wasn't in Toledo. It was a stone's throw from the Ohio Turnpike in Maumee, Ohio, a good drive from downtown Toledo, which might help to explain why so few Toledo natives were able—or willing—to find it. Hell, it was almost as easy to drive from downtown Toledo to Tiger Stadium in Detroit as it was to get to the Lucas County Recreation Center.

But it wasn't just the apathy of the fans that got you down; it was the league the Mud Hens played in. Of organized baseball's three

Triple A leagues—the Pacific Coast League, the American Association and the International League—the latter was the one that looked as if it had one "A" too many. Oh sure, there were—and are—some good franchises and some good ball parks. The Rochester operation flourished; the stadium was old but nice, and the fans came out. Then there was the Tidewater ball park, clean and modern with an attractive stadium club directly behind home plate.

On the other hand, there was the Pawtucket, R.I., Triple A farm club of the Boston Red Sox. When Bunning's Mud Hens played there the facilities were borderline Double A, at best. The visiting clubhouse had to be one of the worst in any Triple A league, although Sec Taylor Stadium in Des Moines, Iowa, might give it a run for its money. The Pawtucket clubhouse was small, and it wasn't very clean, and it gave off a rather unpleasant odor, probably because the urinals didn't flush properly. One night during Toledo's visit Bunning looked up in surprise as a man, wearing slacks and a sports jacket, sauntered into the Mud Hens' dugout. Jim stared at him as the guy fiddled with the water cooler for a while, then headed for the clubhouse. There was a game going on; what did this character think he was doing?

Turned out, he had a very good reason to be there. He was from the local board of health, checking out reports that conditions at the ball park left something to be desired.

Larry Christenson had started the game for the Mud Hens that night and been knocked out of the box. He was sitting in the clubhouse, soaking his arm in a bucket of ice, when our friend walked in.

"Gee," the man from the board of health said, gaping at Christenson, "what'd you do to your arm?"

"Well, you see," Larry told him, "you throw that little round ball and. . . ."

The man was so fascinated that he left without sticking a "condemned" sign on the clubhouse.

Even the happy moments had a way of backfiring when a person had to wear a uniform with "Mud Hens" on the front. Let's face it. Jim Bunning of the Toledo Mud Hens just didn't have the right ring to it. Jim Bunning of the Detroit Tigers, OK. Jim Bunning of the Philadelphia Phillies, fine. Jim Bunning of the American or National League All-Stars, great. But Jim Bunning of the Toledo Mud Hens . . .

On one very damp night in Pawtucket Mud Hens' shortstop Ron Clark came up with the bases loaded and sent a long fly ball curling down the left field line. If fair, it would be a grand slam home run, something the Mud Hens could definitely use. If foul, it would merely be a long, loud, frustrating strike, just another case of rudely crushed hopes in the life of Toledo's No. 1 professional baseball team.

Jim Bunning happened to be coaching at third base at the time. He whirled and watched Clark's long drive soar toward the fence, curving closer and closer to the foul pole as it went. As he watched, Bunning edged closer to third base—he wanted the best possible angle—and he leaned forward, supplying the ball with all the body English at his command.

Miracle of miracles, the ball stayed inches fair, hurtling over the fence just inside the foul pole. Bunning thrust out his arms in a fit of ecstasy, and then he let out a yell.

The yell, it developed, had nothing to do with the fact that the ball was fair. Mike Rogodzinski, the runner at second base, had also been watching the flight of Clark's grand slam and now, as the ball disappeared, Rogo ran over his beloved manager, spiking him in the foot in the process. "Lee [Elia] told me it was dangerous down there [in the third base coaches' box] and I didn't believe him," Bunning said after the pain subsided.

That wasn't the only time Jim felt physical as well as mental pain managing the Mud Hens. There was the time the bat sailed out of catcher Larry Cox' hands on a hit-and-run play and hit Bunning in the leg. And then there were the other occasions when his friend, Rogodzinski, nearly put him out of his misery.

"In Toledo one night he was feeding the pitching machine [putting baseballs in it]," Mike recalled. "I hit a rocket that went right through the screen [protecting Bunning on the mound]. It hit him in the chest. He kinda waddled back and went, 'Uh-h-h-h-h.' And then one time in Syracuse, I think Larry Gura was pitching and I lined a ball in the dugout. Jim ducked, put his arm up and the ball hit his watch and broke his watch band. I stood there watching it slide down his arm."

Hey, nobody ever said managing in the minor leagues was going to be easy. And besides, some good things happened as the season moved along. One of the best was the arrival of John Stearns.

If ever a manager and a ball player were made for each other, it was Jim Bunning and John Stearns. The one-time football star at the University of Colorado matched Bunning's intensity, his drive, his desire to succeed. Jim took one look at Stearns—they called him "Bad Dude" because of a national magazine article devoted to his exploits as a hard-hitting defensive back—and he knew the tough, young catcher was something special. "Look at him," Bunning would say as Stearns prepared for a game, the intensity, the determination showing on his face. "There's a kid who's not the least bit awed. He wants to do it for John Stearns, and he's going to do it."

Stearns did it, too, becoming the first-string catcher of the New York Mets and a National League All-Star. But then, in Toledo, he was just a raw kid. And he wasn't the only catcher with big league potential on the ball club. Jim Essian was there, and you might have expected a conflict between the two young men. But Essian, even if he was forced to play out of position to make room for the kid, learned to admire Stearns' attitude, too.

One night in Syracuse Stearns was crouching behind the plate when a bat accidentally leveled him. John took an awful wallop and Essian, playing first base, was one of the first Mud Hens to reach the fallen catcher.

Exuding sympathy, Essian looked down at the prone body of the bruised catcher sprawled behind the plate. "Dude sees me," Essian said, "and he says, 'A catcher's got to be tough.' I said, 'Hey, John, take it easy. Take it easy.' He said, 'Essian, you just want to get back [behind the plate].' "

With that Stearns slapped his hands together, jumped up and prepared to resume catching. Essian couldn't believe it. "I love the guy," he said.

Bunning loved him, too. Stearns played baseball the way Bunning had always played it, and the way he managed it: all out all the time. "I don't key down," John Stearns said. "I stay hot during the game. That's the way I am. I don't know how to play any other way. When I play I've got to think of the opponent as my enemy. It's a professional attitude, nothing personal, but that's when I do my best."

Stearns had some trying times that summer after making the jump from A ball to Triple A, but Bunning knew it was just a matter of time before the confident, young man became a starting big league catcher. Later, he would plead with the Phillies not to trade him to the Mets (in the deal that brought relief ace Tug McGraw to Philadelphia).

Triple A baseball had been different when Bunning was a kid. "When I was in the International League as a player we never rode a bus," Jim said. Now, they frequently rode buses. You couldn't tell the International League from the Eastern League without a road map.

The Mud Hens got saddled with some dandy trips: Pawtucket to

Syracuse, Rochester to Toledo. Only when they played the Southern teams in the league, going to such places as Tidewater and Richmond, did they normally go by air.

On a typical junket that started after a night game in Pawtucket, the Mud Hens rolled into Syracuse at 4:45 in the morning, bleary eyed and out of sorts. Their destination was a rather venerable establishment known as the Hotel Syracuse that has undergone rather extensive remodeling in recent years. This was before the remodeling.

The bus pulled up at the back entrance and Larry Christenson jumped out. In a moment or two he was back. "Don't get off," he advised. "This entrance is locked."

"How's the hotel?" Essian asked him.

"The worst," Christenson said. "Sagging twin beds."

"Well," announced Essian, "I'm going to sag right into one of them."

Most of the others were too hungry to hit the sack, or the sag, or whatever it was they expected to hit at the Hotel Syracuse. The alternative to starvation was a White Tower hamburger joint across the street. The mob headed for it, transforming that little diner into a beehive of activity at five in the morning. "Don't let the sun come up," Mike Rogodzinski said as he placed his order for a hamburger. "Please don't let the sun come up." In this place it was advisable to eat your hamburgers in the dark. Besides, there was something disconcerting about seeing the sun come up before you went to bed.

Bunning's job was made considerably tougher that year by the arrival of Jay Johnstone, a line-drive-hitting outfielder who had been in the American League with limited success and would go on to become a fine hitter in the National League. Johnstone could hit. No doubt about that. But he didn't fit into the Bunning mold. Jim demanded that his players hustle at all times, run out ground balls, fly balls, all balls. Johnstone had other ideas.

One thing about Jay, though. He had a sense of humor. Practical jokes were the name of his game, and when you played for the Toledo Mud Hens it helped to have a sense of humor. But occasionally Jay carried things a little too far.

There were times he appeared to go out of his way to get on Bunning's already-frayed nerves. If there was an anti-Bunning article in a Toledo paper—no rare occurrence—Johnstone would clip it out and post it on his locker. Most of Jay's jokes were harmless. One night Toledo outfielder Jerry Martin trotted out to his position unaware that the glove he was carrying was stuffed with peanut shells. Poor Jerry. He turned to face the batter, stuck his hand in his glove and—damn!—in a flash he knew the awful truth. Jay Johnstone, practical joker, had struck again.

Finally, came the last straw. Johnstone was scheduled to bat in the bottom of the first inning. But he didn't go out on deck. And when his turn came to hit, no Jay.

"He was the third hitter in the inning," Dave Wallace recalled, "but when the top of the first was over he ran from right field into the clubhouse to go to the bathroom. The first two guys made out. So we're waiting for Jay. And waiting. And waiting. . . ."

"Jim wanted to know where he was," Lee Elia said, "but Jay hadn't said anything to anybody, not even the trainer. So we sent the clubhouse kid into the clubhouse after him, and sure enough he was in there."

"I'd told the pitcher on the way in," Johnstone would explain later.

But the pitcher had neglected to inform the manager. Bunning had a choice. He could stall, or he could send up a pinch-hitter for his No. 3 batter. Not surprisingly, he chose the latter course.

"Now here comes Jay," Dave Wallace said. "You know that Jay Johnstone walk. Well, he comes out of the clubhouse [at considerably less than Olympic sprint speed] and Jim says, 'Jerry Martin, hit.' So Jerry's up there and Jim hollers at Jay, 'You're suspended and fined $100.' "

"At that point," said Elia, "Jay Johnstone was really a cancer for the ball club. Until he got there the old guys—the ones who knew Jim and respected him, the Dick Wissels, the Tom Silicatos, the Dave Wallaces—they had kept everything kind of at bay. Then Johnstone arrived. . . ."

"A lot of people tried to play it up," Jay said after escaping from Toledo. "He [Bunning] had the authority. It was his show. He was trying to make me a better ball player by doing a lot of little things. Hustle to your position, run out ground balls, run out fly balls."

"He's a major league player," Bunning argued. "He's got major league talent . . . but he really hasn't looked at himself in the mirror. He hasn't asked himself, 'Why was I in the minors, why have five organizations said I can't do it this way?' There's a right way and a wrong way. Jay tried to do it Jay's way. I just tried to get him to reflect on what he did."

Before Bunning got through trying the two men almost came to blows.

"Jay struck out one night and the ball got by the catcher," Elia remembered, "and Jay never ran to first; he just walked to the bench. He wouldn't have made it if he *had* run, but it was just the idea. Now, about two or three innings later, he hits a line shot—a one-hopper to the second baseman—and went right to the bench (instead of running to first). When the game's over Johnstone's sitting in front of his locker and he's got all this paraphernalia, pictures of Jim hanging there, all this cheap bull. Bunning went up to him and said, 'Look, I had enough of your stuff. If you've got something to do or something to say, say it now like a man. Get up and say it so I can knock you on your ass.' That was the first time I saw Jim get mad, I mean *that* mad at a ball player. I tried to grab him, get him out of there. If Johnstone had gotten up, Jim would've hit him."

Dave Wallace remembered it this way: "Jay started questioning him. He told Jim, 'I think you're wrong [taking me out of the game].' As soon as he said that, Jim went right over to him, right up in his face and started. 'I'm running this ball club. Neither you nor anybody else is going to run it. If you're trying to show me up in front of everybody, I'll give you your opportunity right now because I'm challenging you. Let's go.' Jay said, 'You'd love for me to hit you.' 'You bet your ass I would,' Jim told him."

Johnstone decided that taking a swing at his manager wasn't the wisest move he could make. He started to take off his uniform instead. Bunning stood there for a while, then—still burning—went to his office.

What happened next should tell you all you need to know about Jim Bunning. "He's in his office," Lee Elia said, "and he's on fire. I closed the door, and just then the phone rings. There's a three-way hookup from Philadelpia. Paul Owens is on, and [Phillies manager] Danny Ozark and I think [Phillies president] Ruly Carpenter, or maybe it was Dallas Green. 'Who do you have right now who can help us with the bat?' they asked Jim.

"Jim sat there fuming; his eyes were a bright red. I mean, he just wanted to break this guy's head in half, and you know what he said to them? He said, 'Jay Johnstone.' I'll tell you, I don't think I could've done it. Maybe two days later I could've said, 'Johnstone's the guy you want,' but not right then. Yet that's the kind of man he was, and sure enough two days later Johnstone went to the big leagues."

Where he's been hitting line drives ever since. It should come as no great surprise that he and Bunning became quite friendly in the years that followed. Neither was the type to hold a grudge.

At the time, the departure of Johnstone was a blessing for Bunning. So was the arrival of George Culver, one of the most genuinely funny men ever to put on a baseball uniform.

Culver had been a big league pitcher; in 1968, working for the Cincinnati Reds, he pitched a no-hitter against the Phillies at Connie Mack Stadium. Even more remarkable, after the game he sat down and wrote thank-you letters to the newspapermen who had written stories about it. There aren't many George Culvers around.

His humor ws practically non-stop, like those Merle Haggard tapes he played on the seven-hour bus rides. "Around George you can't help but have a good time," Larry Christenson said the day after he was sent down by the Phillies in 1975. "I'm almost looking forward to going to the minor league camp just to see him."

"He shows up," said Dick Wissel, "and the whole place lights up."

One in a million, that's George Culver, or the "Grand Funk" as he came to be known. He lured Bunning out to a golf course on an off-day in '74, and they set up teams. It was Jim Bunning and Ron Clark, an excellent golfer, vs. Lee Elia and George Culver, an excellent golfer. It figured to be a pretty hot match. After three holes, much to Culver's obvious displeasure, Bunning and Clark were leading. The situation called for desperate measures.

"Jim was on the fourth tee," recalled Culver, now a minor league pitching coach in the Phillies' organization. "He was getting ready to hit. I said, 'Hey, did you hear about Danny Ozark's new two-year contract [to manage the Phillies]?' Jim blew up. He didn't hit another good shot all day. Must've shanked six in a row."

OK, so the man probably has a tendency to exaggerate, but he *is* funny in a thoroughly delightful way. Nothing, it seemed, could rob him of that sense of humor. Not even getting shipped down to the minor leagues. When that happened to George in the early '70s, the Phillies had a slogan, courtesy of second baseman Dave Cash. "Yes We Can," Cash kept saying, over and over, in an effort to breathe life into a long-dead ball club, and pretty soon the city was inundated with bumper stickers that said, "Yes We Can."

In the opinion of the Phillies' brass, though, George Culver couldn't and he was sent down in the spring of '74. Undaunted, Culver walked up to Lou Kahn, who was running the minor league camp, and said with a straight face, "If you were managing the Phillies this year, do you know what the slogan would be?"

"What?" asked Kahn, a man not famous for his sense of humor.

"Yes We Kahn," Culver told him.

Here was a guy who had spent eight years in the major leagues, eight years living in first-class hotels, flying from city to city, enjoying the good life. And now he was back in Triple A, playing for the Toledo Mud Hens. You'd have expected a man in that situation to be bitter, to exert a negative influence on the ball club. Not George Culver.

"Baseball's my life," he said. "I made up my mind when I went down I wasn't going to complain about penny-ante stuff. I made it fun for myself."

And for those around him, including Jim Bunning. Thanks to the Grand Funk, the long, tiresome bus rides became sing-alongs. They became comedy shows. They became a showcase for Culver's zany, catching humor. "I try to make funny things happen," he said. "That's the only way to play this game. It's like a family. You live together six, eight months. You have to keep everybody loose. You've got to have fun."

With Culver's considerable help, they all had more fun than they thought possible that year. George went out and had special T-shirts made up. Bright, garish, ridiculous things, they had the words "Mud Hen Mania" across the front.

Mania or no mania, Jim Bunning still ran a tight ship. "Gene Garber [a righthanded relief pitcher who went on to make it big with the Phillies, then with the Braves] and I were rooming together in Syracuse," Mike Rogodzinski said. "We're in bed, and there's a knock on the door."

It was Bunning conducting one of his early-morning curfew checks.

"Who's in the room?" he hollered through the locked door.

"Who's at the door?" they bellowed back.

The sound of their voices wasn't enough. Bunning wanted to see their smiling, innocent, sleepy faces. Again he pounded on the door.

"Gene couldn't believe it," Rogo said. "Jim *had* to see us. He *had* to be sure."

Finally, they had little choice but to open the door for their beloved manager, and Jim peered inside the room and checked off their names. Through it all, his face remained stern, unsmiling. Mission completed, Bunning turned and started to leave. He was almost out the door when he suddenly stopped, turned and reentered the room.

"Thank you, gentlemen," he said with a straight face, "and good night."

Boys will be boys, though. It takes more than a strict manager to make them get a good night's sleep if they're not in the mood for it.

On one trip to Syracuse trainer Ted Zipeto, who lived there, invited Lee Elia to his house for the evening. "I don't care where you go after the game," Bunning told Elia, "but get back here in time to have a bed check."

"So we came back for the bed check," Elia recalled. "When that was done, I was going to go back to Zip's house and spend the rest of the night there."

The players had been well warned in advance. All were present and accounted for at bed-check time.

"Fifteen, 20 minutes after I left Jim, I went down and got in the car with Zip," Elia said. "We were sitting there waiting for one of his friends, and you could see the players coming out of the hotel. Three or four of them came out while I was sitting there. Shows you, if they wanted to go out they'd find a way."

Actually, Jim Bunning was beginning to soften up a bit. It was just that not everybody realized it. Lee Elia was sound asleep one night after a tough ball game. The telephone rang. It was the Mud Hens' secretary. She wanted some phone numbers.

"What time is it?" Elia grumbled.

"It's 11:15," she told him.

"Why are you calling me? Why didn't you call the manager?"

The young lady seemed surprised by the question. "I didn't want to bother him," she said.

Elia didn't really mind all that much. He understood the respect people had for Bunning, and the fear some had of him. Lee had a tremendous amount of respect for Jim, too. "If Jim could ever find the right combination of players," he said one day, "I mean guys who come to play the game every day, he'd have the same effect on them as Vince Lombardi. Guys would love to play for him. There isn't a thing Jim wouldn't do for a player."

"I had a dream last night," George Culver said as he walked into the clubhouse at Syracuse's MacArthur Stadium. "It was the bottom of the eighth inning in Philly. We [the Phillies] were winning. Lefty [Steve Carlton] said to me, 'C'mon, let's go to the stadium club and have a beer.' So we go and I'm sitting there, and I hear them announce the final totals and I jump up and I say, 'Dammit, Lefty, I had another inning to pitch.' "

Had Culver had that dream about MacArthur Stadium it would have been easy to understand how he might have missed the last inning. In 1974—a year before they improved the lights there—it was so dark a man could be excused for not knowing a ball game was in progress.

That was the year Mac Scarce, the lefthanded reliever, came down to Toledo after flopping in Philly. Strangely enough, Scarce seemed glad to be with his old manager and his old friends again. "It isn't as bad [coming back to the minors] as I thought it would be," he said. "You don't have people waiting on you. Your rooms aren't air-conditioned. You take those seven, eight-hour bus rides. But you still have your friends."

Nowhere are friends more important, more plentiful, or more genuine than in the minor leagues.

It was a big day for Dick Wissel. After all those years in the minor leagues, he was about to get his 1,000th hit. Pitcher Ed Farmer was reminding him about it on the short bus ride from the hotel in Providence to the ball park in Pawtucket.

"You ready?" asked Farmer.

"Don't put pressure on me," cautioned Wissel. "I've been playing 10 years and I never felt pressure. I'll give my usual 110 percent. That's all I can do."

"There's no such thing as 110 percent," Farmer told him. "One hundred percent is all you can give."

Wissel gave him a hard look. "Listen," he said, "I always play as hard as I can. Tonight I'll play a little harder."

He got his 1,000th minor league hit, and that's no small accomplishment. A man had to survive a lot of bus rides, a lot of dingy clubhouses, a lot of dreary ball parks to accumulate 1,000 minor league hits.

Dick Wissel never did make it to the big leagues, not even for a day, and that's a shame. The closest he came to Veterans Stadium was a room in Methodist Hospital, a mile or so away. That's where they operated on him for the clavicle he cracked diving for a fly ball, an injury that cost him an opportunity to earn a spot with the Phillies as a lefthanded pinch-hitter. Wissel was one of those players who brought a special quality and spirit to minor league baseball. It was no wonder that as tough a competitor as Jim Bunning came to admire him and respect him.

"I enjoy putting the uniform on," Dick Wissel reflected after smashing his 1,000th hit in Pawtucket. "It's embarrassing to tell people, 'I've been playing 10 years,' and then, when they ask you, 'Ever been in the big leagues?' you have to say no. But I'm proud when people ask me what I do and I say, 'I play professional baseball.' "

Wissel had played the game under all conditions. Eight-hour bus rides were short hops to him. "I remember my first year in the Mexican League," he said. "We had a 25-hour bus ride one way. You put that many miles on a bus, it just wears you out. It's hard on your back, hard on your spirit. . . ."

But he survived all those years in the minor leagues, just as Bunning survived them. Barely. "The players bounce back pretty good," Jim said one day in Rochester, "but the trips bury me. Just bury me. It takes me three days to recover, and by then we'll be back on the bus again."

He stuck it out, though. The frequent light moments helped. Like the time utility infielder Rusty Klobas, one of the free spirits on the team, was sitting at the counter of a Rochester, N.Y., diner, waiting to order lunch.

"Are you a Red Wing?" the waitress asked him, assuming he played for the home team.

"No," Klobas replied, "I'm a Mud Hen."

The girl gave him a funny look.

"Well," Rusty told her reassuringly, "we're all birds, anyway."

It was the last Saturday in August. The Mud Hens were nesting in the visiting clubhouse in Rochester, watching the Game of the Week on television. Joe Garagiola just happened to pick that day to explain to the nation why pitchers don't make good managers, a theory held by many that, understandably, drove Jim Bunning wild.

"They play only once every four days," Garagiola was saying.

Bunning shook his head as the clubhouse grew suddenly silent. "I'll probably get a call from Ruly Carpenter," the pitcher-turned-manager said. "All he'll say is, 'See.' "

Jim must have been doing something right, though. His Mud Hens put together a late-season, 10–game winning streak *on the road*. Win No. 10 featured a pair of Dane Iorg home runs and was followed by the annual team party.

"This is a lot more fun than the big leagues," George Culver lied at the height of the festivities. "Isn't it Erskine?"

"I don't know," pitcher Erskine Thomason replied. "I'd like to get there and find out."

Erskine, now a coach in the Cubs' farm system, was the lucky guy who drew the starting assignment for the Mud Hens' first game of the season-ending home stand. There's nothing like sitting up all night on a bus, then pitching that night.

"Let's see," he said, "I pitched the first game in Pawtucket after a five or six-hour bus ride, the first in Rochester after a six or seven-hour bus ride, and I'll pitch the first in Toledo. Last year, in the Eastern League, I pitched five times after Canadian trips. I'm a specialist. I pitch after bus rides."

That final, Rochester-to-Toledo bus ride had added significance for Bucky Brandon. He was retiring from baseball at the end of the season. This was his last road trip. By three in the morning George Culver and Brandon were in high gear, warbling at the top of their lungs as the Merle Haggard tapes echoed through the bus.

We don't smoke marijuana in Muskogee,
We don't take our trips on LSD,
We don't burn our draft cards down on Main Street . . .

Louder and louder their voices got as the hour grew later and later. It was almost 4 A.M. when the bus arrived on the outskirts of Toledo. The party was almost over. "Bucky," hollered Ron Clark, "you're only 1,500 yards away from the end of your last road trip." Brandon looked as if he were going to cry.

Most player have their names and numbers above their lockers. George Culver didn't stop there. Next to where it said, "15— Culver," above his locker in the Toledo clubhouse were the words "Minor Leaguer" in parentheses.

"George was getting all over me in spring training when the Phillies sent me down," Brandon explained. "He told me, 'You're a minor leaguer now.' "

So when Culver came down, Brandon added that neat, little touch to the name and number above the new arrival's locker. It was typical of Culver that he didn't remove it; if anything, he seemed to take pride in it.

That final road trip of '74 was a high point in Jim Bunning's managerial career. Everybody was pulling together; what figured to be a difficult trip when it began turned into a great one. It was no accident that those 10 happy days were spent on the road.

The Fourth Year (1975): Manager of the Toledo Mud Hens (62–78 in the International League)

The attitude of the Mud Hens may have changed in the closing weeks of the 1974 season, but the atmosphere in Toledo didn't. And it was that atmosphere that Jim and his team had to return to in 1975.

If it was tough for the kids, think how it must have been for the men with big league backgrounds—for Wayne Simpson, a righthanded pitcher who had briefly achieved stardom in Cincinnati; for Dick Ruthven, another righthanded pitcher who had been rushed up to the big leagues by the Phillies before getting the opportunity to sharpen his skills in the minors, and for Alan Bannister, who had such a fine spring with the Phillies in 1975 that he broke camp as the team's starting center fielder. Before long, all three of them were teammates—on the Toledo Mud Hens.

Simpson was a steadying influence on the younger players. Arm trouble had cut short his big league career, but he tried mightily to get back. And along the way he helped the kids who were trying to get there, too.

One night in Richmond a struggling Dick Ruthven, recently farmed out by the Phillies, failed to get through the first inning. Dick was despondent . . . until Simpson set him straight.

"He came up to me in the clubhouse," Ruthven said, "and he told me, 'Don't you ever quit. I went through the same thing you're going through. Don't give up. If you do, it's going to be you and me, one on one.' I'm telling you," Ruthven added when he told the story, "I love the guy."

"He's a man," Jim Bunning said about Simpson, "a real pro."

And on a June night in Syracuse that year Wayne Simpson, no longer the overpowering fireballer that he once was, pitched a seven-inning no-hitter in the first game of a double header. It was a big moment not only for him, but for his teammates and his manager.

Dick Ruthven had been charting the game in the dugout, keeping a pitch-by-pitch record of Simpson's performance. As Wayne approached the latter stages of his no-hitter, Ruthven's charting became scrawling; he was too worked up emotionally to write legibly. The last two Syracuse hitters he didn't even attempt to mark down.

"I told him [after the game], 'As badly as I want to go back up, they should take you,' " Ruthven said. "Wayne looked at me and said, 'Don't ever say you'd rather have somebody else go up. You can get buried down here.' "

Ruthven was also a very special person to Bunning. Perhaps that was partly because the young man often reminded the manager of himself at a similar stage in his career. The worst thing that happened to Ruthven was that the Phillies put him in the big leagues before he was ready to be there. Instead of developing confidence in those early years, Dick developed doubts about his ability—doubts that weren't totally erased until he went to the Atlanta Braves in 1976 and made the National League All-Star team.

That was a confused, upset kid the Phillies sent to the Toledo Mud Hens in the spring of '75, but Bunning knew Ruthven had the talent to become an exceptional pitcher. Helping him find himself became one of Jim's chief projects.

It wasn't easy. "I'm not going to let this game kill me," Dick said after one early-inning kayo in Toledo. "I'll quit before it kills me."

In the course of that year, however, Ruthven actually learned to see the positive side of pitching in the minor leagues. Bunning was there. And Simpson. And Alan Bannister. And several others who treated him with a respect he never felt he got during his first stay in the big leagues.

"The bus trips don't even bother me," Ruthven said late in the season, just before the Phillies recalled him. "I just climb up in the luggage rack and go to sleep."

But there were some problems that major league ball players didn't have to worry about. One time his fiancee, Sue Harper—now

Mrs. Dick Ruthven—was supposed to join him on a road trip in Charleston. It all seemed simple enough. Sue would fly to Charleston, and take a limousine to the motel where the team was staying. One problem, though. Dick didn't tell her which Charleston. Sue flew to Charleston, S.C. The team was playing in Charleston, W. Va.

Dick Ruthven managed to get through all of that. Down here, he had a manager who kept telling him how to win. Up there, through those first two losing seasons in the big leagues, he had people who kept telling him why he lost. "The only thing that bothered me coming down here," Dick said, "is that it disorganized an already disorganized life that I was trying to organize."

Ruthven would succeed beautifully in the years to come, and the process started in Toledo. "I'm having more fun here than I had there [in the majors]," he said one day. "I felt cheated not going to the minors before."

He'd make a comment like that and you'd look at him to see if he meant it. Fun in the minor leagues? Fun trying to sleep on a baggage rack during an eight-hour bus ride from Toledo to Syracuse? Fun playing for the Toledo Mud Hens?

The mere mention of that name was often enough to get him started. "Sue thought they were called the Hub Caps instead of the Mud Hens," he said one time. "I said, 'Hub Caps? No, we're the Mud Hens.' She said, 'That's worse than Hub Caps.' I said, 'You know, you're right.' "

As the season went on, the name across his uniform shirt made Ruthven grimace more and laugh less. "I hear 'Mud Hens'," the California native said, "I think of sea gulls covered with oil, flopping on the beach, dying."

Dick was standing in the Norfolk Airport one morning after a series against Tidewater and a little boy, seeing all those athletes, asked him the name of the team. "Toledo," Ruthven told him. "Toledo?" the boy said. "Toledo," Ruthven repeated. He simply wouldn't say "Mud Hens".

But pitching for Bunning was another story. "I love pitching for Jim," Dick said midway through the season.

"I think more of Dick and his ability than he thinks of himself," Bunning said. "That's the problem."

If so, Ruthven overcame it, building up the confidence he needed to be a successful big league pitcher.

Jim Bunning's 1975 Toledo Mud Hens, or Hub Caps, or whatever, were never able to recapture the fleeting magic of the closing weeks of the previous season. Jim's second season there wasn't at all pleasant. He lost his two bullpen stoppers, Dave Wallace and

Eddie Molush, with injuries. His defense was terrible. The team, as a whole, was short of manpower. Lee Elia was gone, having taken over his own club in the farm system. In Elia's place was Scott Reid, who had played for Bunning and briefly for the Phillies. He found Toledo a little hard to take, too.

"I counted 78 fans in the stands one night," Reid said. "Jim told me, 'Oh, they'll announce 200-something.' He said they never announced less than 215, and he was right. They announced 218."

Things happened in Toledo that would drive anybody up a wall. There was the second game of a double header against Pawtucket. The visitors were leading, 2–1, in the last inning when Bill Nahorodny, the Mud Hens' power-hitting catcher, led off with a double.

"I get to second base," Nahorodny said, "and I see Jim and Scotty arguing."

The problem was one of the umpires had seen an apple flying out of the stands just as the Pawtucket pitcher went into his windup, and decided to call time out. Nahorodny's double didn't count. Bunning screamed and hollered and pleaded. No use. Nahorodny was made to return to the batter's box. He flied out, and another game went down the drain.

Maybe the '75 Mud Hens didn't play very well, but their manager was determined to see they got their beauty rest. Room checks were still a common occurrence.

Dick Ruthven had his first experience with a Bunning room check in Richmond, Va. Dick thought the whole thing was pretty funny. Where, he wondered, did the manager think he was going to be at one o'clock in the morning?

Bunning pounded on the door of the room Ruthven was sharing with Andy Kosco, who was sound asleep. Dick let the manager cool his heels in the hall for a while, then opened the door and gazed out through sleepy eyes. There was Bunning, standing there, pad in hand.

"Are you kidding me?" Ruthven asked. "Is this really a room check? C'mon in. Let's talk a while."

Bunning declined the kind offer. After all, there were more rooms to check.

Next trip the Mud Hens made to Richmond, Jim struck again. This time Ruthven was ready for him. By now, Kosco was on the injured list and Dick had Alan Bannister as his roommate. The minute they heard the "and-you'd-better-be-in" warning delivered by coach Scott Reid, they went into action. When Bunning arrived at their room he found this note on the door:

"He who checketh this room will suffer immensely. [Signed] Al The Outcast and Dick The Dummy."

Bannister and Ruthven were right. Jim Bunning did suffer immensely that season.

Occasionally, the trials and tribulations of managing the Toledo Mud Hens would get to him. Like the Sunday afternoon in Richmond when his team was getting whipped, 6–0, in the top of the ninth and the plate umpire, Joe Searles, called an obviously low pitch to the Mud Hens' leadoff batter a strike.

"It was in the dirt," raged Bunning, who felt that the umpire's primary interest at that point in time was to get the game over with. "You're a great umpire," screamed Jim, his voice fairly dripping with sarcasm. "All you want to do is go home."

The ump couldn't let that last remark pass unnoticed. "And you're a great manager," he yelled back at Bunning. "That's why your team's in last place."

The team kept losing, so Jim called an 11 A.M. workout in Metropolitan Stadium in Norfolk, where Tidewater played, and pitched batting practice himself. Bill Nahorodny came to the plate, took a hard swipe at one of Bunning's big, sidearmed curve balls, and didn't come close. The power-hitting catcher took a deep breath and prepared to crush the next pitch. Whoops. Another sidearmed breaking ball. Another swing and a miss.

Nahorodny was disturbed now. He stepped out of the box and looked at the tall, fortyish man who was making him look so bad. "He's not that good," Nahorodny said in a voice that carried to the mound.

Bunning's next pitch was a fast ball at Nahorodny's belt buckle. The kid just managed to jump out of the way.

"I guess I shouldn't have said that," he murmured after catching his breath.

The series in Norfolk finished, the Mud Hens prepared to fly to Toledo for the start of a home stand. The trouble with traveling by air in this league was that non-stop service between cities was virtually non-existent. On this particular morning Jim Bunning and his players were flying by way of Cleveland, where they had to change planes. So there they sat, sleepy-eyed, groggy, in the Cleveland airport, waiting for their flight to be called. Bunning, George Culver, Dave Schneck and Quency Hill were playing cards; the others weren't doing much of anything.

Finally, the announcement they had been waiting for came blaring over the loudspeaker. But the guy didn't simply announce the flight. "At this time," he added, "will members of the Toledo Mud Hens please board the plane."

Dick Ruthven shuddered. "Mud Hens," he claimed. "God!"

Minutes later they were aboard the plane, and a stewardess approached trainer Ted Zipeto.

"What's the name of this group?" she inquired.

"The Toledo Mud Hens," Zipeto replied.

Ruthven was sitting close enough to hear. "Please," he said to Zip, "don't use that name."

What Dick didn't realize was that the name had special meaning to the folks in Toledo. Take the gal behind the desk at the Ramada Inn. She greeted Eddie Molush as he walked in the door to reclaim his room by saying, "I could tell the Mud Hens were back in town before you even got here. All I had to do was look up and see all the dark clouds and I said, 'The Mud Hens are home.' "

Golly, it made the members of the team feel warm all over to know they were appreciated.

One of the hardest things about playing for the Mud Hens was to get motivated. The crowds were so small, the atmosphere so grim. . . .

Alan Bannister came up with a way, though. For three and a half years players had complained about the fines Jim Bunning made them pay. Then along came Bannister, who went to Bunning with his own schedule of automatic fines and asked the manager to make him pay. An 0-for-4 or an 0-for-5 would cost Alan five dollars. A checked-swing ground ball would cost him $25. Failure to score a runner from third with less than two out meant another $25.

"I'll play in this league for nothing if I have to in order to hit .300," Bannister said. "I'll make it up later. This league can destroy you, if you let it. You sit there, and you watch people strike out with the bases loaded, and you can be contaminated by it. I just had to do something to make sure I was motivated. I'm one of the best players in this league and I'm playing like one of the worst. It makes me sick."

Not many athletes have the ability or the inclination to look themselves in the mirror and come up with an honest evaluation. Alan Bannister was one of the rare ones, which might explain why, two years later, he became a valuable member of a Chicago White Sox team that made a serious run at the American League West pennant. And why he's still in the big leagues now.

On Father's Day that year the Mud Hens were looking for a banner crowd; the general manager had arranged with the Gillette people to give away free razors. Naturally, the black cloud that followed the Mud Hens on their journey around the International League arrived on schedule. An hour or so before the game it became apparent that a storm was on the way.

GM Charley Senger stared sorrowfully at the darkening sky. "What am I going to do with 2,000 razors?" he asked.

You'd have thought a man who was general manager of the Toledo Mud Hens would have more sense than to ask a question like that.

Since there was some doubt that the game would be played, the players turned to the radio for guidance. Presumably, the station that carried the Mud Hen games would be the first to know, but that station was hard to get at the ball park in Maumee. Of course, you could always get in your car and drive a few miles to a place where the station came in loud and clear.

"That's what the minor leagues are all about," Dick Ruthven said. "You have to find out on the radio whether the game's rained out or not, but you've got to be out of town to hear the station."

The sky was so dark, the weather forecast so ominous that Charley Senger finally threw up his hands in surrender and decided to postpone the Father's Day extravaganza, even though it hadn't started to rain yet. Outside the Toledo clubhouse a young lady sat in a car, watching the players come off the field.

"Is the game off?" she asked.

"Yeah," Alan Bannister told her. "It was postponed because of lack of interest."

From the looks of it, the dark clouds were planning to hang around until the end of the home stand. Senger took a look at them the following Tuesday night and decided another postponement was in order, prompting Bannister to ask, "When are they going to build a dome on this place?"

Dick Ruthven didn't take the latest postponement lightly. He was scheduled to pitch that night. He wanted to pitch. The weather wasn't *that* bad.

Much to everybody's amazement, the following day—the last of the home stand—arrived bright and clear. The weather man must have miscalculated by 24 hours. Anyway, at 4:30 P.M. Jim Bunning was standing on the mound, bathed in something that veteran Toledo natives identified as sunshine, throwing batting practice.

"Hey," Ruthven hollered at him, "have they called it off yet?"

"Not yet," the manager assured him. "If a cloud comes over, then they'll call it."

Ruthven sought out general manager Senger to see what the chances were. "It looks like rain," Dick told him, looking up into a cloudless, blue sky.

Senger nodded. "With our luck," he said, "it probably will."

But it didn't rain, and Ruthven won, 3–2, on a home run by Bannister. The eight-hour bus ride to Syracuse that night seemed slightly more bearable.

It was close to 8 A.M. when the bus arrived at the Hotel Syracuse. Ruthven jumped up, smacked his head on the overhead rack and let out a string of profanities. "And you can quote me," he said.

Go through a trip like that and you find yourself wondering how ball players can possibly perform decently the next night. And then you get the answer: they can't.

The first game in Syracuse was a travesty. After three innings the Mud Hens were eight runs behind and Bunning's primary concern was saving his overworked pitching staff for future games. He did it by letting Blas Santana, his starting third baseman, pitch the middle three innings, then called in right fielder Dave Schneck to finish up. The fans got a big laugh out of it, but the night did little to instill pride in the hearts of the Mud Hens.

"I was so embarrassed," Ruthven said, "that when the game was over [an 11–5 Syracuse romp] I didn't want to leave the dugout and walk across the field."

Bannister knew the feeling. "There was an instant I said, 'What's going on? Is this a circus or what?' " he said. "Then in another instant I decided if the ball comes out here I was going to get it if I had to dive for it, and people would say, 'Look at that guy. Eleven runs down and he's still diving for the ball.' "

The Mud Hens' black cloud outdid itself later in the series against the Syracuse Chiefs. Ex-Yankee Jerry Kenney, playing shortstop for the Chiefs, hit a ground ball up the middle. Bill Dancy broke quickly to his left, made a fine stop behind second base and whirled to throw to first. As he did so, his cap went flying off his head. Dancy threw, the ball hit the cap in mid-air, knocking it inside out, momentarily disappeared, then spun out and sailed crazily in the direction of the right field foul line.

"The old hit-the-hat play," said Dancy, who wound up being charged with a throwing error. "I actually thought of batting the hat away with my hand, but then I thought, 'I can't hit that. That's impossible.' "

When you're a Mud Hen, nothing's impossible.

"Twenty-seven years in the game," Jim Bunning said, "and that's the first time I ever saw that."

"Hey 'Dance'," yelped Dick Ruthven, "you just pulled a hat trick."

Bunning saw a few things that season he had never seen before. There was the night in Rochester when lefthander Chuck Kniffin was pitching with runners on second and third. Kniffin was young then, and inclined to be nervous. When Bunning spoke to him it was hard to tell if Chuck was nodding or quaking. Jim had that effect on some people.

Jim Hutto, a one-time big leaguer, was the batter and Bunning ordered an intentional pass. The manager stood in front of the dugout, that cold, determined look on his face, and pointed to first base. Kniffin nodded, then threw the first intentional ball. It was wide, all right. Also about 10 feet too high. Bunning watched in horror as the ball sailed to the backstop, a run-scoring wild pitch.

To Bunning, one of the most difficult chores he had to face that season was working with Charley Senger, the general manager. The two men simply didn't get along. It reached the point that Senger told the local press he was going to fire Bunning at the end of the year, and the story went coast to coast, even though it was up to the Phillies—not a minor league GM—to decide who managed their Triple A farm club.

In the end, Senger got rid of the Phillies. Since it was clear that Bunning wouldn't be welcomed back in Toledo, and since it was equally clear that the franchise there left something to be desired, the Phillies moved their top farm team to Oklahoma City in the American Association. On the surface it appeared to be a rousing vote of confidence for their Triple A manager.

"It showed me what Philadelphia thought of me," Bunning said at the time. "Well, maybe not Philadelphia, but Dallas [Green], anyway. They weren't going to let someone from outside the organization dictate to them who their manager was going to be because they thought I was doing the job they wanted done at Triple A."

At least, that's what Jim Bunning thought they thought.

The Fifth and Last Year (1976): Manager of the Oklahoma City 89ers (72-63 in the American Association)

Tommy Lasorda, the effervescent manager of the Los Angeles Dodgers, tells a story about his minor league managerial days in Ogden, Utah. "The game's about to start," he says, "and the foul lines aren't down. So I get hold of the groundkeeper. 'Hey, Pop,' I say, 'what happened to the foul lines?' 'Oh,' he says, 'the wind blew 'em away.' "

Well, that same wind swept across the Oklahoma plains, just as Rodgers and Hammerstein said it did. Anybody looking for missing foul lines at All-Sports Stadium in Oklahoma City would have been well advised to start the search on the other side of the left field fence. The wind always seemed to be blowing in that direction, especially if you were a lefthanded pitcher and there was a righthanded batter at the plate.

That was an interesting ball club, the 1976 Oklahoma City 89ers.

The roster was liberally sprinkled with college graduates, highly intelligent, interesting men who didn't have to play baseball for a living but rather chose to play the game. Among them were lefthander Larry Kiser, a gentle giant of a man nicknamed Bear who majored in marketing at the University of North Carolina; catcher Jack Bastable, a football and baseball standout at the University of Missouri; third baseman Jim Morrison, who had received his degree from Georgia Southern the year before; shortstop Mike Buskey, an English major at the University of San Francisco who was obtained by the Phillies in a winter deal, and righthanded reliever Dave Wallace, a business administration major from New Haven (Conn.) College.

These guys wanted to play baseball, and enjoyed playing baseball. Sure, some of the traveling was less than first class. That diploma from North Carolina didn't prevent Larry Kiser from making a total of seven—count 'em, seven—bus rides to Canada and back in his Eastern League days.

"Three in '73," said the Bear, "two in '74, two in '75."

"Well," Dave Wallace told him, "I had to go to Hawaii five times. That's six hours one way on a plane."

"O-O-O-O-O, that breaks my heart," retorted Kiser. "A plane bounces a little bit, but it doesn't make right and left turns, and it doesn't stop at stop signs."

Two of the closest friends on that '76 Oklahoma City team were, on the surface at least, as dissimilar as two men could be. Dane Iorg was a quiet, introspective, low-key first baseman-outfielder from Brigham Young. Randy Lerch, four years younger than Iorg, was a tall, slender, lefthanded pitcher with a can't-miss label and an outgoing, at times even cocky approach to life. Their backgrounds were different. Their personalities were different. And yet they became almost inseparable.

"Dane loves life and he loves to help people and he's just a fine human being," Randy Lerch said.

They met in the winter instructional league Lerch's first year with the organization. A year later they got apartments next to each other in Florida, and the two summers after that they roomed together on the road—with Reading in '75, with Oklahoma City in '76.

"My first year Dane Iorg really helped me [in Reading]," Lerch said. "He was on me all the time. 'Randy, you can do this. Randy, you gotta win; you throw better than anybody.' You know, he was building up my confidence all the time. He had a lot to do with my good year down there, and so the next year, when we were in

Oklahoma City, I had it in my mind that this was the year I was going to help him."

Iorg was so soft-spoken, so easy-going that he sometimes gave others the impression that he didn't want to make a full commitment to the game. It was a false impression, but surely it was the impression Bunning got. Not surprisingly, Dane had great difficulty playing for Bunning at that time.

It reached the point that Iorg wrote a letter to the Phillies following the 1975 season, in which he said he could never again play for Jim Bunning. Something happened over the winter, though. Dane Iorg did a lot of thinking, a lot of self-examination. Late in spring training of '76, he made up his mind he would play for Bunning, if Jim still wanted him. Jim did. Their past differences quickly forgotten, Dane went on to enjoy an outstanding season on the way to becoming a solid major league ball player with the Cardinals.

"I was on his butt all the time," Randy Lerch said. "Heck, if he'd get one hit in a game and seemed satisfied, I'd say, 'Big deal. Maybe some other guy who isn't as good a hitter as you should be happy with one hit, but you shouldn't be.' I'd climb all over him, get him mad."

By the time the smoke cleared, Dane Iorg was the fourth leading hitter in the American Association at .326. Later, without Lerch to prod him on, he added nearly 50 points to that average to lead the American Association as a member of the Cardinals' Springfield (Ill.) farm club. But it was that '76 season that got him moving in the direction of the big leagues. During a remarkable, late-season spree the lefthanded, line-drive hitter ran up a consecutive game hitting streak of 24 games. Long before the season ended Jim Bunning had become a solid Dane Iorg booster, and Iorg had done a 180-degree turn, landing in Bunning's corner. "I didn't change," Iorg says now. "Jim changed."

There were some good players on that Oklahoma City team, men with big league futures. In addition to Iorg and Lerch, there were Lonnie Smith, a fleet outfielder just up from Class A; outfielder Rick Bosetti, a free-spirited Californian who could steal bases, challenge fences and make wise cracks with the best of them; Wayne Nordhagen, a strong, righthanded-hitting first baseman-outfielder, catcher Bill Nahorodny and pitchers John Montague and Willie Hernandez.

Bunning's relationship with the players on this, his fifth minor league team, contrasted sharply with his relationship with players on his first couple of teams. With few exceptions, these men understood what he wanted and enjoyed playing for him. For quite a while that season, the 89ers led the league. The crowds were large and responsive. It was a good year—and it would have been better if he hadn't lost Nordhagen, his big RBI man, because of a mid-season trade engineered by the parent club.

"You can actually hear the fans yelling *for* you here," Larry Kiser said. "In Toledo they waited until you screwed up to holler."

If the town was an improvement, so was the league. Mile High Stadium in Denver was big league all the way, right down to the electronic scoreboard high above the rightcenter field bleachers. And Rosenblatt Stadium in Omaha, annual site of the college World Series, was a fine minor league facility. Granted, there were some not-so-good facilities, too. But all in all, that year in Oklahoma City seemed like a big step up.

One thing all leagues have in common, though. Manage in them and you can go out of your mind. There was the night in Omaha when Bob McClure, a lefthander with a tremendous pickoff move to first base, was starting for the home team. Before the game Bunning walked through the locker room, warning each man in the 89ers' starting lineup to be careful if he got on first.

They sat there, and they listened, and they nodded. And then the game began. Lonnie Smith, the third batter, reached first base. Cleanup man Bill Nahorodny was at the plate. Zap! McClure picked Smith off first.

Now it was the third inning. With two out Rick Bosetti grounded a single past second base to become the second 89er to reach first. Zap! McClure picked him off before the next batter could take a swing. If not for the fact John Montague picked that night to pitch a 1–0, seven-inning no-hitter, Jim Bunning might have lost his sunny disposition.

The trouble with traveling in the American Association was that it seemed you spent half your time sitting in the Kansas City airport, waiting to catch a plane to some minor league town. "Maybe one of these days we'll be coming in here to play," Larry Kiser said during one such wait. "I'm tired of cruising through these towns. I'd like to stay a while."

"All I ever see in the inside of airports," Rick Bosetti complained. "People back home mention a place to me and I say, 'Oh yeah, I've been there. They've got a nice airport.' "

Tulsa, Okla., was in the Association that year. The Tulsa airport was fine. It was the ball park, and the clubhouse in that ball park, that left something to be desired. Oiler Park gave the impression of being on its last legs in 1976. Considering that part of the stands collapsed during an exhibition game there in '77, that impression wasn't too far off the mark.

First day in town Bunning checked with Tulsa manager Ken Boyer, who informed him that the playing field was in brutal shape. "He said it's a disgrace," Jim reported.

The visiting dugout was no bargain, either. It made the one in Chicago's Wrigley Field look roomy by comparison. "Look at that first step," said Rick Bosetti, "You need a ladder to climb out of there."

You also needed ear plugs to get through a Saturday night game. It wasn't the baseball crowd of some 1,800 that made the racket; it was the mob watching the stock car races just beyond right field, and the VROOM-VROOM-VROOM of the engines as the cars came hurtling around the near turn.

The clubhouse wasn't as bad as the health menace in Pawtucket, but it wasn't very good, either. The wooden lockers were old and small. The players, and the manager sat on stools that were screwed to the floor. Larry Kiser walked in the night he was supposed to pitch, looked around, slumped down on his stool and murmured, "What some people have to do for a living."

Taking a shower in that clubhouse could be an exciting experience, as relief pitcher Jesus Hernaiz discovered. He was standing under the water when somebody flushed a toilet, an act that robbed the shower of cold water for a few seconds—just long enough for Hernaiz to get scalded.

Without Wayne Nordhagen, the 89ers didn't have a chance to keep pace with the red-hot Denver team that went on a tear the second half of the season. Still, it was a summer that had more than its share of laughs, victories and fine individual performances. Jim Bunning felt strongly that he was ready for a big league managing job. He had paid the price. He had learned how to manage the hard way.

Howie Bedell, then the Phillies' assistant farm director, had joined the 89ers on their final road trip. One night, over dinner, he and Bunning discussed Jim's future. It was agreed that if Bunning didn't get a big league job he'd return to Oklahoma City. It wasn't until a month and a half later that Jim wished he'd had a witness to that conversation.

Major league baseball teams do a lot of peculiar things. What the Phillies did to Jim Bunning has to rank among the most peculiar.

It was nearly big league playoff time. The 1976 Phillies, winners of the National League East, were getting ready to play the world champion Cincinnati Reds. Jim Bunning planned to fly to Philadelphia for the first two games, then return to Cincinnati for the conclusion of the best-of-five series. He'd ordered playoff tickets

from the Phillies for the games in Cincinnati, and they hadn't arrived yet. So he called to make sure nothing had gone wrong.

"I talked to Howie [Bedell]," he said. "He told me not to worry
about it. They'll be sent."

Jim stopped worrying. However, the following Tuesday there
was a message at home to call Bedell. Thinking that perhaps his
playoff tickets had been lost in the mail, Bunning phoned the assistant farm director.

"I made some decisions," Bedell informed him. "You're not going
to be retained next year as manager of Oklahoma City."

Bunning was dumbfounded. This was the man who had told him
during that dinner meeting in Denver in late August that the job was
his, if he wanted it.

"It was my understanding we agreed I'd be back," Jim told him.

"Well, it wasn't mine," Bedell replied.

Incredible. After that dinner they had gone up to Bunning's
motel room and continued the conversation. They had discussed
plans for the following season. Surely, Bedell remembered that.

"Did you or did you not offer me the job?" Jim asked him over
the phone.

"I did not," said Bedell, who himself would get the ax from the
Phillies following their 1980 world championship season. (He now
works for the Kansas City Royals as minor league Coordinator of In-
struction.)

So many things about his sudden, unexpected firing were difficult for Bunning to believe. If they'd wanted to unload him, why
had they waited until a week before he was scheduled to leave for a
winter ball managing job in the Dominican Republic? Why had they
told him one thing in August, another thing—the exact opposite—in
early October? Why had they stayed with him during the tough
years, then lowered the boom on him after his best year? And, above
all, why hadn't Dallas Green, the man who had hired Jim, done the
firing?

The more Jim thought about that unbelievable telephone conversation with Green's assistant the more perplexed and angry he
became. Only two years before Bunning had asked Ruly Carpenter
how he stood with the Phillies organization, and the owner had
answered: "If Danny Ozark crossed the street and got run over by a
car you would be our manager in Philadelphia."

And now the Phillies had elected to run over Jim Bunning instead.

The "reasons" Bedell gave Bunning for his dismissal were that he
wasn't "offensive-minded enough" as a manager—an opinion that in
no way seemed supported by the facts; that he didn't communicate

well with the players—a charge that might have been leveled early in his managing career but seemed contrary to the facts now, and that his desire to become a big league manager was a detriment. The last one took the cake. Of course, Bunning wanted to manage in the big leagues. He hadn't endured those last five years of 12-hour bus rides and bad hotels and crummy clubhouses in the hope of spending the next decade in the minors.

"I don't have the answer," Bunning said. "I wish I knew the answer. I suppose a lot of people resent me. They resent the fact that I was a successful player who decided to go down [to the minors] and do my thing and learn my job to get back to the major leagues. 'How can he do that?' they want to know. 'Why doesn't he go home and count his money? Why doesn't he get the hell out of it?' Not all people obviously, just some people. I feel used. It's as if they [the Phillies] said, 'We've picked his brain for everything he can do. Now let him get out of here . . . That's the way I feel."

Why did Jim Bunning get fired when he did, and the way he did? Maybe Mike Buskey, his shortstop that final season at Oklahoma City, had the answer. "I couldn't believe it at first," Buskey said, "but then when I thought about it I could believe it. I don't think the front office could handle Jim. They didn't like him. He was too honest."

Too honest. And too intelligent. And too opinionated. Or a combination of the above. The suspicion grows that the men up front were simply waiting for the right time to unload him. And what better time than the week the Phillies were about to participate in their first post-season playoffs?

It was—and is—Bunning's feeling that Phillies general manager Paul Owens played a major role in his firing. A third party told him that Owens had said he didn't want Bunning around.

If true, Owens never gave Bunning any hint that he felt that way in their personal relationship. In fact, shortly after the firing, Bunning was sitting in Ted Zipeto's hotel room in Philadelphia during the playoffs when Paul Owens and Dallas Green walked in.

"Paul came over to me, and he slobbered all over me," Jim said. "He's kissing and hugging me, saying, 'Jim, you know how it is, some things just happen. . . .' I got out of there as quickly as I could."

But the thing that really upset Bunning was the failure of his long-time friend, Dallas Green, to stand up and be counted. "The thing about the firing that bothered me the most was the fact that the guy who hired me didn't have enough guts to do it himself," Jim said.

It bothered him because Jim and Dallas and their wives had been very close—surely too close for Dallas Green to assign an assistant the task of telling Jim Bunning he was fired. Mary Bunning felt so strongly about it that she wrote Dallas a letter without Jim's knowledge. The answer did little to solve the mystery or erase the hurt.

"Dear Mary," Dallas Green wrote in longhand, "I've hesitated writing this letter for so long but I hope you'll hear me out. I know the hurt, frustration and possibly bitterness you felt towards Howie and I [sic] on our decision on Jim. Maybe you could care less about how we came to a decision and why, but I'd like to try and explain some of our thoughts as honestly as I can. I explained these to Jim and rightfully so he seemed more upset at the way it was handled than that we came to our decision not to hire him back. . . . I explained my position to him and why I was not the one who told him. I still hold I was right on this judgment, but do realize the hurt he felt because I did not tell him.

"Mary, although I was on the road solidly the last month of the major league season. Howie and I wrestled with the decision as to the direction to take that was best for Jim Bunning and for the organization. . . . All people have plusses and minuses and both Howie and I realize Jim has some strong plusses. Maybe we can see his minuses better than his wife but believe me please, both of us feel strongly that Jim Bunning can manage in the major leagues and I've told Ruly and Paul I feel (and still do) this way. . . .

"I sincerely felt we had to make a change for the best of the organization . . . But even more than this, Mary, I told Jim he was stagnant in our organization and was being billed to the outside world as a 'Phillies man' and this made it tougher for him to get a major league job. . . .

"Mary, I value your friendship and that of your family's a great deal. When friends are in positions like this it never is pleasant for anyone—most people think how terrible it was for Jim but fail to realize it was very painful for me and for Howie also because we do have feelings above our job. Yet we must always do our job and what we feel is best for all or I feel we cheat ourselves and our profession and I won't do this no matter how much it does hurt me personally.

"May I ask your understanding and your prayers as always. [Signed] Dallas."

So they had fired Jim Bunning to free him to find another job, even though they considered him top managerial material. Jim nearly threw up when he read Green's letter. About four months later the ex-minor league manager stopped off to see Phillies president Ruly Carpenter in Philadelphia, still in search of some answers.

"It's just, we don't think you can manage," Ruly told him. "I can't personally say that; I've only seen you manage a few games, but my field guys tell me you can't manage."

Yet one of those "field guys"—the one who was closest to Bunning during his five years as a minor league manager—expressed the belief that he *could* manage, even after the firing.

Confusing business, baseball. But maybe Jim Bunning should be grateful to the people who determined that his five-year plan to become a major league manager should fail. It got him out of baseball and into another, more important field, in which his competitive instincts could come in just as handy.

In retrospect, the Phillies did Jim Bunning a large favor. Certainly "Senator Bunning" has more of a ring to it than "Manager Bunning", unless you happen to be a Kentucky Democrat.

"I never thought about running for anything," Jim said. "I'd been in the public eye for 27 years as a ball player and had no idea I'd ever want to get back into the public eye."

But in Fort Thomas, Ky., where the Bunnings lived, they were trying to put together a ticket for city council. Jim got a call. "If you're interested," the caller said, "call back."

It required considerable discussion between Jim and his wife. "We started hammering it out back and forth," he said. "I thought I should make a contribution to my community. I'd lived in it 23 years. So not knowing anything about it, I committed myself to running for city council."

Bunning had been involved in one other political campaign. He'd worked on the Athletes for Nixon committee in 1968. "We all make mistakes," he would say with a wry smile years later. Actually, that "mistake" was quite understandable. A few years before, when Bunning, Robin Roberts and Harvey Kuenn were trying to get the Major League Players Association moving, they had considered—and interviewed— Richard Nixon for the job of heading it. Bunning spent three hours with Nixon in his New York law office, and the future President of the United States impressed him. "In three hours," Jim said, "you can't judge people."

Anyhow, Bunning found himself running for political office a year after baseball knocked him out of the box. "My basic contribution," he said, "about a month before the campaign was over we decided as a group to send a sample ballot to every registered voter in Fort Thomas with our candidates on it, and to write a personal note to each person."

Since there were close to 11,000 registered voters that was quite an undertaking. In the next two or three weeks Jim wrote approximately 5,500 personal notes. It took him every spare moment he had. "I wrote and wrote and wrote," he said. And then he waited to see what happened on Election Day.

It was a landslide. Bunning received more votes than any city councilman in Fort Thomas history. So it came as no great surprise when the state Republicans asked him to take a shot at running for higher office. Next thing he knew he was a candidate for the state Senate running against an incumbent Democrat in a strongly Democratic area. It was a lot of hard work—hour upon hour of door to door canvassing—but Bunning stuck with it, and in a very close race he won—something not very many Kentucky Republicans did in 1980. Now, the man who would have been a big league baseball manager is thinking about running for the United States Senate. "If somebody asked me now to manage in the major leagues I'd say no," Bunning said recently. "I think I have more important things to do than manage a major league baseball team."

But how about those last five years in the minors prepping for a job that wasn't to be? Does State Senator Jim Bunning regret spending—wasting?—those five years riding buses and battling umpires and getting frustrated and doing all the things minor league managers have to do?

It may come as a jolt, but the answer is a firm, sincere no.

"The only thing I can remember is the guys," Bunning said.

At least those are the people he remembers best. Some of them he went on to represent when they made it to the big leagues. At various times in the last five years Bunning has been the agent for such major league ball players as Jim Morrison, Dick Ruthven, Randy Lerch, Lonnie Smith, Rick Bosetti, Jim Dwyer and Warren Brusstar, some of whom he still represents. In most cases, they got to know him as a manager, and the respect they gained for him in that capacity led them to seek his advice after he left baseball.

Bunning also associated with some people he didn't like during his five years as a minor league manager and that experience also proved helpful in preparing for life as a politician. Jim had never been very good at hiding his feelings. If he didn't like you, you found out in a hurry. He could be sarcastic, abrupt, downright offensive. In the minor leagues he learned to work with some people he would have preferred to avoid. It was a lesson a politician has to learn.

"There are a lot of people I don't like to associate with in politics," he said, "but I'm able to do it and keep a straight face and do my thing and not be offensive, where I couldn't do that a while back . . . It's my personality that I'm sharp and abrasive. I can't help it. That's just me. If I think that somebody's wrong and I'm right I'm not too easy to live with."

But, with the help of that humbling minor league experience, he has learned to live with it.

His firing by the Phillies still rankles him. "There always will be [bitterness]," he said. "I react poorly to things that are handled that way."

And yet, in a way, the firing—and, in particular, the way his long-time friend Dallas Green went about doing it—prepared him for an incident early in his career as a State Senator. A battle developed over reapportionment and "a friend, a fellow Republican" turned on Jim in the heat of the battle. "I told him," said Bunning, " 'You're not a friend. I don't want you to ever be called a friend again. I'll associate with you and work with you, but don't you ever try to be my friend.' That's just me. I can't help it. I found that out in professional baseball. It was a repeat of when I was fired—by a friend who didn't have the guts to come up and say it himself. I'm a loyal person, and when I trust someone as a friend and they betray the trust, boy, I react badly."

Bunning frequently talks about his "pleasant memories" of managing in the minor leagues, and of the close relationships developed in the minors. Like most men who went through the minor league experience as a player, then made it to the big leagues Jim has grown apart from most of the friends he made in those early, formative years. "I think," he said, "the minor league players who do not get to the major leagues make a heckuva lot closer and more lasting relationships than those who do. Once you get to the big leagues, you kind of split up. Some of the closest relationships I had in the major leagues—Frank Bolling and Rocky Colavito were my roommates longer than anyone—I very seldom hear from or see any more. The closeness that you once had disappears. But I still hear from some of the guys I managed. I think it's a spirit of trying to get there [that makes minor leaguers so close]."

In Jim Bunning's case, he batted .500. As a player, he got there. As a manager, he didn't. It might have been a blessing in disguise.

5

LAUGH, CLOWN, LAUGH

He is a clown, a funny-looking, 62-year-old man with a big nose who wears a baseball uniform with a questionmark on the back and baggy pants. And he is as much a part of minor league baseball as early-morning plane trips and all-night bus rides and ball parks with dim lights and crummy, undersized clubhouses, and bad hotels.

The minor leagues owe a lot to Max Patkin.

No man connected with baseball puts up with more than he does. Do you think making people laugh, putting on that ridiculous uniform, taking pratfalls in the coaches' box, doing all the things that Patkin does more than 70 times a summer are easy? Not when the entire season is one, long road trip made up of one-night stands. Not when you show up in a town and wonder why nobody's at the airport to pick you up, and find out that your show has been canceled because they never received your signed contract in the mail. Not when you have to put up with all the grief, all the loneliness, all the headaches that are part of being the Clown Prince of Baseball.

He was a pitcher once upon a time—a minor league pitcher with a high kick and a pretty darn good fast ball. "I was always a goof off the field," he said. "I liked to clown around when I wasn't pitching."

As time went on, he did less and less pitching, more and more clowning. "You know how it is," he said. "They call it 'color' if you're great [and you do funny things]. If you're lousy, they call you a clown."

They've been calling him that for 37 years, from coast to coast, from border to border, and beyond. They know him in Billings, Mont., and in El Paso, Tex., in Vancouver and in Mexico City. And in some towns you probably never heard of.

"They talk about consecutive game streaks by guys like Pete Rose and Steve Garvey," Patkin said. "Sure, it's fantastic. But these guys live first class, they travel by plane, they stay in the best hotels. I've done over 4,000 shows [in minor league ball parks] and traveled over 4 million miles and I've never missed a performance. *That's* phenomenal. I've been sick, had fever up to 103, 104 so many times; I've had a broken rib, broken toes, broken fingers. I've had hamstring pulls. I've had trouble with my knees. I've had mental problems. To go out there and try to make people laugh is hard when you're not mentally up to it."

But he still does it, and he plans to keep on doing it as long as his health permits. Have clown suit, will travel: That's been the story of a career that spans five decades. He began doing all those nutty things on the baseball field in the '40s and he's going strong in the '80s.

Not as strong as the San Diego Chicken and some of those other "barnyard characters" who frequent ball parks, mind you. The Chicken, Max discovered, makes $4,000 plus expenses for a minor league appearance. "He'll make between half a million and $600,000 this year in baseball alone," the clown said, not bothering to mask the envy he felt.

Patkin gets anywhere from $600 to $1,000 for a performance (although his expenses usually come out of that). With 75 minor league bookings in '82, Max should gross somewhere in the neighborhood of $50,000. It isn't a bad neighborhood, but no man connected with baseball works any harder.

It all started during the Second World War. Patkin was stationed in Honolulu, pitching for a service team called Aiea Barracks. "I only weighed 145, 150 pounds," he said. "I was 6–3, long and lean. They used to laugh at me, the servicemen."

You couldn't blame them. There was the big nose, and the skinny neck, and the supple body, and that flair for the ridiculous when he was in the coaches' box.

"One time they brought me in in an ambulance to first base," Max said. "Everybody was asking, 'Where's Max Patkin? Where's the clown? Where's the coach?' Then here comes a siren and the center field fence opens and here comes an ambulance. They brought me right into the coaches' box all wrapped in bandages, head to foot. They put me down on a stretcher. I got up with crutches and I started coaching. Then I took my bandages off and they all started cheering. They went crazy. It was the funniest thing you ever saw. From then on, I started to do all these goofy things on the [coaching] lines."

Little did he know he'd still be doing them four decades later.

Max' biggest day in Hawaii, though, involved pitching, not clowning. "We were playing the 7th Air Force team," he said. "They had Joe DiMaggio in center, Ferris Fain on first base, Joe Gordon on second base, Gerry Priddy at shortstop. . . ."

Patkin got the nod to pitch against that all-star lineup, no small assignment for a man whose professional baseball experience consisted of two years in the Wisconsin State League.

"Red Ruffing was pitching against me that day," Max said. "I struck DiMaggio out the first time up; I had about six, seven strikeouts that game. I struck out Gerry Priddy three times. I had a good fast ball. When I lifted that leg up in the air, reared back and threw that ball, them guys would say, 'Shit!' "

It must have been a rare experience having that funny-looking fella with the big nose and the skinny neck firing fast balls at you. "First time up, DiMaggio was too busy wondering what I was," Patkin said. "He looked at me and he couldn't get it all together. I slipped a fast ball by him. I really did. The second time up he almost knocked the third baseman into left field with a single. Third time up I threw him a change. He hit it into the South Pacific almost. I think they call it memorabilia. It's still bounding around out there somewhere. I followed him around the bases from the pitcher's mound. When we got to home plate, everybody came out of the dugout—*his* dugout. They were shaking *my* hand, and about 20 of them walked me back to the mound, patting me on the back. And there was DiMaggio sitting in the empty dugout."

They didn't call him Max Patkin over there. And the "Clown Prince of Baseball" tag hadn't been born yet. They called him "Elmer" because he reminded them of the character Joe E. Brown played in a comedy baseball picture, "Elmer The Great." Max went along with the gag. [The gag hasn't been invented that Max won't go along with.] He signed autographs "Max (Elmer) Patkin".

Besides being a very funny fellow, he was an accomplished dancer. Max performed with Ray Anthony's band in Hawaii, and with Bob Crosby's band. "I used to dance on battleships and in service clubs," he said. "I did eccentric, comedy dancing—like Ray Bolger."

He was so much like Ray Bolger that some folks thought he *was* Ray Bolger. Invited to perform at the University of Hawaii, he walked into the gym, where the show was to be held, and saw a big sign, "Welcome Ray Bolger". Max, overcome with honesty, went to see the president of the university and revealed the awful truth: he wasn't Ray Bolger. Heck, to this day he doesn't know all the words to "Once In Love With Amy".

The president was most understanding. "Well," he told Max, "if anybody asks just say you use the nickname 'Ray Bolger', say they call you that."

The ersatz Ray Bolger was introduced and the 500 or so spectators gave him a big hand. Patkin did his comedy dance. "To this day," he said, "I guess they think I'm Ray Bolger."

When he wasn't pitching, and he wasn't clowning, and he wasn't dancing, Max gambled. "Gambling killed me," he said. "Buried me. I never bet horses, but I bet everything else. You name it. Golf, gin rummy, everything that moved or crawled. I've given up gambling completely now. Honest to God, I don't bet baseball, basketball. . . ."

But in those days he bet wildly, and a clown and his money are soon parted. There were times, though, when he won. One such occasion involved a table tennis showdown with Bobby Riggs.

"Bobby Riggs was a hustler," Max said. "He used to shoot baskets. He could shoot fouls better than anybody I ever saw. He played all those great athletes stationed over there, and he won enough money to buy himself a car."

Riggs was also an accomplished table tennis hustler. Fearless Patkin took him on. "He gave me 13 points, which was too many," Max said. "I was playing him for $100 a game. I beat him for 2,000 bucks. To this day he owes me $1,500. He always says, 'I'll take you to dinner, Max.' "

Poor Max. The losses, he paid. The winnings, he's still waiting to collect. And his pitching days were numbered. "I had a bone chip operation on my elbow," he said. "I got hurt in Green Bay, Wisc., my second year of pro ball. A guy slid into me at home plate when I went to cover and tore up my right arm."

Patkin was a free agent when the war ended, but that was no era for free agents in baseball—least of all free agents with funny faces and sore arms. Max signed with Cleveland's Class A farm club in Wilkes-Barre, Pa. His arm still wasn't coming around, though, and the president of the club, Mike McNally, got a bright idea. "He started telling Dick Porter [the manager], 'Why don't you put him out on the coaching lines, where he does all that goofy stuff?' " Max said.

Porter obliged, and Patkin immediately became a hit. "I built up a great rapport with the fans," he said, "but I was getting angry. I didn't want to do it. I told Dick, 'I want to pitch.' He said, 'You've got a bad arm.' I said, 'I know, but it's starting to feel a little better.' "

While Max was trying to talk his way back to the pitcher's mound, Mike McNally came up with another idea. Connie Mack's Philadelphia Athletics were playing an exhibition game against the Harrisburg Senators of the Interstate League. Since Wilkes-Barre was on the road, Patkin's services as a clown were not needed. "Let's go down there [to Harrisburg]," McNally said to Max. "Do a couple of innings."

Patkin went. "Connie Mack was sitting with the dignitaries in the lower box seats," Max said. "I did my routine and he was hysterical. He almost fell off his seat."

It was becoming increasingly evident that Max had a better chance to make people fall down laughing than strike out swinging. His popularity as a clowning first base coach was such that the Wilkes-Barre club decided to give Patkin "a night". Max was thrilled, doubly so when he saw the size of the crowd that turned out to honor him.

"They had 400 or 500 people the night before," he said. "The night I was honored they had 5,500—a full house, standing room only. My folks came up from Philadelphia. . . . Dick Porter said to Mike McNally, 'I think we ought to pitch him.' We were playing the Hartford team for second place [in the Eastern League]. Scranton was running away with the league that year.

"Anyway, he pitches me. I look down at the bullpen, there's a guy warming up. I ain't thrown the first pitch yet. I'm cussing. 'That's a lot of gosh darn guts,' I'm saying. You want to know something? I won that damn game. I went the full nine and I won, 6–5."

Ah, but that was nothing compared to the highlight of the evening: the Max Patkin Night ceremonies at home plate. Nowadays, a guy gets a night and they give him a car, a stereo, a television set, a video cassette recorder and an expense-paid trip to Acapulco. But this was 1946 and to be honest about it, Patkin didn't do quite that well.

"They gave me a night," he said, "they advertised it, they brought me up to home plate, and they gave me a plaque. That's all, a plaque. A piece of crap. I don't even have it any more. I must've thrown it away, I was so mad."

Next day, as Max roamed around Wilkes-Barre, people stopped him, shook his hand, told him what a great night it had been and wanted to know what he got. "They figured I got money or something," Patkin said.

Max, of course, set them straight in a hurry. All he got on his gala night was a crummy plaque. "The word got back to Mike McNally," he said.

McNally had spent 10 years in the big leagues with the Red Sox, Yankees and Senators. He'd been in three World Series, roomed with Babe Ruth. He was a big man in town and he didn't like the idea that some clown was going around insinuating that he was cheap.

"He called me in the office," Patkin recalled. " 'What's this I hear about you saying you should have gotten something on your night?' he said. I said, 'Yeah, I told people that.' He said, 'I'll tell you what I'm going to give you. I'm going to give you your release.' And that's what he gave me."

Oh well, at least—like the plaque—it was suitable for framing.

Poor Max thought it was the end of his career. Instead, it was the beginning. A couple of days later he got a call from the Harrisburg Senators. They were playing another big league exhibition—this one against the Cleveland Indians—and they offered Patkin $100 to repeat the routine that had reduced Connie Mack to helpless laughter. Max, of course, did it. Lou Boudreau, player-manager of the Indians, told Bill Veeck, their new owner, about him. Never one to let a promising promotion slip by, Veeck summoned Patkin to his office.

"He says, 'I'd like to sign you, put you on before the game,' " Max recalled. "Boudreau says, 'No, I want him as my first base coach. I want him to come out there for two innings of every game, that's all.' Bill Veeck says, 'Are you sure?' "

Boudreau was sure. Along the way, Patkin would run into several old-line baseball men who objected strenuously to having a clown perform while a game was in progress. Not Boudreau, though. And surely not Veeck. The '46 Indians were a sixth-place ball club that finished 18 games under .500 and 36 games out of first place. The fans in Cleveland needed a good laugh.

"The first night I went out there to perform, it was hard to believe how scared I was," Patkin said. "It was a Sunday afternoon game. They're honoring Ty Cobb, Tris Speaker and Babe Ruth. They've got 80,000 people there. I never saw so many people in my life. . . ."

Not even Max Patkin Night in Wilkes-Barre had drawn *that* well. The flop sweat appeared on Max' forehead, started the long journey down his nose. "I was scared to death," he said. "The first inning went by, the second, the third. The ball players are all coming over to me. 'When are you going out there, Max? C'mon, get out there.' "

Finally, about the fifth inning, Max made his appearance. The act he did then before that huge crowd in Cleveland wasn't much different from the act he does now in front of more modest gatherings in Davenport, Iowa, and Reading, Pa. One sure-fire laugh getter was to stand just behind the first baseman and mimic his every move while he warmed up the infielders.

"I go through this routine," Max said, "and the crowd went ape."

Some of the finest first basemen in the business would play straight man for Patkin's pantomime routine that year. Ferris Fain did it. "He was great," Max enthused. Hank Greenberg did it.

Along the way, of course, Max would improvise. When the Indians were playing the Yankees and Joe DiMaggio came off the field at the end of an inning, Max would follow him into the dugout. "Little Phil Rizzuto, he'd laugh like hell," Patkin said.

Rizzuto had a sense of humor. His Yankee teammate, Frank Crosetti, didn't. "Rizzuto almost got Crosetti to kill me," Max said.

"One time at Yankee Stadium—we got a full house, Bob Feller's pitching against Hank Borowy—Rizzuto came out to me and he says, 'Max, Crosetti's got a great sense of humor. He's got this habit. When he goes over to third base he picks up his glove [in those days, players left their gloves on the field] and he spins it. He'll get a kick out of it if you follow him to third base.' "

It sounded like a swell idea to Patkin. "I didn't know that Crosetti was a red-ass," he said. "I didn't know he hated guys like me. So now I follow him. He knows I'm in back of him because he hears the fans laughing. He can feel my breath. He got to third base to pick up the glove and instead of spinning it, he wheeled around and hit me right across the nose. I thought he broke it. He knocked me right on my ass. Everybody in the stands was hysterical. Rizzuto, he couldn't play shortstop. He's standing out there, hiding behind that glove, laughing. And I'm standing in the dugout holding my nose."

Max, you might say, had his hands full.

There would be other big league appearances in the years that followed. When Veeck bought the St. Louis Browns, he sent out the call for Patkin. Max joined them in 1951, on the day that Eddie Gaedel, a midget, was sent up as a pinch-hitter in one of Veeck's best-remembered stunts. "I always say, 'My nose weighed more than the midget,' " Patkin said.

Traveling with a major league team was a joyride. "It was like heaven to me," Max said. "You traveled by train [in those days]. You lived great. The ball players all knew me. I had people to live with and talk with. Johnny Berardino [an infielder who went on to become a TV soap opera star] was my roomie many times."

And the ball club was so bad one extra clown, more or less, hardly mattered.

But Max' major league clowning days were cut short by Veeck's decision to hire Rogers Hornsby as his manager. "They brought him in the last game of the season," Max said. "He was in the pressbox and I'm going through my routine. Writers told me what he said. The first thing he did, he pointed down there [to the first base coach's box] and he said, '*That's* got to go.' So it was either Rogers Hornsby or Max Patkin." In case you wondered, Max lost.

He had toured the minor leagues in the late '40s with Eddie Gottlieb, the owner-coach of the pro basketball Philadelphia Warriors, handling his bookings. Now he returned to the minors, where he has been ever since—with the exception of an occasional late-season appearance for a struggling big league team in need of a boost at the gate.

Traveling with a big league team had been fun. Traveling alone from minor league town to minor league town, sitting in a bus terminal in the wee hours of the morning was no fun, at all.

"I'd get to the point where I'd almost want to commit suicide," Max said. "I'm talking about years ago [the early '70s] when I was having problems with my ex-wife."

There was a Mexican tour that opened with a two-night stand in Mexico City. Just before he left home, Patkin's wife told him she was leaving him. "It almost broke my heart," Max said.

The show must go on. He flew to Mexico City, went to the ball park, changed into that baggy-pants baseball uniform and suddenly it hit him. "I just came apart," he said. "I'm laying in the clubhouse, getting ready to go on, and I got the shakes."

Bobby Maduro, one-time owner of the Havana Sugar Kings in the pre-Castro years, handled Latin-American baseball for the commissioner's office, and he was at the stadium that night. "I told him I couldn't go on," Max said. "Luckily, the game was called on account of rain."

He was ready to fly home, ready to give up a week's worth of bookings. Maduro convinced him to stay. "Bobby took me out to dinner that night," Max said. "I couldn't eat. I just had some soup. But I went on the next night and the show was terrific. Once I get on the coaching lines I forget about the whole world. It's like the whole world stops. I go out there, I become another person."

One person travels by himself, sits in hotel rooms, stares at the four walls and grows depressed. The other person puts on a funny uniform and makes people laugh.

Max Patkin likes people. He needs people. Being alone for long periods of time is sheer torture to the man. One day, a few years ago, he made a long-distance phone call from a phone booth in a bus terminal in Baton Rouge, La., to a newspaper office in Philadelphia. Loneliness had caught up with him, nearly overwhelmed him. He needed to hear a familiar voice. It was sad . . . and revealing. The public saw only Max Patkin, the clown. This was Max Patkin, the man. His next stop was Lafayette, La., but his bus wasn't scheduled to leave for another hour. Time was dragging, the way it almost always does for him on those long, lonely trips through the minor leagues.

Traveling can be tough on baseball players, particularly in the low minors. And it can be even tougher on umpires. But at least players travel with other players, and umpires travel with other umpires. A baseball clown travels alone, and nothing is tougher than that.

"People think I love this work," Patkin said that day over the phone. "Nobody knows the mental anguish I go through between bus stops and plane stops. Nobody knows the mental anguish I go through sitting in a hotel room by myself."

His worst experience came in the '50s in Chicago. Eddie Gottlieb had booked him to do a sports show that was to run for 53 days. Max would be appearing with such big names as Ted Williams and Jim Thorpe at $150 a show.

"I had never done an indoor show," Max said, "and I had a leg with a boil about that big on it, and it was bothering the hell out of me."

Depression was setting in fast as show-time approached on opening night. "I was scared to death about going on," he said. "I'm thinking, 'This is my first one. I've got to do 52 more.' I said, 'Geez, I don't know how I'm going to do this.' "

They had stuck him in a room on the outskirts of Chicago. The longer he sat in that room the more depressed he became. "I actually stuck my head into an oven and tried to commit suicide," he said. "I swear to God, I actually stuck my head in the oven for two or three minutes. Then I pulled it out. I got scared. I couldn't breathe. I didn't want to die *that* much."

Now, for the most part, he only performs on weeknights, returning home on weekends to see his daughter, Joy, and his brother, Eddie. The first couple of days of each road trip are the toughest. As the weekend approaches, his spirits rise dramatically. But happy or sad, he does his routine.

"Sitting in the bus stations or the train stations is murder," he said. And sometimes making people laugh is murder, too. It took Max years to gain the widespread acceptance that he enjoys today. And even now there are managers—and an occasional pitcher or two—who would just as soon not see his smiling, funny face.

"It was tough [in the early years], let me tell you, going around to these towns, trying to get on the coaching lines," he said. "This kind of stuff was unheard of then."

The baseball comics had always done pre-game acts. Until Patkin arrived on the scene, nobody had dared to go for laughs during a ball game.

"I had a lot of trouble," he said. "I had to cancel out of some places [because a manager refused to give him permission to perform], jump on the train, go to the next city. I had to clear it with the umpires. I had to clear it with the manager of the other ball club. By the time I got done clearing it, I was exhausted. Then I'd go out there and I'd have to be funny. Luckily, I looked twice as funny as I do today. I was so skinny then and I had this old-fashioned bathing suit underneath. I'd lose my pants and run around with the bathing suit. It was strictly stupid. To be funny, it *had* to be stupid. If I had class, there'd be no act. My act has no class. It's just a funny looking act."

And Frank Crosetti wasn't the only guy who didn't laugh at it. Patkin could stand on his head, fire off a barrage of Bob Hope one-liners, drop his pants, do anything within reason and several things beyond reason and Jim Bunning, for one, wouldn't crack a smile. Especially if his team happened to be trailing at the time.

Jim remembered Max from the not-so-good, old days. "In 1952 I was pitching for the Williamsport Tigers and Max Patkin was there," Bunning said. "I'm getting massacred and the people are laughing. I was a young man, not 20 yet. . . . I didn't make any special vow or anything that I'd get back at him because I didn't think the opportunity would ever come. But I just don't believe—and I still find it difficult to handle—that during a professional baseball game there is someone other than a professional on the coaching lines involved in the outcome of the game."

It just so happened that Max was booked to appear in Reading when Bunning was breaking in as a minor league manager there. "I didn't want him in Reading," Jim said, and to prove the point he had Jimmy Bronson, the general manager, write Max a letter telling him to please stay home.

Patkin remembers it as a phone call, not a letter, but it's the thought that counts. Max was upset. And hurt. He placed a call to Bunning, who was in West Haven, Conn., at the time. "You know what he said to me?" Max asked. "He said, 'Max, do you remember 20 years ago when I was pitching for Williamsport? You were coaching at first base doing your act and I was getting creamed and I said if I ever managed any ball club I'd never let you in my ball park.' "

So Patkin got canceled in Reading that year. Not that it made much difference. Hurricane Agnes hit the town, turning the ball park into a lake and forcing a series of postponements. Never underestimate the power of an angry clown.

And that wasn't the end of it. Max was scheduled to perform in both ends of a day-night doubleheader that season in Quebec City. As luck would have it, the Reading Phillies were in town.

"That was one of the funniest things I ever saw," Bunning's minor league trainer and friend, Ted Zipeto claimed. "We lost both games of a split doubleheader. You should've seen the expression on Jim's face when Max came out to perform."

Hah-hah-hah. It must have been a barrel of laughs. Talk about your tough audiences. Max could have introduced the freshest, fun-

funniest routine in the history of clowndom. He could have had the French-Canadians rolling in the aisles. No matter. Bunning would have stood there, arms folded, glaring.

"He got creamed those two games," Max remembered cheerfully. "He got killed. He was so mad he was boiling. He refused to look at me. He turned away when I went to the coaches' box. He ate the ball players out for laughing on the bench. They told me, 'Max, it was pure hell you being there.'"

A year later, Bunning didn't stand in the way of Patkin performing during a Pacific Coast League game in Eugene. But he still didn't like it.

"I got there," Max said, "and the first thing I walked in the [Eugene] clubhouse and Jim says, 'I'd rather you didn't dress in my clubhouse.' 'I always dress in the home team's clubhouse,' I tell him. 'Well, you don't dress in *my* clubhouse,' he says."

Bunning remembers it well. "There was a room right next to the clubhouse," Jim said. "He dressed there. You know where he wanted to dress? In the manager's and coaches' room. I said no. Zip [trainer Ted Zipeto] put him over in the bat room, where they stored the bats. That's asking a little much when you don't want someone there and they ask to dress in your room."

So Max changed in the bat room. It could have been worse. "He let me go over the routine with the ball players," Patkin said. "And he let me coach the way I usually do."

Better yet, Max had a surprise ending for his comedy skit that night. Bunning's team won. To hear Patkin tell it, he was the most valuable player. Or, at least, the most valuable clown.

"What happened," he said, "we"—with Max, the home team is always we—"won the ball game while I was coaching at third."

Bob Spence, a lefthanded power hitter, was at the plate and Patkin bellowed "fast ball" as the pitcher went into his motion. "I usually wait until the pitcher throws a bad curve ball," Max explained, "and then I stick my neck down with my feet wide apart and make out like I'm stealing the sign, and I'll say, 'Fast ball . . . fast ball,' because very seldom does the catcher ever come back with a curve ball after that. Well, I did it, and Spence hit it out, and we won, 3–2. Spence told me, 'Max, I really did look for a fast ball on that pitch.'"

Okay, so it didn't take a genius—or a clown—to figure out that a fast ball was coming. But a win's a win, even if Max Patkin is coaching at third base when the winning run crosses the plate. By the time the night was over Bunning may not have been laughing on the outside, but at least he was smiling on the inside.

Max, still bubbling over Spence's home run, found the courage to enter Bunning's office after the game. A photographer saw the clown approaching the manager and asked Jim if he'd mind posing for a picture. Bunning, obviously mellowing in his old age, agreed to do it.

"It was a good picture, too," Max said. "Later [in 1976] when I got to Oklahoma City and Jim was managing there, there's my picture on his deck. I said, 'What's this?' He said, 'Max, I want to tell you something. You wouldn't believe it, but I often look at your picture.' I said, 'And what do you do, throw up?' He said, 'No, I look at that picture and I say to myself, 'Jim, don't take this game so seriously.' "

Actually the closest Patkin ever came to getting a genuine smile out of Bunning was during a Toledo-Tidewater game in Tidewater in 1975. There was Max, giving it his best shot before a good crowd, and there was Bunning standing in the front of the dugout, arms folded, glaring out at the clown, refusing to show the faintest hint of amusement.

Patkin couldn't take it any more. He trotted over towards the Toledo dugout, looked the glowering manager in the eye and hollered, "That's the trouble with you, Bunning, you don't take this game seriously enough."

Max' problems with minor league managers started long before Bunning tried his hand at managing, however. If Jim didn't go for baggy-pants comics during a baseball game, how do you think Gene Mauch felt? Mauch was managing in Minneapolis in the '50s when he and Patkin crossed paths—again and again and again. And again.

"I got Mauch four times on the road one summer," Max said. "He hated my act. Three times he lost. Finally the fourth time he got me in Denver. Bob Howsam was the owner of the Denver Bears then. He had 21,000 people in the stands and Mauch refused to let me go on. He said, 'I won't let him coach.' Howsam said, 'You've got to let him go on. These people love him in Denver.' He talked Mauch into letting me go on and he lost that ball game, too. I never got him again after that. Thank God."

Normally, Patkin does his coaching bit only when the home team is batting. Back in the late '40s, though, Paul Richards had other ideas. Max was booked for a three-game stand in Buffalo, where Richards was managing. When he found out what Max wanted to do, he raised a rumpus. No blankety-blank clown was going to coach for him. Finally, a compromise was reached. Max could perform—but only if he coached for the visiting team, the Newark Bears, as well. "So I had to coach for both teams," Max said. "I'm running back and forth between the two dugouts and when Newark is scoring they're booing the shit out of me. I didn't know what the hell was happening."

Max Patkin walks into a big league clubhouse these days and he's virtually certain to run into several players who remember him from their minor league days. Recently, he popped in the St. Louis Cardinals' clubhouse, where the mere sight of that big nose and smiling face was enough to start Bob Forsch telling about the night in El Paso, Texas, when Max kicked off his shoe—as he does routinely during his act—and it went soaring through the air and hit an umpire squarely on the head. Talk about your big laughs.

"The funniest thing I ever did in my life," Max called it. "The umpire was a big, fat guy. His name was Scotty Harris. He must've weighed 400 pounds. He was behind the plate and he didn't see the shoe coming. Luckily, we were good friends. You know what he did? He motions to me; he makes me walk down to him. He's got this serious look. I don't know what he's going to do. As we come together he hits me with his belly and knocks me right on my fanny."

Then there was the time in Eugene when Max went through his batting routine, in which he hits the ball and runs to third base, where the umpire calls him out. "This little, short umpire was at third," Max said. "I slide into third and I jump up to argue with the umpire, like I always do, and he's got his hand in his back pocket and he takes a gun out and he puts it that far from my nose and he says, 'I've had enough of your crap all these years, Patkin,' and he goes bang-bang. He shoots me twice right between the eyes. When I heard the second shot I knew I was okay. I froze. I thought to myself, 'What do I do?' Then I said, 'Fall backwards, you dummy.' So I did and the crowd went crazy."

Sometimes one of the athletes goes a little crazy, too. One time in Syracuse, perhaps 20 years ago, the home team scored "about seven runs" the inning Patkin coached at third. The fans thought it was great. The Syracuse team thought it was great. The guy who was pitching for the other team wasn't nearly as enthusiastic about Max' performance.

"He confronted me between the two locker rooms," Patkin recalled. "He wanted to punch me out. When I finished my act, he was waiting for me. Luckily, there was a clubhouse guy back there, and he grabbed him. Boy, I never saw a guy so fiercely, intently ready to kill me."

The Frank Crosettis, the Paul Richards, the Gene Mauchs, the Jim Bunnings, the angry pitchers, the wise-guy umpires notwithstanding, Max still survives, a relic of simpler times when a guy didn't have to dress up as a chicken or a furry animal to get laughs at a ball park. With each passing year, the job gets tougher. "It's not easy out there," he said. "Some nights it's awful hard."

Certainly, the physical end of it is no picnic for a man in his 60s, as Max keeps finding out. When minor league baseball returned to Louisville in 1982, Patkin was there, playing to a crowd of 22,705.

"While I was coaching first base they scored six runs," he said. "The other team changed pitchers twice. I'm thinking, 'What am I going to do to kill time?' "

Max' roving eyes spotted Stan Musial and his wife sitting near the home dugout. It was made to order. He'd dash over to the railing, climb over, kiss Stan's better half and give her a big hug. The fans would love it.

Well, Max did it, and the fans loved it, all right, but in leaping over the railing he gave his left arm an awful crack. Days later, it was still black and blue and throbbing. All part of being a clown. Which, to Max, is a heckuva lot better than being a chicken or a furry animal.

"I'll put it this way," the Clown Prince of Baseball said, "they're not baseball. I'm baseball. But I appreciate talent. The Chicken is good, and the [Phillie] Phanatic is good. They're starting to costume everybody in ball parks, though. They're starting to make a farce out of the whole thing. Somebody without talent goes running around as a mascot, you're not proving anything. I'm not going to knock it because it looks like sour grapes. I'm not jealous of these guys that are making all that money. I'm envious.

"I always look at it this way. They don't hurt me. They're different acts, and they've got to have outfits. They don't have any identity. I feel as if I've got identity. They want to fire those guys they can put another body in there. Nobody can fire me. I am baseball. I love baseball. It's my life. I'd say 90–95 percent of the ball players are my friends, and that includes umpires, managers, general managers. You know why? They know what I've done for baseball and they know I'm not trying to hurt them on the field. Now, wherever I go in the minor leagues, they love me."

And, once the show begins, the other Max Patkin—the showman, the clown, the one who'll do practically anything to get a laugh—has himself a wonderful time. It's only before the show starts, and after it's over, that the real Max Patkin—the lonely man hopping from one-nighter to one-nighter, from airport to bus terminal to train station—goes through hell.

"Oh God," the real Max Patkin said, "when I lay in those hotel rooms, when I get in a town at 11, 12 o'clock and I lay on the bed and look at the ceiling [waiting for the long afternoon hours to go by], it's so boring. I don't like to watch TV. Those soap operas are depressing. I turn 'em off. I look at the game shows. Game shows at least make me laugh. But those soap operas, everybody's crying.

"As the years wear on, it gets lonelier. The ball players get younger and I get older, so I can't travel around with them. In the old days I roomed with all these guys—the Tommy Lasordas, the Chuck Tanners. I stayed with Tommy on the road when he was managing at Ogden, Utah, and at Albuquerque and at Spokane. I roomed with Chuck when he was managing El Paso. They used to say to me, 'C'mon, Max, room with me.' "

But they're managing in the big leagues now, and he's still clowning in the minor leagues. How much longer? Just as long as he's able to do it. So what if it's a tough way to make a living? So what if he starts each long road trip feeling a little bit sorry for himself? So what if there are nights when the home team is losing and nobody—not even a guy with a big nose and baggy pants—can make the people laugh?

"It's just a great feeling to know who you are," he said. "It's a great feeling to be *somebody*. I was in St. Louis a couple of years ago and a guy came up to me and he said, 'Max, I played ball 20 years ago,' and he shook my hand. Now he's a surgeon. I was flattered. Made me feel good. And then another guy came up to me in Houston. He used to play for the Hawaii baseball team. He's a pilot now. He was walking through the airport and he recognized me and he said, 'Hey Max. . . .' "

The man they call the Clown Prince of Baseball smiled. "Once you see me," he said, turning his face so the full profile was in view, "you remember me. I have the type of face you don't forget."

And he subjects himself to a schedule that only could have been mapped out by a Greyhound vice-president gone mad. In August of '82, for example, at an age when most men are contemplating retirement, Max Patkin chose to run himself ragged instead, committing himself to 25 minor league appearances that carried him to (in order), Oneonta, N.Y.; Midland, Tex.; Phoenix, Ariz.; Tuscon, Ariz.; Salt Lake City, Utah; Vancouver, Canada; Billings, Mont.; Butte, Mont.; Wausau, Wisc.; DesMoines, Ia.; Shelby, N.C.; Bridgeton, N.J.; Fort Myers, Fla.; Miami, Fla.; Vero Beach, Fla.; Orlando, Fla.; Daytona Beach, Fla.; Reading, Pa.; Syracuse, N.Y.; Erie, Pa.; Auburn, N.Y.; Bristol, Conn.; West Haven, Conn.; Waterbury, Conn., and Utica, N.Y.

And that, as the Clown Prince of Baseball knows only too well, is no joke.

6

WHEN BEING BLACK ISN'T BEAUTIFUL

It was August 24, 1976, a rainy Tuesday night in Oklahoma City. But even as the clouds gathered, so did the crowd. Over 2,400 showed up to honor the home team as it neared the end of a good season. It was Awards Night, and the Oklahoma City 89ers, who finished nine games over .500 that year, had several players worthy of recognition. Among the big league-bound athletes on that Triple A team were first baseman Dane Iorg, who put together a 24-game hitting streak and batted .326; third baseman Jim Morrison, who hit .289 with 18 homers and 71 runs batted in after making the big jump from the Carolina League to the American Association; right fielder Rick Bosetti, an excellent defensive player who hit .306 and scored 82 runs out of the leadoff spot in his first Triple A season; catcher Bill Nahorodny, a long-ball hitter who was immensely popular with the fans, and a young center fielder named Lonnie Smith, like Morrison fresh out of "A" ball.

Obviously, there were plenty of players to honor on that night—the last scheduled home game of the season for the Oklahoma City 89ers. And there were lots of awards handed out during the pre-game ceremony at home plate. You know, all the usual things: most valuable player and most popular player and most improved player and outstanding rookie, and more.

One by one, the Oklahoma City players marched up to home plate to receive their awards, and their applause. But Lonnie Smith never got out of the dugout.

Nahorodny was the "most popular." Bosetti was the top rookie. Lonnie Smith, the 20-year-old kid who had batted .308 and scored a league-leading 93 runs, wasn't even mentioned.

Big deal, you say. Well, to Lonnie Smith it *was* a big deal. He felt hurt, left out, unappreciated. And he couldn't help wondering if he'd been overlooked on this night because he was black.

"It was difficult for me because I was still young," he said. "I wasn't used to being away from home. Baseball was still a [relatively] new experience for me. It was only my second full year. I was away from all my friends in "A" ball. I was up with a bunch of new guys. I had to kind of feel my way through."

Some of his Oklahoma City teammates went out of their way to help. "Guys like Dane Iorg and Bob Oliver [a black first baseman with big league experience] and [pitchers] Dave Wallace and Chuck Kniffin, they made it a little easier for me," Lonnie recalled. "But it just seemed like whenever there were opportunities for players to do interviews or sign autographs up on top in the booth they set up, they always went to the white players. It probably wasn't meant that way. It just seemed to turn out that way. All the Latin players felt like they were left out. And the black players felt like they were left out."

It's doubtful if anybody knew the depths of Lonnie Smith's feelings as the young man stood in the dugout on that Awards Night waiting to hear his name called.

"All the white guys got the awards," he said. "They had beauty queens there, and all the white guys got to escort them."

By the time the last beauty queen had been escorted, and the last award winner had been applauded Lonnie Smith was in no mood to play a baseball game. "I was looking forward to something," he said. "I expected something. When I didn't get it, I felt pretty bad. It took me a while to get over it. I thought I would at least get some kind of mention. I thought maybe I would win the rookie of the year award because I was 20 and I made the jump from "A" ball to Triple A, but it just wasn't meant to be."

Later, Lonnie would realize, although his offensive statistics compared favorably to Bosetti's, that Rick "had played a much better outfield" and probably deserved the award. But at that moment, on that night Lonnie Smith was simply a deeply hurt young man. "I was hurt real bad," he said. "I thought I would at least get a mention or a certificate or something. I was still young and I acted like a child afterwards."

The game began. Lonnie was in center field, as usual, batting third. Where he wanted to be, though, was any place but in that ball park. He didn't want to play a baseball game. He wanted to pack his bags, jump on a plane and fly home.

"I came pretty close to just calling it quits that day," he said. "Actually, that year had started out kind of shaky, but I roomed with

Bob Oliver and he helped me out a little bit, so I was able to function better. But after that night, I don't know; I just didn't give a shit anymore."

He played like it. In the top of the third inning, Tony Franklin of the Wichita Aeros hit a fly ball to center field. Lonnie had to come in for it, but it was little more than a routine play.

He slowed down, though, and—instead of making the catch—he casually trapped the ball, fielding it on one hop. It was obvious from the press box that he hadn't made the catch. Lonnie, of course, knew that he hadn't. But Joe West, who was umpiring on the bases, signaled the batter was out.

What ensued had to be one of the most astonishing arguments in baseball history. An outfielder, given credit for a catch he hadn't made, charged the umpire to protest the call. "Joe West [now a National League umpire] said I caught it," Lonnie recalled. "I was so mad at everything that I told him he blew the call. What I actually said was, 'You must be a horseshit umpire because no way did I catch that ball.' He threw me out of the game and I said, 'Thank you.' I wanted to get thrown out. I didn't want to play. I just felt so bad that day. I felt like everything I had done was worthless. Plus I'd gotten kind of big-headed. My first year in rookie [league] ball, I tied for rookie of the year. The next year I won a bunch of honors playing "A" ball. Then to play up there and to hit .300, I thought I really accomplished something."

Shortly after he was thrown out for arguing that he *hadn't* caught the ball, the rains came pouring down and the game was called. Lonnie wound up closeted with his manager, Jim Bunning. "He asked me if I was disappointed in not winning an award," Lonnie said. "I lied to him. He told me he wasn't going to play me until I realized what I had done and until I came up to him and told him I was ready to play again."

Three nights later, at Denver's Mile High Stadium, Lonnie singled, tripled and doubled on his first three at-bats to lead the 89ers to a lopsided victory. He did a lot of fast growing up in the days following that Awards Night in Oklahoma City. The talk he had with Bunning resulted in a far closer relationship between the two men—one that led Lonnie to choose Bunning as his agent after Jim's managing days were over. In the Triple A seasons that followed, Lonnie's feelings about Oklahoma City and the people there changed, too. "My last two years there I really enjoyed," said the present-day St. Louis Cardinals outfielder. "Everything just seemed to be a lot nicer."

It's certainly understandable that a young black man would have some difficulty adjusting to life in Oklahoma City, and that he would feel "a little bit of racial pressure at times." But imagine how tough it must have been for the Lonnie Smiths of the '50s and '60s to fight and claw and scratch their way to the big leagues.

There's still prejudice, of course. Now, however, it's largely hidden, simmering beneath the surface. Then, it was out in the open, blatant and ugly. You have to wonder how many Lonnie Smiths were unable to handle the racial pressures of earlier times and never made it out of the minor leagues as a result.

"I've heard a lot of stories about those types of things," Phillies center fielder Garry Maddox said. "The players that make it through those situations and go on and enjoy some success and also become good human beings, those are really strong, special people."

Indeed they are. Ask Dave Bristol, a minor league manager in the Cincinnati Reds farm system two decades ago. He saw first hand what it was like for a young black trying to make it in professional baseball in a Southern town.

"It was tough, I'll tell you," Bristol said. "They got after us with shotguns in one little, old town in Florida."

Bristol and some of the white players were in a restaurant. The black players were outside, waiting in cars. "We'd order for them," Dave said. "You know, get the food and take it out to them. Some [white] guys were just sitting in the place. They went to get a shotgun. We just loaded up and took off."

Bob Gibson, who blazed his way to a Hall of Fame pitching career with the Cardinals, remembers how it was when he was coming up.

"I went to Columbus [Ga.] for a month in '57," he said. "It wasn't very much fun."

He was 21 then, and it was his first experience living away from home. "I stayed in the YMCA with a bunch of fags," he said. "One guy used to follow me all over. But you can handle anything if you wanted to. If you wanted to play ball, you handled it. The problem [bigotry] still exists. It's not open, but it's still there. People have become sophisticated in their bigotry."

There was nothing sophisticated about the bigotry in some of the towns that comprised the old Sally League. "You had a lot of name-calling and stuff you don't have nowadays," Gibson said. "It was really common then. I remember one night—in Augusta [Ga.], I think—some guy was yelling out of the stands. He called me 'Alligator Bait,' and I'm laughing. I didn't know what the hell it was."

Years later, Gibson found out. "I was discussing it with a doctor friend of mine. He was from the South somewhere. I said, 'You know, it always was on my mind about this guy calling me that name. What the hell did that mean, Alligator Bait?' He laughed. He said, 'Back in the days of slavery they used to take black people and throw them in the water with a rope around them. When the alligator would come up they'd snatch 'em out of the water and catch the alligator.' It was 10, 12 years before I found out what that meant. Then it wasn't so damn funny."

Perhaps the hardest part was not being able to stay where your teammates stayed, eat where your teammates ate. The first time Gibson ran into that, he was still in college, the first black to play baseball and basketball at Creighton in Omaha, Neb., Gibson's home town.

"We took a trip to Tulsa [Okla.] on the train and the coach didn't tell me until we got halfway there that I wasn't going to be able to stay in the hotel with the rest of the players," Bob said. "I asked him how come he didn't tell me before we left and he said because I wouldn't have gone and he knew it. I cried. I was 18 years old, and I cried. We stopped at the train station in Oklahoma City and the guys got off to get something to eat in the restaurant, and they were going to take me back in the kitchen to feed me. I said bullshit, so nobody on the team ate. We all left."

Gibson became hardened to it in the years that followed. He had no choice. "When you're doing it for a living, it makes a difference [in your attitude]," he said. "There are a lot of things you have to deal with when you're dependent on that job. . . . I guess that's one of the reasons why they always talked back in those days about the durability of the black ball player because of all the other things we had to do along with playing. A lot of people would crack under those circumstances. I was fortunate. I had the ability to take all kinds of problems and put them aside until I finished playing. I can do that regardless of whether it was that type of problem or anything else. I remember a guy asked me about retiring. He said, 'When did you realize you were going to retire?' I told him I was standing on the mound one day. I had the bases loaded and I was thinking about my ex-wife. That's when I decided it was time for me to retire. I was no longer concentrating on what I was doing."

Somehow, in those early, minor league years, Bob Gibson was able to block out the things that could have eaten him up alive. It took a lot more than name-calling to make Gibson lose his concentration.

"Those kinds of things, they teach you to be hard," he said. "If you can handle that, you an handle almost anything.

"People say, 'While you're growing up, you're bitter. You've got a chip on your shoulder.' Probably so. That's the only way you could really handle that stuff. You had to be tough."

Bill White was tough. White, who recently concluded his 12th season as a radio-TV broadcaster for the New York Yankees, had a long, successful big league career as a hard-hitting first baseman with the Cardinals and Phillies. Originally, though, he signed with the Giants, who let him train with the big club in Phoenix in '53, then shipped him out to the Carolina League, of all places.

Bill's first unpleasant experience occurred during spring training. He had gotten to know movie actor Stewart Granger, who was a Giants fan. Granger worked out with the ball club on occasion and White, then 19, and the actor became good friends.

"We came back from a road trip once and I picked up a paper and I saw *Cochise*"—a Granger movie—"was playing some place in Phoenix," White said. "So I decided to go. I went to the ticket counter—I was about five people back in line—and finally I got there and the girl gets suddenly busy and I say, 'Hey, I want a ticket.' She says, 'I'm sorry. I can't sell you a ticket.' I say, 'Why?' She says, 'I just can't sell you a ticket.' All of a sudden the manager shows up. He says, 'Well, we don't have a balcony.' I say, 'I don't want to sit in a balcony.' Then I found out they had a racial policy in Phoenix then. . . ."

He'd been permitted to stay in the same spring training hotel as his white teammates, but he couldn't buy a ticket to see a movie. Bill went back to the hotel and told Monte Irvin, another black member of the Giants, what had happened. "Monte just read the facts of life to me," White said.

Compared to towns in the Carolina League, the facts of life in Phoenix weren't all that bad. You have to wonder why clubs would send their top black prospects to Southern cities in those days. Why did the Cardinals send Gibson to Columbus, Ga.? Why did the Giants send White to Danville, Va.? Both men had the same, quick answer. The parent clubs were insensitive to the special problems of the black athlete. To put it simply, they just didn't give a damn.

It would be hard to imagine anybody breaking into pro ball under more difficult circumstances than Bill White. He was not only the lone black player on the Danville team, he was the lone black player in the Carolina League.

"We'd get in [a town] at two o'clock in the morning and I'd have to find a black cab to go to a black hotel," White said. "I always had to find my own way to the ball park and from the ball park. And I had to put up with the crap from the fans, which had never happened to me before. I was called names I had never heard."

A man can take only so much. One night, in Burlington-Graham [N.C.], Bill's temper boiled over. "I just got tired of it," he said. "I gave 3–4,000 people the finger."

It didn't take long for White to find out who his friends were.

"The one guy that really was with me was a guy named Bob Knight from New Orleans," he recalled. "As I was going down in the dugout some lady put her hand on me and said, 'Nigger, you can't come down here and do that to us.' He took her hand, threw it off, and said, 'None of you is any good. Leave him alone and go back wherever you came from.' Then, of course, when we came out [of the clubhouse after the game] they had about 2,000 of them supposedly ready to jump us. So we came out with bats and they let us by and then they threw rocks at the bus. They were allowed to call me anything they wanted, but I couldn't do anything back, you see."

Like Bob Gibson, Bill White didn't let the racial badgering interfere with his performance on the playing field. "I took it out on the baseball," he said. "I never had that much respect for Southern whites anyway. So I wasn't affected that much by them. I just figured they were ignorant sons-of-bitches and they had nothing else to do. They either went to work all day in the steel mills or they went to work all day in the hosiery mills and they came out [to the ball park] and they yelled and screamed. They weren't going anywhere. They were going to be there all their lives. I was just passing through. I had a chance to do something. So I really didn't let it get to me that much."

White thought he had left all that behind him when he moved on to the Western League the following season. The Giants sent him to Sioux City, Iowa, which was an improvement over Danville, Va. But the road trips still left a lot to be desired. He still couldn't stay with the team in Lincoln, Neb., and Wichita, Kan.

A night in Wichita remains etched in his mind. Even now, nearly three decades later, he can remember details. "Dave Garcia was my manager," White said. "We all went into a restaurant to eat. We were sitting in there—a place called Edna's, a diner, really—and the waitress says, 'I'm sorry, I can't serve you.' There's a guy in there with grease all over him, no shirt on, eating at the next table. Dave Garcia got us all up and we left.

"As far as letting them break me, I couldn't and wouldn't do that. But this one time I did get disturbed—out of frustration. I mean, to sit there, halfway decently dressed, and to see some guy I would consider an animal—I wouldn't allow him to come in, he was so dirty—be allowed to eat in peace simply because of his color while I couldn't eat. . . . I think that's the only time in my life I cried."

Garcia, who would go on, years later, to become manager of the Cleveland Indians, left a lasting impression on White because of his sincerity and his kindness that summer. "Dave roomed with me for a while," Bill recalled. "I guess he figured I was lonesome, so he spent a week with me on the road, which I've never forgotten."

If there was one thing the Gibsons, the Whites, most of them discovered, it was that their fellow players—even the ones who came from the Deep South—were largely sympathetic. Gibson put it this way: "I've always said, if everybody in the world were like athletes this would probably be a marvelous place because, as athletes, you learn to deal with adversities and you learn to play and live with each other day in, day out, and you really get to find out what a person is like."

In Jackie Robinson's day it was different. "It had to be really tough for him in '46," Bill White said, "because he had to deal with [prejudice from] the players. But for some reason I never had to deal with that—with being thrown at and being spiked."

Ironically, White can recall the first time in his professional baseball career that an opposing player went out of his way to "run over" him on the bases. That player was Jackie Robinson. "But that," said Bill, "was the way he played."

What of the man who many consider the greatest player, black or white, who ever played the game? For a moment now, let's go back to 1950, when a teenaged black athlete from Alabama rode the rails to Trenton, N.J., to become a minor league baseball player. They called Willie Mays "Junior Mays" then, and until he stepped on the field the people who followed the Trenton Giants of the old Interstate League had no idea they were about to see a diamond in the rough.

Bus Saidt, now a sports columnist for *The Trenton Times*, did the play-by-play broadcasts of the Trenton games then. "The lights were very bad in Trenton," he recalled. "They were brutal. It was pitch dark in the power alleys. In one of the first games he ever played in Trenton a guy hit a long ball to left center field and Mays, on the dead run, caught it with his bare hand. Very few people have seen anything like that before or since."

Playing conditions may have left something to be desired, but being the first black in the Interstate League was considerably easier than being the first black in the Carolina League. In most of the towns Mays was permitted to stay with the rest of the team. Not in Wilmington, Del., though.

Herb Clark, now a writer for *The Trentonian* whose son, Alan, umpires in the American League, remembers Junior Mays' first trip to Wilmington. "They wouldn't let him stay at the Hotel Rodney," Clark said. "They (the management of the Trenton Giants) asked me to take him to a rooming house in the black section."

Herb looked the place over, gave it the official Clark Seal of Approval, then drove Mays there. If Willie was upset by the "special treatment," he didn't show it. Compared to what the Gibsons and the Whites and so many others went through, his initiation to organized baseball's minor leagues was mild.

Willie Stargell's wasn't. One of the most admired men in all of baseball, Stargell closed out a 20-year career with the Pittsburgh Pirates in 1982. A gentle giant of a man, he led the Pirates to the 1979 world championship at the age of 38 and won the hearts of a city—and much of the nation—in the process. In Stargell's final year as an active player it became commonplace for his every pinch-hitting appearance to be saluted by a standing ovation. The people loved him for what he did, and they loved him for what he was. But as a teenager starting out in professional baseball in 1959, Willie Stargell felt more hatred than love.

He still remembers his first spring training. The Pirates sent him a plane ticket that said "Jackson" on it. Willie boarded the plane in San Francisco without even knowing that Jackson was in Mississippi and without realizing how blacks were treated in the Deep South in those days.

"I went to spring training with two white fellas," Stargell said. "All we talked about was we couldn't wait to get to Jackson to get something to eat because we were hungry. All they served us on the plane was hot chocolate. Well, we got off the plane in Jackson the next morning and we went right to the restaurant and this guy said, 'You Niggers, get out of here. You know we can't serve you.' Then this black red cap came over and he said, 'Hey, boy, you know better than that. If you want to eat something, boy, you've got to go around back.' The guys I was with said, 'Look, if you can't eat something we're not going to eat.' I said, 'Hey, no, no. We've been flying all night. You guys go ahead and eat. I'll go around back.' So I did, and they had this big meat chopping block, where they chop up the meat, and they had flies and excess meat sticking to it and blood, and the guy put down some napkins and I said, 'No thank you. No-o-o-o thank you.' That was the beginning."

Welcome to professional baseball, Willie.

His first season, in Roswell, Texas, was quite a test for a young man who had never been exposed to that kind of thing to any great degree. "I was quite taken aback by it," he said. "You know, eating in the back of those restaurants and drinking from those special water faucets. I'd heard about it. But it's like you tell a kid, 'Don't touch the fire because it burns.' A kid doesn't know what the hell you're talking about. Sooner or later you've got to touch it. *Then* you have felt what somebody has been trying to tell you."

So young Willie Stargell felt it for the first time. "I used to really have to cry myself to sleep every night," he said.

The Roswell team had a quota system, a maximum of three blacks on the roster. "The towns, I guess, said what they wanted," Stargell said, "and they had to comply. That's just the way it was."

Willie's two dark-skinned teammates didn't provide much companionship, however. One was from Cuba, the other from the Dominican Republic. They didn't speak English. He didn't speak Spanish. "And a lot of times they were fighting each other," Stargell said, "because they were away from home for the first time in this kind of environment and they got very bitter. It was never a case they got angry at me because they didn't know what I was saying and I didn't know what they were saying."

All in all, that was some introduction to professional baseball. It had to take a lot of inner strength to get Willie Stargell through that first season.

"I think what was my salvation at that time was my parents," he said. "I'd call and tell them what I was dealing with and I can still hear the echoing of their words. If I wanted to come back to the projects, they'd say, if I wanted to be subject to a lot of gangs and fights and muggings and prostitution and gambling, the whole bit; if I wanted to come back to that, fine. But if I wanted to play baseball, they told me, I had to do the best I could and, hopefully, I'd become a man out of all this."

Willie listened, and he plunged head-first back into that chamber of horrors, and in time he became one of the most beloved and successful men in his chosen profession.

"There were some tough moments," he said. "The way I like to look at them—the so-called troubles and problems and obstacles— they were things you just had to deal with. You can look back and say it allowed me to get to a point where I had to decide that I would let nothing or nobody stop me from being able to do what I'd always wanted to do.

"I couldn't understand the things that I had to deal with because other people [the whites] didn't have to deal with that. It got to be very frightening at times. So I got, I guess you might say, a small third of what Jackie Robinson went through. I only had my life threatened as a result of being a black ball player once. Oh, I've had phone calls, but I'm talking about where I was looking down the barrels of a double-barreled shotgun."

It happened in a little town in Texas called Plainview. Stargell will never forget the experience.

"I'm going into the ball park," he said, "and this guy came up and he said, 'Nigger, if you play tonight I'm going to blow your brains out.' You talk about scared. That's why I guess getting a hit or not getting a hit isn't that important. I guess if every day you had to come to the ball park and somebody put a gun to your head and said, 'You have to get a base hit,' it wouldn't be as much fun."

Surely, that night in Plainview, Texas, wasn't much fun. Stargell has had some bad nights in baseball. There have been nights when he had trouble getting his bat on the ball, and nights when he made costly errors in the field, and nights when his team lost tough ball games. But there was never a night as bad as that one in Plainview, Texas.

"I had to make up my mind that this was what I wanted to do," Willie said, "and if they were going to kill me, then I'd be doing exactly what I wanted to do when I died. A couple of times there were backfires—you know, motors out in the parking lot—and I urinated all over myself a couple of times. But I made it through that and I think that was the crossroads in my life."

The remarkable thing is, there's no rancor in Willie Stargell's voice when he talks about those early baseball experiences. "I didn't know who to be mad at," he said, "because I was playing with some white guys and they certainly weren't like that. It wasn't like every person I met had that bitterness or hate, so I couldn't associate everybody with that. I still kind of look at it in a way that God said, 'If you really want to be a ball player, then I'm going to test you. I'm going to put you through some things that are going to be very challenging.' I'm glad in a way that I had to do a degree of suffering and see things that weren't so pleasant. It kind of makes you put things in perspective, see what things really are and how you like to try to live with people. I still try to find something pleasant in everything and everybody.

"I had baseball on my mind that first year. That was probably the one thing that kept me afloat because I never could wait to get to the ball park. I just felt I had so much to learn."

A professional baseball career, Willie Stargell said one day last season at Three Rivers Stadium in Pittsburgh, "is like jumping on a train in New York and you get a chance to ride to California and then that train sort of turns around to come back. It's always picking up new passengers. The thing you want to do while you're riding that train is enjoy yourself. So don't complain about how the train is riding or about the weather you run into and all that. Certain things happen, but the thing I always wanted to do is enjoy it."

And, to his everlasting credit, he did enjoy it. His long "train ride" began with a shotgun pointed at his head in Plainview, Texas. It ended with a rousing, loving, standing ovation in Pittsburgh, Pennsylvania. The people pouring out their hearts to him on that final day weren't concerned with the color of his skin. Whites and blacks alike were on their feet to salute a very special man.

How special? Bill Robinson, a teammate of Stargell's for seven-and-a-half years, can answer that as well as anybody. Robbie is a pretty special person himself—a guy who had one of the greatest throwing arms in baseball until he seriously injured it in winter ball, a highly touted young player who came to the New York Yankees with a gigantic buildup and hit .196, .240 and .171 in his three torturous years there, got sent back to the minor leagues and had the courage and the determination to fight his way back.

Bill Robinson became an outstanding big league player with the Pirates, and it was only fitting that when Willie Stargell hit the two-run homer that beat the Orioles in the seventh game of the 1979 World Series in Baltimore, Robbie was on base.

They became exceptionally close friends during their Pirate years. "Bill Robinson," said Stargell the day after his friend was traded to the Phillies in June of '82, "is one helluva man, nothing but a plus in anybody's life. He's a caring, concerned man. He does things without boasting or letting people know about it."

In short, Willie Stargell and Bill Robinson have a lot in common.

"It's tough to put into words the gut feeling I have about Will," Robbie said. "There's just no greater person. I think maybe [we grew so close because] he and I are both older and both black and know how tough it was on us earlier to make it to the major leagues. A lot of the younger people nowadays have it made or have it given to them. Maybe Will and I both had to battle extra hard and play in the Deep South. When we first broke into baseball it wasn't the easiest thing for a black person. You learned to appreciate maybe where you are a little bit more."

Robbie played in Waycross, Ga., and Dublin, Ga., as a kid. He heard all the names. He experienced all the adversities. Like Stargell, he grew up in an area where racial prejudice was fairly well hidden. For the young Bill Robinson, raised in Pennsylvania, those Georgia towns were a jolt.

"I remember asking a manager, Jim Fanning, to send me down [to a lower classification]," Bill said. "I was playing in Eau Claire, Wis., and I wasn't doing well and I wanted to go where I could play. He asked me, 'Where would you like to go—Cedar Rapids, Iowa, or Dublin, Ga.?' Naturally, I said, 'Cedar Rapids.' Next day I was on my way to Dublin."

That's the way it was. "The only thing I can say is, if you can survive those days you can more or less survive anything," Robbie said. "When I think about the things I had to go through then to make it now I honestly believe I might've had to be three times better than a white player to make it to the major leagues."

Listen to the stories the Gibsons, the Robinsons, the Stargells relate and you can't help wondering if baseball organizations were insensitive to the problems of the blacks in those days or actually determined to make life as difficult for them as possible. Bill Robinson's first spring training—in 1962—was an example of the apparent lack of concern baseball teams had for the young black players who were coming into the game.

"I had a Triple A contract with the Louisville Colonels," Robbie said. "My family took me to the Greater Pittsburgh Airport. It was my first time on an airplane. I jumped on the plane and I went down to Brandenton, Fla., a place called, I think, the Manatee Hotel."

There he was, far from home for the first time in his life. He walked up to the desk and said, "I believe you have reservations for Bill Robinson of the Louisville Colonels."

He believed wrong.

"I'm sorry," the guy said, "no reservation."

"What do you mean?" Robbie asked. "I'm with the ball club. They told me to report here."

The man stared at him coldly. "We don't have any reservation for you," he repeated.

At that point, 18-year-old Bill Robinson felt very much alone. "Maybe there was a tear or two," he said, "because hey, what do I do now? This guy's not going to give me any information."

Think about that for a while. They give a kid a contract, send him a plane ticket, have him fly from western Pennsylvania to the west coast of Florida . . . and then they let him wander around, lost. Not even a club representative on hand to tell him what to do, where to go.

"I'll never forget a player named Lee Tate," said Robinson. "He just happened to be in the lobby. He saw me and he said, 'Bill, that's the way it is down here. You're not staying here, but I know where the rest of the guys are. I'll take you down there.' "

Tate, a white infielder, drove the black outfielder to the other side of town. "Hank Aaron was there and Tommie Aaron and Rico Carty," Bill said.

Bobbie belonged to the Braves then. In '63 minor league spring training was in Waycross, Ga. "It was an old, converted army base," he said. The buildings—barracks, really—where the players lived were called "Braves' TeePees."

"They had five 'TeePees'," Bill said. " 'TeePee' No. 5 was for the blacks, and it was out away from the rest of the guys. I remember one night where they literally locked us in. After 12 o'clock or so they locked the door from the outside, and I literally kicked the door down. I said, 'What if there's a fire or something in here? You have us locked in from the outside. Don't do that.' They stopped doing it, too."

Chances are, it was management's way of preventing the blacks from coming in after curfew.

"Those were the days that made a person what he is today," said

Bill Robinson, echoing the sentiments of his friend, Willie Stargell. "Certainly my son [Billy, a fine, young athlete who graduated from high school in '82] won't have to go through what I had to go through. I just thank the Good Lord for letting me be able to keep going through those years and get to the point where I am now. You just play your ball, play as hard as you can, and get the hell out of there. There were two ways of getting out—hitting your way out or just quitting. Fortunately, I hit my way out. I know there were a lot of guys that just quit."

As bad as it was for a black player in a Southern minor league, though, they actually held a Bill Robinson Day in Waycross in 1963. "They collected money," said Robbie. "I remember them throwing in dollars and quarters and stuff. It was very surprising, a nice, little tribute."

A remarkable tribute, really, but it couldn't erase the memories of all the unpleasant incidents—the night in Moultree, Ga., or maybe it was Thomasville, Ga., when there was a fight on the field involving most of the players and when it was over the police grabbed Robbie, the only black player, and started to take him to jail. "Only me. Nobody else," said Robinson, who was playing for the Dublin, Ga., team then. "Our manager told them, 'If you take him to jail, when your team comes to Dublin I'm going to have them all put in jail,' " Bill recalled. "So they let me go."

You have to marvel at the men who were able to go through that without becoming deeply embittered. You have to admire the strength, the self-control, the understanding of a Bill White or a Bill Robinson or a Willie Stargell.

"I thank the Good Lord that I was able to have a level head," Robbie said. "What good does it do to be bitter towards people? You can't condemn all society for a few ignorant people. . . . I just feel that this world is going to get along with me or without me and I'd love for it to get along with me. I don't care about leaving a mark in the world, but just playing my part. And I can only do that by working hand in hand and side by side with everyone I come in contact with. Life is too short to go through it bitter and mad at the world."

So some gained strength from their experiences, while others fell by the wayside.

If some black players have had lonely, difficult times, think how National League umpire Eric Gregg felt when he got his start in the Florida State League.

"In '72," recalled Gregg, "my partner, Dallas Parks, went to a barber shop in St. Petersburg [Fla.]. He said, 'Wait for me.' I said,

'I'll go across the street and buy some things and meet you after your haircut.' So I finished early. I got back and he [Parks, who happens to be white] was just getting into the chair. I walked in and the guy [the barber] looked at him. He said, 'Is he with you?' Dallas said, 'Yeah'. He pulled the sheet off him and he said, 'I can't cut your hair.' Dallas said, '*He's* not getting a haircut. I am.' 'I don't care,' the guy told him. 'He's with you.' "

It can happen almost anywhere—on an awards night in Oklahoma City, in a ball park in Augusta, Ga., in a movie house in Phoenix, Ariz., in a diner in Wichita, Kan., in a barber shop in St. Petersburg, Fla. Unfortunately, it's part of the game, too, part of the struggle to get to the big leagues and the men involved—whether an outfielder named Smith, a pitcher named Gibson, a first baseman named White, an umpire named Gregg—remember those incidents as vividly as any game-winning hit, any game-saving play. Nobody has an easy time of it in the minors. For some, though, through no fault of their own, it becomes especially hard.

7

BASEBALL AND BOOZE

The game ends at 10 P.M., maybe 10:30. The bars stay open to 1 A.M., maybe 2. there's nothing much to do the next day but sleep, and watch television, and kill time. In the big leagues, some players get in the habit of going to the ball park early. If the game starts at 7:30, they might grab a cab, run out there early in the afternoon and spend two, three hours playing cards. You can do that in most big league clubhouses. They're big and they're bright, nice places to pass the time. It's different in most minor league parks. The clubhouses there are often small and dingy. No way a man goes there before he *has* to go there.

It's difficult getting accustomed to the pro baseball lifestyle: the long road trips, the three, four, even five days spent at a single place, the seemingly endless hours of sitting around, waiting to go to the ball park. Add to that the pressure of playing night after night after night, of sinking into one of those devastating slumps that even the good hitters go through, of making one bad pitch in the ninth inning and having it cost you a ball game or, even worse, of having somebody make a bad play behind you or getting a bloop hit off you with the game on the line.

Is it any wonder that baseball and booze go together like ham 'n' eggs, like George Steinbrenner and turmoil, like scotch and soda?

To put it bluntly, there are a lot of men who develop drinking problems in pro baseball, and some out-and-out alcoholics. You'll find them in the dugouts, on the playing fields, in the front offices.

A young man just starting to coach in the Phillies' farm system told me this story: each night, after the game, a fellow coach would lead the way to the nearest pub. Finally, the new man balked. He didn't want to spend all that time in bars, and he said so. "You know

114

what he told me?" asked the young coach, a man named Glenn Gregson, who now works in the Chicago Cubs' organization. "He said, 'You've got to learn to drink. It's part of the game.'"

Sadly enough, it *is* part of the game—at least, a big enough part to rank as a serious problem. And that problem often begins in the minor leagues, where young ball players first find themselves with all that pressure to handle and all that time to kill.

"That's where it all began for me," St. Louis Cardinals catcher Darrell Porter was saying recently. "I remember exactly [where it started]. I was on a road trip in Appleton [Wisc. in the Midwest League]. I never drank in high school. I never smoked. I didn't do anything like that because I didn't think athletes were supposed to do it. My dad was an alcoholic and I didn't want to turn out like he was. I began playing for Clinton [Iowa], my first pro team [1970] and, heck, I was used to being the star in high school. Then I got over there and everybody was as good as I was. Most of them were better because they'd already played a year or so of minor league ball."

Darrell Porter was 18, fresh out of Southeast High School in Oklahoma City, where he was all-Oklahoma in baseball and All-America in football. "I could've played college ball and made more money than I did in the minor leagues," Porter said. "I had an offer [from the University of Oklahoma]. I could've made $1,000 a month and a car and an unlimited expense account at a clothing store."

But he chose professional baseball instead. "I felt like I would've let a whole lot of people down if I didn't," Porter explained. "So I went. Man, I was lonely. Anyway, I got to struggling. I was hitting like .205. I was real down in the dumps and a couple of guys asked me if I wanted to go out and have a few beers and just relax. I did, and I couldn't believe how good I felt when I had those beers. I started drinking and I found out I sure didn't worry about hitting .195 or .200. And I wasn't lonely any more. I kinda found a way to relax."

It's a way too many of them find. Alcohol—and later, drugs—nearly destroyed Darrell Porter, the all-American boy who never drank, never smoked before becoming a pro baseball player.

"It's hard in the minor leagues because you're in these old, rotten towns playing in real bad ball parks," he said. "I played in better ball parks in high school than we did there. You go away from home and you go to bad hotels with no air-conditioning, and the clubhouses, you might as well not take a shower because you're going to be as hot when you finish."

One thing led to another, and suddenly the non-drinker was a heavy drinker. The older guys on the team gave him the same line that Glenn Gregson heard: "You've got to learn to drink. It's part of this game."

"Exactly," Porter said. "That's what I was told, too. But I also saw it. You see, it *is* a part of baseball."

He had been such a gung-ho, idealistic kid when he signed. Before they shipped him to Clinton, Iowa, the Milwaukee Brewers—his first pro employers—brought him to the major leagues to work out with the big club for a couple of days. "Here I am," said Porter, "bug-eyed, always believing that athletes didn't drink and didn't smoke cigarettes and didn't do things like that. I walk into a major league clubhouse for the first time and guys are getting dressed in their uniforms smoking cigarettes. It blew my mind. I could not believe it. It really messed me up. After the game I came back in and they weren't only smoking cigarettes, they were drinking. In the clubhouse! After a game! It was a shock to me."

The shock wore off. Before the end of that first pro year at Clinton, Iowa, Darrell Porter was one of the boys. He only spent two seasons in the minors, but that was plenty of time to find out that a cold beer or two, or three, tasted awfully good after a hot ball game and even eased—at least numbed—the pain of an 0-for-4. And then later, in the big leagues, he got involved in the drug scene. It says a lot for Darrell Porter that he was eventually able to face the terrible truth—that he was a man in deep trouble—and leave the alcohol and the drugs behind him.

"I never saw drugs in the minor leagues. Never," Darrell said. "Well, I saw marijuana, but that's the only thing I saw. At that time, though, I was still a little bit leery of drugs. I guess nobody would've felt comfortable using drugs around me at that time because it wasn't something that was really out in the open—not like it is right now."

Porter started using drugs in the big leagues the same way he started drinking in the minor leagues. It began with amphetamines. "Greenies," the ball players call them. "I got to struggling a little bit there," Darrell said, "and one of the players came up to me and said, 'Try this. This'll make you feel better.' I popped one of them things. It did make me feel better. I don't know if I did any better, but I sure felt good out there.

"I'll tell you what it is, though. With me it was a real psychological dependency. I don't think in the end those things did much for me. But I'll guarantee you, I'd go to the clubhouse and I would feel rotten, I mean *rotten*, until before infield [practice]. That's when I'd always take my 'greenie', and I would feel just terrible until that time and when I put that thing in my mouth all of a sudden I felt better. I know that stuff didn't have time to get in my system, but I'd feel better."

Darrell Porter's story, up to that point, is not at all unusual. If booze and baseball go together, "greenies" and baseball are just as close.

Like Porter, Yankee broadcaster Bill White remembers his first drink. It, too, came in the minor leagues. "I was 19," he said, "and we're on a trip from Colorado Springs to Sioux City. Another ball player said, 'Hey, here, I'm going to give you a sleeping pill. Drink a glass of beer with it.' I did, and I slept all the way. That was my first drink."

In White's playing days, though, hard drugs weren't nearly as common—or accessible—as they are today. "We didn't have the hard drugs that these guys can get," he said. "We couldn't afford them. Now you have hard drugs plus alcohol."

"Greenies" have been around for years, though. "I was introduced to them by the trainer," White said. "My daughter had an operation. My wife stayed up with her all day. I'd go all night. I couldn't sleep. I'd come to the ball park, lay down, get an hour or two of sleep, get up and the trainer would give me a 'greenie.' Damn, I'd feel like a million. I played with a guy in Philadelphia [outfielder Johnny Callison] who took that 'red juice.' It's a super upper. He gave me that one day when I was feeling down. He said, 'Now go out and work.' I went out and sweated, got it in my system. I came back and he gave me another little sip. I went out there and I hit that damn ball all over the place. For three days I couldn't close my eyes. I said, 'I don't need that.' But I can see why those guys [the Phillies] ran down in '64 because I understand they were all on that stuff.

Some guys get hooked on alcohol and drugs. Some guys don't. Darrell Porter was one of the unfortunates who did.

"I don't think I was an addict [in the minor leagues]," Porter said. "Probably when I crossed that line was in about '74–'75 when I became dependent on that stuff—on drugs and alcohol. I didn't realize [at first] that my problem was drugs. I thought I was becoming mentally ill from different things that happened in my life. I thought they were driving me crazy. I didn't give drugs and alcohol that much credit."

By the mid–'70s Porter was not only drinking heavily and compulsively, he was "doing cocaine and Quaaludes and 'Speed' and marijuana and a lot of different things."

"I knew in about '76 I had a problem," he said. "I was so miserable. Something was wrong. My attitude toward life and toward myself and everything else had changed so much. I knew I was a sick man. It just got to the point it was unbearable. I was in misery all the time, from the time I got up to the time I went to bed, and I just didn't want to go on like that."

Then, one spring, Don Newcombe came to spring training and gave a talk on the subject. Newcombe, once a strong, hard-throwing righthander for the old Brooklyn Dodgers, had fallen into the alcohol trap as a player . . . and climbed out.

"When Newcombe talked to us about it, I thought maybe this isn't my problem, but I'm going to give it a chance. I'm going to find out," Porter said.

Newcombe's talk, and the action Porter took as a direct result, "saved my life," the Cardinals catcher said. "It didn't take much courage (to fight the alcohol and drugs) because I was so down. I was gone. And unfortunately that's what usually has to happen to us before we're ready to deal with it. We've got to hit that complete bottom. If we could only raise that bottom up for people so they didn't have to go that low to hit it."

Porter's successful fight against alcohol and drugs, and similar fights waged by other baseball players, rank among the most dramatic "victories" in sports.

"The biggest part of it was getting my head straight after I quit," Darrell said. "I just look at this game now as a game. I don't care if I hit .150 . . . No, I *do* care if I hit .150, but if I do hit that I'm going to enjoy every hit it takes me to hit .150. That's just the way I look at it now. When I was doing all that drugs and stuff the only thing that I really had in my mind was baseball. Success in baseball to me was the only thing that would bring me happiness. I found out that success in baseball definitely doesn't bring you happiness and that all the torment and pressure you put on yourself trying to succeed and worrying about all this crap, it just ain't worth it. This game was not meant to be taken that seriously."

As he spoke those words Darrell Porter was a key man—a catcher and a cleanup hitter—on a contending ball club. Now when the game is over and he's thirsty, he drinks water, not beer—even if the team he plays for *is* owned by Anheuser-Busch.

Today Darrell Porter is, quite frankly, "afraid" to have a "social drink." He has been through too much to risk going through that nightmare again. "I know where I was at," he said, "and I don't ever want to be there again. What I miss—I don't miss the high, I don't miss the feeling that I got from drinking, but I like the taste of beer. The only thing I miss is having a good, old, cold beer after a hot ball game. I go in and everybody else is having a beer . . . But I try not to dwell on it. That's when I get in trouble.

"It's fun again playing baseball. I'm having the time of my life in this game. And last year, even with the kind of year that I had [a rotator cuff injury that put him on the disabled list in mid-May and a final, .224 batting average for 61 games] I have never enjoyed the game of baseball as much. I really think if people would try to have more fun out of it they would perform better, anyway."

To Porter, the problem that he had to lick isn't simply a baseball problem, but a problem that confronts all of society and reflects all of society. "I think sometimes that everybody wants to make a big deal out of drugs and sports, and out of alcohol and sports," he said. "But it really is no different than it is in society. We are the same as everybody else. We screw up, too."

But the pressure of trying to make it in pro baseball. . . .

"What is pressure?" Porter retorted. "I think of pressure as being a man that's struggling with a nine-to-five job and he's got four or five kids to feed and he's only making $25–30,000 a year. Now to me, that is pressure."

Very true. But there *is* a special pressure, an overwhelming pressure that builds up in pro baseball, a game in which everything can be measured down to the last decimal point. A man's batting average sinks below .250 or his earned run average soars above 4.00, there's no escaping it. *That's* pressure.

And then there's the peer pressure that leads to so many problems, the "it's-part-of-the-game-so-you-better-do-it" pressure applied by the guys who have been around, and who seem to know.

Above all, though, there's the pro baseball lifestyle.

"The thing that kills us as ball players is all the idle time that we have," Darrell Porter said. "We're in the perfect situation for something like that to happen."

Travel around the minor leagues for a while, observe the players on and off the field, and the extent of that problem becomes evident. There's hardly a club that doesn't have one, or two, or more heavy drinkers. Baseball people don't like to talk about it, but it's there, an ever-present threat that should be discussed openly and frankly and frequently.

As we've seen, the threat occasionally surfaces. A Darrell Porter, a Don Newcombe, a Bob Welch talks publicly about the problem. For the most part, though, drinking is something baseball men would rather do than discuss.

Want to know what drinking can do to a young man? Ask Dickie Noles of the Chicago Cubs. To know Dickie Noles—I mean, to really know him—is to like him, and to root for him. He's the type of person who'll give a friend the shirt off his back. But even Dickie's friends have learned to keep their distance when he starts drinking the hard stuff.

The Noles story is a hopeful one. He's trying to beat the drinking problem before the drinking problem beats him. "I learned," he said during his first spring training with the Cubs in March of '82, "liquor just tears you down. You start going into shots, then, next thing you know, you don't know what you're doing."

Dickie found that out the hard way. When the guys wanted to have a post-game drink, he went along. Peer pressure again. It can destroy a man. Especially a man who can't handle his liquor.

"Liquor just changes me," Dickie said. "I get liquor in me, I don't know when to stop. First thing I want to do is nail somebody."

Noles did some of his heaviest drinking in '81, after the Phillies sent him to Oklahoma City. It was hard going back to the minors for a pitcher who had been in a World Series the year before. It was easy to fall into the drinking habit down there.

"You have a bad night or something," Dickie said, "I'm going to pound 'em. The hell with my body. You have a good game, it's, 'Hey, let's celebrate.' Drinking eats your liver up. It eats your mind up, too. When I drink liquor I'm a different person. I'm a Dr. Jekyll and Mr. Hyde. It took me a while to learn it. Guys would say, 'Is Dickie drinking liquor? Stay away from him.' "

That was sound advice. "Trouble finds him," Phillies minor league pitching instructor Bob Tiefenauer was saying recently. "It's like that old cartoon—you know, the guy with the black cloud hanging over his head."

The stories of Dickie Noles' close calls are legend. In Venezuela one winter they had to sneak him out of the country—"put a wig on him and dress him up as a woman to get him out," Tiefenauer said. That's how much of a disturbance Dickie stirred up after having too much to drink.

Then there was the time early in Noles' minor league career with the Phillies when Tiefenauer heard a knock on his door at two in the morning. "You've got to help us, Tief," the man at the door said. "Somebody's got a .45 against Dickie's head in the parking lot."

Tiefenauer threw on some clothes and he and one of the Phillies' minor league trainers rushed down. Sure enough, a guy was standing over Noles in the parking lot of the Royal Inn in Clearwater, Fla., pointing a gun at him and saying, "Move and I'll blow your head off."

Dickie? He was too drunk to be frightened. Fear wasn't in his vocabulary at times like this. Instead of cowering on the ground, pleading for his life, he was talking back to the guy, telling him, "You might as well shoot because if I get up I'm going to kick your ass again."

Somehow, Tiefenauer and others managed to convince the man

holding the gun not to pull the trigger. Finally, the police arrived and Noles walked away unharmed.

"People kept telling me all these years that sooner or later something was going to happen to me [if he didn't stop drinking]," Dickie said. "Finally, it all got me in one year. Last year [1981] was a pretty rough year to go through."

There was a fight with a man in a Des Moines hotel. And a run-in with Phillies general manager Paul Owens in a bar at a Chicago hotel. Owens, like Noles, is not the friendliest of drunks. The police had to be called before that skirmish was broken up.

Drinking can do that to people—to players, to general managers, to minor leaguers, to major leaguers, to anybody. The smart ones find out before it's too late that drinking . . . and drugs . . . don't have to be a part of the game. But anybody who thinks they aren't is simply fooling himself.

There isn't much doubt that the drinking problem, when it arises, often begins early in a young man's minor league career. On the use of amphetamines, though, judgments seem to vary. Darrell Porter talked about getting hooked on them in the major leagues, not the minors. But that doesn't mean "greenies" haven't been made available in minor leagues clubhouses.

Eddie Molush, a promising righthanded relief pitcher in the Phillies organization whose career was cut short by a sore arm, didn't have to make it to the major leagues to see "greenies" in use. "One of the things that upset me at the Triple A level was when I saw guys using 'greenies'," said Molush. Later, after his pitching career had ended, Molush went to a game at Veterans Stadium and visited the clubhouse to see a former teammate. "Just looking at him," he said, "there was no doubt in my mind he was 'buzzed' beyond all belief. 'Christ,' I thought, 'is that what you've got to do to be here?' "

For some, sadly enough, it is. The pressure doesn't end when a man gets to the big leagues; frequently, it intensifies. Getting there is tough; staying there can be tougher. "There's a lot of pressure on them to stay where they are," Molush said, "and they're going to take something to keep them up there."

It would be naive to think that the idea of using artificial means to get "high" is unknown in the minor leagues. I remember vividly how upset Lee Elia got on one trip with his Reading team to West Haven when he caught several of his players smoking marijuana under the stands after a game. "One year in Rocky Mount," said Molush, "it got to be a big joke. It was the bullpen staff—the relievers—and the 'dopers'. That was our pitching staff. All the starters were the 'dopers'. They'd smoke 'pot' before the game."

That's hardly astonishing news. High school kids smoke it. College kids smoke it. Kids on street corners smoke it. Of course, some professional ball players smoke it. The pressures of the business being what they are, it would be absurd to assume otherwise. A young player sees his teammates using it, chances are he's going to try it, too. Maybe he'll like it, maybe he won't. And maybe he'll become dependent on it—or some stronger drug—as Darrell Porter ultimately did.

Certainly the follow-the-leader syndrome, so common in baseball clubhouses, adds to the danger. If a young player sees a respected veteran swallowing "greenies" before a game, is it surprising that he begins gulping them down, too?

Randy Lerch explained it this way: "I just think it's a learning experience, and you have to learn yourself. They didn't work for me, so we'll go on to the next page. It gave me a sense of a laid-back attitude, where I wouldn't go after the hitter aggressively. The problem was, it gave me a sense of throwing the ball so well that I didn't have to pitch any more. A lot of times I'd just throw pitches right down the middle and I got hurt."

So much of baseball is played in the head, so much of the struggle to become—and remain—a major leaguer is waged mentally that it should come as no surprise that many ball players are tempted to try something that's supposed to make the daily grind seem easier. It seems safe to say that professional baseball's drug problem isn't as serious as professional football's drug problem, which became headline news in the summer of '82 when it became evident that a significant number of National Football League players had switched to cocaine for their "pre-game meal."

Darrell Porter read those reports with more than passing interest. He knew what Don Reese and George Rogers and all the other admitted "coke" users were going through. He'd been there, too.

"I know one thing," Porter said, "at least I feel like we don't have that kind of problem in baseball. We've definitely got a problem, but I think our problems are more alcohol than anything."

Alcohol *and* uppers, that's baseball's most serious problem, the deadliest double play in the game. Baseball players don't have to peak, get sky high for that one, big Sunday afternoon effort. They don't have to play a game in which painful injuries are the norm. You can see why a football player might go for the "hard" stuff, and why a baseball player, whose greatest challenge is getting through the long season and filling all those idle hours away from home, might be more inclined to get hooked on booze and uppers.

"Guys get to where early in the season they take one [upper],"

Darrell Porter said. "Then by the middle of the season they get to two—every day."

It may not be as dramatic a problem as that faced by pro football, but it's a serious problem just the same, one that fairly cries for major corrective measures, not the head-in-the-sand approach that seems to be favored by so many baseball people.

In a general sense, we contribute to the "delinquency" of our athletes in this country by placing them on a pedestal. We coddle our sports heroes. As long as they hit home runs, or throw strikes, or score touchdowns, or crash the boards for rebounds we put them in a special category. We let them—even encourage them—to get away with murder. As Darrell Porter found out the hard way, we're not doing them any favor.

"One thing I know," the Cardinal catcher said. "Guys [athletes] aren't afraid. Nobody's afraid to do drugs. I wasn't because I knew one thing: If I got caught somebody was going to bail me out. I've seen it happen too many times before—athletes getting caught with marijuana and nothing happens. Just like when one of us is driving down the road going 90 miles an hour. They don't write us a ticket. They let us off. That was one of my problems, too. Nobody ever made me be responsible for what I was doing. They'd always get me off the hook some way. So consequently I said, 'Hey, I can get away with this stuff."

The Darrell Porters, and the Don Newcombes discovered from firthand experience that they really weren't getting away with a thing. By closing one eye to what was going on, the men who ran their sport—and society in general—weren't helping them a bit. The artificial highs the drug users experienced were too often followed by devastating lows.

It took a long time for pro football to get seriously involved in a drug prevention program, but over the last few years the NFL has significantly stepped up its efforts. Now it's baseball's turn to face the problem squarely—and the place to start is in the minor leagues, where habits, both good and bad, are formed.

8

REMEMBERING WHERE
THEY CAME FROM

Down there, in the minor leagues, they played the game of baseball. Up here, in the major leagues, they're engaged in the business of baseball. They're today's big leaguers. They beat the odds—and long odds they are—to make it to the big leagues, to enjoy the benefits of playing baseball in an era when a man doesn't have to be an everyday player to make six figures a year.

Occasionally, you hear people say, "Those big leaguers, they're spoiled. They forget where they came from."

Where they came from, of course, are the minor leagues, 17 of which still operate in organized baseball. Considering some of the shortcomings of life in the minors—the poor facilities, the tough traveling, the low salaries and inadequate meal money—perhaps it's to be expected that today's big leaguers forget where they came from. Human beings have a way of putting unpleasant memories out of their minds.

But have they really forgotten?

Were those difficult, growing-up days in the Pioneer League or the Carolina League or the Eastern League or the Pacific Coast League really all that unpleasant? Or do today's successful, high-salaried big leaguers look back on their minor league days with a smile, a pleasant sense of nostalgia? Could it possibly be that the bad, old days were really the good, old days?

To find the answer to that fascinating question, a number of major league baseball players were asked to reflect on their minor league days. Many of them seemed to enjoy reminiscing about their early years in pro baseball. With very few exceptions, even experiences that must have been unpleasant at the time were recalled with a smile, a touch of humor.

They talked about having fun playing baseball in the minor leagues. Fun playing in bad parks under bad lights? Fun taking eight and 10-hour bus rides? Fun staying in bad hotels? Fun struggling to make ends meet?

Yes, fun. At least, when they look back now they remember the good times they had, the good friends they made. There's something about the friends a guy makes in the minor leagues. People get closer there. Baseball is really an individual game cloaked in a team concept. There's a tendency for players to grow selfish, especially players on non-contending teams. But in the minors—particularly the low minors—a kindship, a camaraderie. Guys actually root for each other, worry about each other, care about each other. Down there, a feeling exists that they're all in it together, waging the battle to make it to the big leagues. When people are struggling, they tend to grow closer.

So let's see what some of today's established big leaguers think about when their minds flash back to a time when they were part of that huge, nameless fraternity of minor leaguers.

There might not be a better ball player in the game today than Mike Schmidt, the Phillies' two-time National League most valuable player. "I'll tell you, he's the best hitter in the game—at least in our league," Bruce Sutter, the Cardinals' ace relief pitcher, said during the '82 season. "If there's a better hitter in the other league I'm glad I don't have to pitch to him."

Yet the righthanded power hitter who terrorizes National League pitchers in the '80s batted .211 in his first season as a minor leaguer. Mike Schmidt, like most of the men who make it in the majors—the Dave Winfields, the Bob Horners are the exceptions—had to put it all together in the minors, where putting it together can be extremely hard.

Schmidt had the unique experience of breaking into organized baseball in a minor league ball park as the shortstop for a major league ball club. Part of the Phillies' enticement to make Schmidt sign—in addition to a rather modest $32,500 bonus—was the offer to fly him to Philadelphia, from his home in Dayton, Ohio, to work out with the big club.

"It just so happened the Phillies had their exhibition game with Reading that week," Mike recalled the day he signed his whopping, $10-million-plus, long-term contract in December of '81. "Larry Bowa was sick. He was unable to play. They asked me if I would want to play shortstop with the big league club. I said, 'Are you sure you don't mean go down and play shortstop with Reading *against* the big league club?' 'No, play *for* the big league club.' "

So off to Reading he went—as a Philadelphia Phillie for a night. "John Vukovich played third," Mike said. "Denny Doyle played second. Deron Johnson was playing first and there I was, playing shortstop. And I hit a home run to win the game—off Mike Fremuth [a righthander from Princeton University who came close to making the big leagues before switching to a career in law]."

Major leaguers loathe playing exhibition games against minor league clubs. In other words, Schmidt was surrounded by players who would have preferred not to be there. "I was probably the only guy enjoying the game," he said. "I was on Cloud Nine. They're all playing the game as an exhibition. They can't stand being there. . . ."

Nobody said much to the kid from Dayton. Then he hit the home run, and as he crossed the plate the Reading catcher said, "Nice hitting, Mike."

That's all. Just, "Nice hitting, Mike." But those three, little words were enough to make Schmidt feel like a million bucks. "I'll never forget the warm feeling I got when he said that to me," Mike said. "I didn't know anybody. The only person I knew in the whole stadium was my dad."

And Bob Boone had not only congratulated him, he had called him by name. It was the start of a beautiful friendship. "From the day he said, 'Nice hitting, Mike,' to this day right here he's the guy I've been together with longest and experienced the most with," Schmidt said shortly after Boone had been sold to the California Angels in December of '81. "We've come a long way together. Guys in the minor leagues have a lot of relationships like that because they've been through so much together. It's experiencing the hard times in the minor leagues, overcoming adversity together and dressing in shifts and traveling in buses at night and scuffling together that makes people become friends."

From the start of his professional baseball career in Reading in '71, the Boones—Bob and Sue—and the Rogodzinskis—Mike, the lefthanded-hitting outfielder, and his wife Jean—"sort of took me under their wing," Schmidt said. "They were the guys who could apparently relate to my position—guys who were drafted out of college and knew what it was for me to come from a college environment to this professional environment. They knew that I'd experienced better uniforms, better locker room conditions. They knew that I was one of the 'big-deal guys' on my college team and now I was thrown into an environment where I was absolutely starting all over,

and I was away from home. You know, it was a real test going right
to Double A."

His first road trip was to Elmira, where he sat and watched.
Then it was on to Pittsfield, Mass., where he played his first official
game. "I couldn't believe these guys were changing in shifts," he
said. "Half the team would go in and dress while the other half
would wait outside." The locker room simply wasn't big enough to
squeeze everybody in at one time. "It was steamy and dirty," said
Mike. "I thought, 'Geez, this is professional baseball.' "

It was a struggle from the start, or at least from the time opposing
pitchers began throwing him a steady diet of breaking balls. "I had
no idea how to hit a slider," Schmidt said. "From the time I got out
of college until almost halfway through my Triple A year I couldn't
hit breaking balls at all. They'd just freeze me at the plate. I had
trouble swinging at them, let alone hitting them.

"Those guys [at Reading] used to get on me unmercifully. I was
the whipping boy on that team. They had all paid their dues. They
had all been there for years, all working their way up, and then been
sent back down. . . ."

Schmidt played for $500 a month that first season. Dallas Green,
then the Phillies' farm director, sent him a contract for $800, or
maybe $850 the following winter. Telling the story, Mike stopped
abruptly when he mentioned the figure. "Was it $800 a month?" he
asked in all seriousness. "It wasn't $8,000, was it?"

This was the day after he'd signed that multi-million-dollar contract with the Phillies. In that context $800 simply didn't sound
right, but that's how much it was.

"I wrote him a letter back," Schmidt said. "I told him, 'Dallas, I
need $1,000.' I talked him into $900."

Things perked up that second year in Eugene, Ore. "I went with
a great ball club," recalled Mike. "That was probably the turning
point in my career right there."

Eugene was a Triple A club loaded with big league prospects.
Craig Robinson was there. And John Vukovich. And Andy Thornton. And Bill Robinson. And Oscar Gamble. and Joe Lis. And Bob
Boone. And Larry Cox. And Bob Spence. Some would go on to make
it big. All would at least make it, if only for a short time.

"Being on that team, that was really when I first realized how
close I was to being in the big leagues," Schmidt said.

Looking back on it now, this five-time home run champion called
his season with the Eugene Emeralds "one of my most fun years in
my whole baseball career." And, he added, "that includes the last
two years, too." That's quite a statement for a man to make a short

time after winning back-to-back most valuable player awards, and one year after being named the outstanding player on a triumphant World Series team. Yet that's the impact minor league baseball can have on even the greatest of big league stars, if they'll only accept it for what it is, rather than fight it every step of the way.

Mention that season in Eugene to Mike Schmidt and the memories come rushing back. "I'll never forget walking into Tacoma," he said. "We played there opening night and I remember riding on the bus from the hotel; I knew nothing about going out to the ball park early and taking cabs out, playing cards and all that. I sat around on pins and needles all day at the hotel waiting for opening day in Triple A, wondering how good these guys going to be. You know how Oscar Gamble is. From the time we left the hotel to the time we got to the ball park, he never shut up. We rode past ball parks with kids playing and he's say, 'That's where it all started. There it is. Out there. . . .' He's sitting in the back of the bus saying, 'I know some of you rookies are nervous. What's that first pitch going to be? Fast ball? Slider?' He's screaming all the way to the ball park, and I mean funny as hell, and then he goes up there and strikes out three times. The guy struck me out three times, too. On the bus going back to the hotel he [Gamble] says, 'That guy struck me out three times [and] I don't even know his name.' "

Ah, the fun of being young and a minor leaguer on the way up. "I remember Joe Lis one night shaking everybody's hand in the dugout *before* he went up to hit so he didn't have to do it afterwards because he was going to hit a home run," said Mike Schmidt, laughing. "And he hit one."

The early going in the Pacific Coast League in '72 wasn't much better than his '71 season in the Eastern League. Mike was struggling to make contact, battling to get base hits. Bill Robinson helped. "He had a lot to do with my career," Mike said. "He was one of the first guys who really gave me a lot of confidence. He would tell me that I was a good player and that I was going to make it some day. But I guess the big turning point in my career was when Seminick [Eugene manager Andy Seminick, who caught for the 1950 Phillie Whiz Kids] came walking out. . . ."

Schmidt leaned back, his eyes half closed. It was almost as if he could still see Seminick walking on the field one day during batting practice, heading for the kid infielder. "I'll never forget," Mike said. "You know, this bow-legged guy, and he's got a big chew in his mouth, and he looks at me and he says, 'You ever play any second base?' I said, 'Sure.' I never played second base a day in my life. But I was hitting like .201 at the time and Paul Owens, as I understand it, was ready to send me back to Double A because I'm struggling so much. Vuk [John Vukovich] is the same way. He's playing second [instead of third, his normal position], and he can't hit because he's concentrating too much on trying to play second base. So I said, 'Sure, I'll play second base. I'd love to play some second base.' 'Okay,' Seminick said, 'how'd you feel about switching with John? He'll play third, you'll play second.' "

Schmidt was only too willing. This was about midway in his second season of pro ball and a change—any change—would have been an improvement. Maybe he'd been worrying about his hitting too much while playing third. Maybe if he had a new position to occupy his mind, he'd relax at the plate and start making contact.

That's exactly how it worked. "I started playing second," said Mike, "and it seemed like I totally concerned myself with my defense and just forgot about the pressure that was on me to learn to hit. I started hitting like crazy. I ended up hitting over .290, which means from that point on I had to hit a good .350 or .360. I hit 26 home runs and I had 90-some ribbies [runs batted in]."

A star—better make that a superstar—was born.

"We go to Albuquerque," Schmidt said. "Albuquerque had [Tom] Paciorek at first, [Davy] Lopes at second, [Von] Joshua in center, [Ron] Cey at third, [Steve] Yeager catching, Doug Rau, Charlie Hough and Buddy Solomon pitching. We played them an eight-game series—they're like the cream of the league—and we beat 'em the first seven games. I just 'smoked' for seven straight games. I hit like five home runs. I made diving plays, barehand charging plays, almost beat them single-handedly. I think that series right there turned my career around.

"I remember Lasorda [Tommy Lasorda, Albuquerque's manager at the time], he's in the dugout and he's screaming at me, going crazy. Next day in the paper, he's saying, 'Best I've ever seen. . . .' They beat us the last game, so we beat them seven out of eight. After that series, I'll never forget, Andy walked over to my locker and he reached into his pocket and he said, 'Here, son, take this $20 and go out and buy yourself a steak. You deserve it.' "

Mike Schmidt isn't about to forget his first trip to Hawaii, either. "We played in that old stadium, Honolulu Stadium," he said. "They've got pineapple in a cooler in the middle of the locker room—slabs of pineapple, already cut. I started eating that right after I got there, one after another after another."

Then the game began. Bloated with pineapple, Mike Schmidt tried to play. "Second inning, I'm out at second base," he said, "and I got to puke. Andy Seminick had to take me out of the game, I was so sick. I went back into the clubhouse and stood in the shower and vomited for half an hour. All pineapple. To this day—*to this day*—I'm scared of pineapple."

And to this day, he remembers those minor league adventures and those minor league friends. "You're experiencing hard times with a lot of guys that you've really become close to and care about," he said. "You spend time with them. You get to know their families. They're pivotal years, and you experience it all together . . . The minor leagues were fun times for me because I got breaks and I moved right up the ladder. I guess I had just enough minor league experience. I was there just long enough to really say I had a good time. If I was forced to be buried in the minor leagues for four, five, six years, who knows what would have happened to me?"

Okay, fair enough. Maybe the shortness of his minor league experience was what made it all so much fun in retrospect. How about the guys who spend six, seven, eight, even 10 years bouncing around the bushes from Walla-Walla, Wash., to Springfield, Ill., from Waterbury, Conn., to Reno, Nev., from Spartanburg, S.C., to Oklahoma City? How about the Dane Iorgs and the Ed Farmers and the Jim Morrisons and all the rest?

Talk about struggling to get to the big leagues; that's what Dane Iorg had to do. He was 27 when the Cardinals sent him to Springfield, Ill., for yet another minor league season. He was 28 when, after hitting .371 to lead the American Association, he finally made it to the big leagues to stay.

"It's a crazy game," Iorg said. "I'm lucky, I'll tell you. Look how close I came to not getting an opportunity. Everything had to fall just right. People talk about pressure in the big leagues. There's no pressure on me now, not after what I've been through. When I was battling for that 25th man on the roster—to be the last man cut or the last man to make the team—*that* was pressure. That was unbelievable. I've had all the pressure.

"I was a pinch-hitter [in the big leagues] for a year and a half. I've hit in a lot of crucial situations where people say, 'Hey, there's a lot of pressure on you.' But nothing during the season can compare to the pressure of having to go out every day of spring training and perform and know that your job's on the line and know that you're either going to make a living or you're not going to be able to make a living. That's like a life and death thing. That's survival and non-survival. This other stuff isn't. Not any more."

Yet from a purely baseball standpoint Iorg came to enjoy the minor league experience. "I mean," he said, "that's baseball, the minor leagues. You don't have the attention from the media. You don't have all the fans you have in the big leagues. It's a whole different ball game. You're still struggling to achieve. You meet some guys you really care about. You have some great times together because it seems you're all depending on one another.

"The year I was sent down by the Phillies the first time, I went down to Oklahoma City and my wife and I had an apartment next to Jim [Morrison] and all my teammates from the previous year and we were like in heaven. If the Phillies had asked me to come back, the only reason I'd have gone would have been because I'd be making a better living for my family. From an enjoyable standpoint I'd have much rather been in Oklahoma City. I remember that very vividly. I got down there and I thought, 'Well, what do you know? I'm finally back to the real world of baseball, so to speak.'

"It *is* a different world. In the minor leagues it's just you against the other people, and nobody cares. I mean, you could play in an empty ball park instead of the 2–3,000 you get and it wouldn't matter that much. There's just a camaraderie among the players. In the big leagues you feel that so many people are trying to get a piece of the pie. That's the frustrating part about the big leagues."

And yet for all those thousands of players fighting their way up the minor league ladder, getting to the big leagues is all that really matters. It's strange. Once they get to the big leagues so many of them look back on the minor league years as the happy years, the "fun" years. But they wouldn't want to go back.

"I think," said Dane Iorg, "like anything else the fun is getting there. That's the real fun. It's like a new car, a new house, making a lot of money, whatever it is. The fun is in achieving it, not in having it.

"Maybe that's it. Maybe everybody in the minor leagues has that same goal, is looking for that same thing. You feel it from everybody and so you develop a real close bond with everybody. In the big leagues—hey, everybody's achieved that dream now and they're all going off in different directions finding out what they want to do next. I know I don't have near the personal relationships with big league players I had in the minor leagues. I mean, I like to play. I enjoy the game. I want us to win and I try as hard as I can. But you're fighting for championships now. You're not fighting to be in the big leagues, and the real struggle is in trying to get to the big leagues. Now you're here. Now you're fighting for championships and it's not as important as getting to the big leagues. It's strange."

And strangest of all is the often startling difference between life in the minors and life in the majors. "Look at the playing situations in Triple A," Dane said. "Look at the ball parks, the clubhouses, the bleachers where the people sit, our dugouts, the bats, the equipment, the uniforms. I mean, it's second rate. You get to the big leagues you're playing in enclosed stadiums with AstroTurf, big clubhouses. Right there, that's enough to intimidate you. At Springfield, we didn't even have a clubhouse [for most of his season there]. We had to dress at home. My wife had to wash my uniform each day before I came to the park." That was a year after Iorg had opened the season in Philadelphia, playing first base for the Phillies. Talk about two different worlds. . . .

"If there was anything that intimidated me more than just playing at Vet Stadium [in Philadelphia], I don't know what it would be," he said. "Just to drive to the ball park and look at that thing. I'd think, 'Hey, look where I've been. I played in Walla-Walla, [Wash.], in Reading, [Pa.], in the Carolina League, in Okie City, in Springfield, and now I'm going to play in this thing. That's my home. That's the office now.' I couldn't get that out of my head for a while because it was so unreal. I couldn't believe they had drink machines and hot dogs and potato chips and tables and chairs and big lockers and all the bats you wanted and free gloves, free shoes, anything you wanted you had. That was the most astonishing thing to me. I'd go across that Walt Whitman Bridge [connecting South Jersey, where he lived, and South Philadelphia, where Veterans Stadium was located] and I'd see that thing and I'd think of the places I played in the minor leagues and I'd go nuts."

Surely, most of them have had similar feelings at one time or another. The big leagues—be it the Vet or Yankee Stadium or Dodger Stadium or Fenway Park—is the promised land.

"You play in these rotten places [in the minors] and nobody caters to you," Iorg said. "Then you get to the big leagues, you're just not ready for it. You're not prepared. I think maybe the best thing they could do when they signed a player is let him go to the big leagues for a week or 10 days. Let him see what it's like. Then he can motivate himself. I'd never stepped in a big league clubhouse before I got there and it just kind of overwhelmed me."

But for all the dream-come-true aspects of making it to the big leagues, a man leaves a part of himself in the minors. Above all, he leaves a lot of very good friends.

As Iorg said—as most of them say—it's different in the big leagues. Friendships with teammates generally aren't as close, as lasting. In part, that may be a defense mechanism set up by men who have learned, the hard way, that here-today, gone-tomorrow is a way of life in professional baseball. Is there a man playing the game who wasn't jolted, early in his career, by the trade or release of a teammate who was one of his closest friends? Perhaps for that reason a ball player learns to build an emotional wall to protect him from getting jolted again and again and again. In the big leagues, there's almost a tendency to regard a teammate who's been cut as a "non-person". He's gone. Forget him.

"That," said Dane Iorg, "is the greatest mystery to me—how that can happen. But it's true. I know myself when one of my friends or teammates is sent back to the minor leagues you come to the park the next day and it's like he's never been there."

Not so in the minors, though. The "wall," in most instances, hasn't been built yet.

One of Iorg's closest friends on that '77 Oklahoma City team was third baseman Jim Morrison. "We'd stay in the same apartment complex," Morrison said. "We'd ride to and from the ball park together. [Pitcher] Danny Boitano, the same way. I really don't have friends like that in the big leagues. I actually depended on Dane. I was struggling to get through the season [after being sent down], and he was a stabilizing force in my life."

And then suddenly, on June 15—the trade deadline—Iorg was traded to the Cardinals organization. One day he was playing baseball with his friends in Oklahoma City. Next day he was going to the airport to meet his new teammates in New Orleans, where the Cardinals' Triple A farm club played at the time. Jim Morrison rode with him to the airport. On the way back, he was in tears. That's how meaningful a minor league friendship can be. Stay in baseball long enough, though, and a man learns to ride with those emotional punches. Last spring, for example, the Chicago White Sox, Morrison's team at the time, traded Greg Pryor. "He was one of my closest friends on the team," Morrison said, "but it certainly didn't affect me the way it did when Dane got traded."

"I think that's the hardest thing—to have friends and have them traded away," said Bob Forsch of the St. Louis Cardinals. "Boy, when Jimmy Dwyer got sent down the first time I was crushed. He was my roommate on the road and all of a sudden I didn't have anybody. Everybody else was older. It was really hard. I was in my room by myself. I didn't really have anybody to eat with."

Forsch had come up through the minors with Dwyer. "We'd go to Tulsa, some place like that," Bob said, "and we'd get our apartments close to each other, ride in to the ball park and back. Then all of a sudden he was gone. I think I kind of learned then that maybe it's not that good [to have close friends in baseball]. Maybe it's better to have friends that aren't in baseball."

One of Bob Boone's closest friends through his early years in

baseball was Greg Luzinski. It was one of those rare baseball friendships that began in the low minors and kept going all the way to the
big leagues. They have finally been separated; Luzinski is with the
Chicago White Sox now, Boone with the California Angels. But the
friendship, built on their life together in the minor leagues, endures.

"We went down to our first big league spring training in 1970,"
Boone recalled. "We're all excited. We're going to go to Clearwater
[to train with the Phillies]."

But they needed a place to stay. "I remember Greg got there a
few days before us," Boone said. "He was going to check the housing.
You know how tough Clearwater is at that time of the year. Greg
ended up standing in line to get a little house on Clearwater Beach.
Cost us $500 a month, and that was way out of our range. We shared
it. A two bedroom house and we each had a baby, and we shared it.
When we look back on it we just laugh. So many things happened.
We started out splitting the groceries. You know who took the short
end of the stick on that. Greg would come in, make a sandwich and
take a whole package of bologna. 'Where's the bologna?' 'Oh, I had a
sandwich earlier. '

"One night Jean [Luzinski] and Sue [Boone] and I are sitting in
the living room watching TV. Greg had two bowls of popcorn. *Two
bowls.* He was in the kitchen making it. We heard it cooking. 'Great.
That's nice. Greg's making popcorn.' He came out, sat down in a
chair without looking at us—and he wasn't kidding—and he started
eating out of the two bowls. We didn't even say anything. All three
of us sat there and just stared at him. Finally, after a little while, he
looked up. 'Oh, would you like some?' We still get on him about
that."

It's great how the laughter starts to flow when established big
leaguers sit down and start talking about their minor league growing
pains, about their first Florida instructional league perhaps. "You
talk about brutal," said Boone. "We were in those Palm Apartments
[on Clearwater Beach]. . . ."

Sounds nice. Palm Apartments on the beach. Has a ring to it,
right? Take my word for it; it sounded better than it looked. Matter
of fact, the year after Bob Boone and friends stayed there, the place
was condemned.

"We got $15 a day and we got the room for free, so everybody
lived right there," Boone said. "We all knew we were getting
shafted, but it was really neat. We were playing ball during the day.
We'd come back and somebody would have the grill going and
everybody would barbecue on the same grill. Then we'd sit on the
lawn and shoot the bull. We got into going to jai alai, too. We'd pool

our money and everybody would buy a two dollar ticket and share the winnings on a quinella ticket. We had a ball."

No money. A terrible apartment. And they had a ball. It says a lot for the resiliency of youth.

"Those are just great memories for us," Bob Boone said. "We loved it. Even the bad part. When I went to Raleigh-Durham [Carolina League], Walter Brock was there. He had to be the tightest man who ever ran a club. He sold bats. We didn't have any helmets. Yet we had a great time."

Tight-fisted operators were—still are, in most cases—a fact of minor league life. But Bob Boone wasn't exaggerating. The late Walter Brock had a tighter fist than most. "Once I pinch-hit with runners on second and third," Boone recalled. "I couldn't find a helmet that fit, so I went up there with this little helmet sitting 'way up on top of my head."

Boone and Luzinski were in Raleigh-Durham in 1969. Greg tore the league apart that year—until a beaning slowed him down. He left a trail of tape-measure home runs throughout the Carolina League. There was one in Red Springs, N.C., that took off over the left field fence, cleared a light tower and landed on a road some 500 feet from the plate. There was another that struck the power wires high above the outer fence in Durham. And a drive that soared high over the center field fence in Raleigh and landed on the highway beyond.

But it took Greg a while to start unloading those moon shots. Walter Brock was impatient. "He wanted to ship me out after two weeks," Luzinski said. Fortunately, Brock didn't get his way. Luzinski stayed. One day he hit three straight home runs. The fourth time he came up the bases were loaded. Greg took three mighty swings . . . and struck out. The fans gave him a standing ovation, anyway.

Yessir, those were the days. The uniforms were hand-me-downs from the parent club. When I joined the Raleigh-Durham Phillies for a road trip in July of that year, Luzinski was squeezing his National Football League-fullback-sized body into a pair of pants that pitcher Joey Jay had worn two years before. His name was still scrawled on the waistband in indelible ink. Meal money was even tighter than the uniforms. The going rate was $3 a day.

Then it was tough. Now it's something to laugh about. "Guys would fight over who would drive when we went over to Raleigh [from Durham]," Bob Boone recalled. They fought for the privilege because the driver received three dollars, and in those days three dollars meant something.

"I'll never forget one year Howie Bedell [who ran the Phillies' minor league spring training camp] sent out a whole pamphlet with a big section on the importance of eating properly and getting a balanced diet," Boone said. "You read the pamphlet, then you get to spring training and they give you something like $29.50 a week to live on—in a resort area."

So much for balanced diets. Unless, of course, Bedell had in mind balancing a hot dog with a hamburger.

The most balanced meal—certainly the most expensive—that Luzinski ate that season was on the night I met him in Raleigh-Durham. Since the games—the triple header, remember?—had been postponed, I called him and arranged to meet him for dinner. Minutes later Walter Brock, the GM, called. "Let's have dinner," he said. "I can't," I told him. "I'm having dinner with Greg Luzinski. He's meeting me at the motel at six." Brock wouldn't take no for an answer. "Fine," he said, "we'll all go."

It wasn't until later that I found out Brock and Luzinski had a deep-seated dislike for each other, and that they'd had a heated argument over Greg's expenses for a medical trip to Philadelphia that very morning. The argument ended, Greg informed me, with Brock shouting, "I never want to see you in this office again." And now, hours later, he practically insisted on taking Greg out to dinner. It was a great example of the power of the press. Brock, trying very hard to make a good impression on the big-city journalist from Philadelphia, must have been scared stiff over what Luzinski would say about him if he wasn't there.

I phoned Greg at his apartment to tell him we wouldn't be alone at dinner. Something told me it would be a good idea to warn him. Greg received the news with the aplomb of a Teddy Kennedy fan who just found out he was going to have to sit through a Ronald Reagan speech on the economy. "If he goes, I won't," Greg told me. But finally he gave in after I pointed out to him that this was really the chance he'd been waiting for—the opportunity to get a penny-pinching minor league general manager to spring for a good meal.

So off to dinner we went, and let me say this for Greg: he made the most of his opportunity.

Noley Campbell, the Raleigh-Durham manager, and another non-fan of the GM's, showed up, too. So the four of us wound up in a very nice, rather expensive restaurant as the guests of the general manager. As I recall, we ran up quite a bill. Greg, just a growing boy at the time, hit all the high spots on the menu. Maybe it was our imagination, but you could almost see Walter Brock flinch every time Luzinski signaled for a waiter. Noley Campbell and I didn't do badly, either, but Greg was in rare form that night. I'll say this for Brock. He never uttered a word of protest. He was either playing the role of the perfect host or—and I lean to the latter theory—struck speechless by the size and quality of Luzinski's order.

Somehow, Bob Boone missed out on that rare treat. But his minor league days left him with some warm memories, just the same.

"I remember staying down on the beach at the Triple A level in a place called The Happy Traveler," Boone said. "We stayed four in a room. Four!"

Two would have been crowded in those rooms. Four in a room was ridiculous. But they put up with it because they had no choice. And really, it wasn't as difficult as it sounds. Teamwork was the key. When two guys exhaled, the other two inhaled.

"You really knew guys then," Boone said. "But now, in the big leagues, you get single rooms on the road and everybody's going in different directions. You may not even see somebody except on the field."

In those days you saw your teammates everywhere—on the field, in the eating joints, in the hotels. No wonder the friendships were so lasting.

"Those friendships," said Keith Moreland of the Cubs, "were built on respect. You grow up down there when you're making no money and you live so close together. The only thing you've got money to do is buy a six-pack and sit in the apartment at night because you can't go out, and you get to know those guys. You get to know them real well. The ones you become friends with are friends for life. I think of all the good times in the minor leagues with guys we got to know for a long time—the Jim Wrights [Kansas City], the Kevin Sauciers [Detroit], the George Vukoviches [Philadelphia]. You build up friendships that you never forget. It seems like you get to know a person better in the minor leagues when he's broke, he's struggling. We're all going for one goal, and that's to get to the big leagues. There were some guys that didn't make it and you say, 'Gosh dang, I thought they were pretty good.' You start to wonder, especially when you're in 'A' ball and you see guys you thought were great get out of the game, 'How am I going to make this?' And then you get a chance and you make it and you look back on it and you say, 'God, it was all fun.' But you never want to go back and do it again."

It was fun because, for all the struggling, all the hardships, those were relatively carefree, trouble-free days for most of them. The minors seemed almost like a continuation of school days. They saw new places, did new things. All for one, one for all.

"Buck Martinez, George Brett and I were playing in Omaha," relief pitcher Mark Littell said. "We had a day off and we fixed a heck of a dinner, a barbecue. The meal was so great that we even took a picture of it. Buck barbecued, I made the salad and George set the table." Even then, apparently, George had the stuff that stars are made of.

Anyway, after dinner the Three Musketeers decided to take in a movie. "We're driving along," recalled Littell, "and here's this carnival. So we decided to pull in and check out what's going on."

One of the games caught their attention. "What we were wanting was a great big stuffed animal for our apartment," said Littell. "So we figured the best way to get one was to win it at the carnival. We each had about 25 bucks on us. The game we were playing was a dollar a throw. We kept playing the thing, kept playing it, and before we knew it each of us had spent 15 or 18 bucks trying to win this big, stuffed animal—a dog or a donkey, something like that. Only we were the donkeys really.

"There started to be a crowd gathering around, so this guy said to us, 'Hey, you guys lost what? Forty or 50 bucks?' We said, 'Yeah.' He said, 'I'll tell you what I'll do. It'll be good for business. If you get the ball in the slot [and win the game] I'll give you all your money back *and* I'll give you the stuffed animal. How's that sound?'"

It sounded absolutely sensational. And then, just to show Littell, Martinez, Brett and the spectators how easy it was, the man took the ball and sent it flying. It landed—kerplunk!—in the slot. Damn, it looked easy. "This guy would do it every time," Little said. "We'd watch him. We'd look at the ball. We'd look at the slots. We'd watch his feet."

If there was a trick, they couldn't spot it. So off they went, throwing more dollar bills into the kitty.

"Before we knew it," said Mark, "we lost 70 bucks. We didn't go to the show that night. No possible way. We didn't have any money."

But they laughed about it. Later, anyway. Okay, much, much later. But eventually they *did* laugh. Even if they didn't see a movie, they had fun that night—something to think about and joke about years later.

"The game's a lot different in the minors," said Keith Hernandez, now one of the top hitters in the National League. "When you're a prospect in the minors you play. In the major leagues it's a production thing. If you don't produce, they'll cut you loose. So there's less pressure in the minors. I enjoyed the minors a lot more. They made me into a man."

Most players talk about the fun they had in the low minors. Not Hernandez. "I think the most fun was Triple A," said the Cardinals first baseman, who got his Triple A experience in Tulsa.

"There's less petty jealousy in the minor leagues than at the big league level," Hernandez said, "although I saw a little bit of it [in his first minor league season]. A lot of people were a little resentful towards me because I was a $30,000 bonus baby. I had friction with some guys. They felt a little bitterness towards me because I was given every opportunity—even when I fell flat on my fact, which I did two years in a row in the minors. That was all behind me in Triple A. There weren't any problems there. But the first couple of years in 'A' ball [St. Petersburg, Fla.] and Double A [Little Rock, Ark.], there were a few petty jealousies, which bothered me. I mean, I can't help it if I got that kind of money. I almost got in a fist fight one time. But I think all in all, I made some great friends down there."

And, despite that rocky first year or two, Hernandez has mostly good memories about his minor league experience. Not that it was easy.

"In the Texas League we went 21 hours on a bus from Little Rock to El Paso," he said. "We slept on the bus. That was rough. I slept on the luggage rack a couple of times. I remember we took off at 11 o'clock at night after a night game, and we bused all night. Everybody got drunk, drank themselves to sleep. I woke up in the morning, the sun was rising, and we just happened to be going by a sign: 'El Paso 690 Miles.' That was a long ride. And then there was Midland, Texas. That was 19 hours. San Antonio was 17 hours. Amarillo was 12. That was a bush league. I swore I would never go back to that league. But you could do anything then. You'd be surprised how far you can push yourself when you're 19. You don't know any better then. You don't know there are plane flights. You don't know your luggage is taken up to your room [in the big leagues]. You don't know $35 or $40 a day meal money. All you know are bus rides and horseshit meal money and barely getting by. Things were a lot more simplified then. Things get more complex up at this level now. It's become such a big money game, and not just as far as salaries are concerned. It's big business. It's Hollywood."

Down there, though, it's Midland and El Paso and Little Rock. The big money, the glamour come later.

"People don't realize what we go through," Hernandez said. "I played with Mike Easler [of the Pirates] in the minors. I'm really very happy for him. He was a hard worker. Somebody put the rap on him that he wasn't a big league player. To see him spend 10 years in the minors and finally get a chance is great. It does your heart good because he's paid his dues more than anybody.

"Every player out here has paid his dues," Hernandez said as he sat in the Cardinals dugout before an exhibition game. "There's a lot of heartache and ups and downs along the road. And mental strain. I mean, people can say, 'Oh, cry on my shoulder,' but they can't relate to what we have to do out here. They have no idea of the mental battle that goes on and the things we have to deal with. The average person—95 percent of the people in the country—couldn't deal with it. They'd fold their tents. It takes a strong man. This game is a game of perseverance, of endurance. It's a test of the will."

And the stiffest test comes in those formative years, when a 19-year-old kid has to get off a bus following a 21-hour trip and play a baseball game, when a "bonus baby" fighting a slump in his first pro season has to overcome the slings and arrows of jealous teammates.

"In high school I hit .500," Hernandez said. "You're not used to making outs. I hit .256 my first year [in St. Petersburg, Fla.]. That was the biggest adjustment—that, and playing every day and learning to accept the fact that you're not going to get a hit every game, and learning to control my temper. I was a red-ass. I'd throw helmets. I threw a bucket of game balls out on the field once after I struck out. The balls were sitting in our dugout in Tulsa and I threw them all out on the field, 50 balls. That's all part of being young."

All that's behind him now. Hernandez has won a National League batting title, shared a most valuable player award. "I have great memories of the minor leagues," he said. "If I didn't make it [to the big leagues] and I played minor league ball until I was 28 and had to get a late start [on another career], I'd still have no regrets. I think everybody should have that experience. I would bet that 90 percent of the guys that go through it feel that way."

If so, Garry Maddox stands tall among the other 10 percent. "If you need the negative part of the minor leagues," he said one day, "talk to me. I hated it."

You won't catch Maddox talking about the "fun" times in Salt Lake City or Fresno or Phoenix. You won't hear him tell stories about the "good, old days." To him, they were rotten days.

Much of his negativism towards the minors stems from the raw deal he believes the Giants gave him when he first signed a pro contract in 1968. "To be a second-round draft choice and to be offered a $1,000 bonus," he said, "then to come down to spring training and find guys that were maybe 10th-round and got more than you. . . . That was my initiation into it. When you're trying to make ends meet, when you never had anything—been on welfare all your life, things like that—then to find out they weren't fair with you, it's bad. Here you are. You know nothing about contract negotiations or free agent drafts or anything and they come and make you an offer like that. I just assumed they're giving me the final offer, [that] if I want to play baseball I'd better take what I can get. My father said, 'Maybe we'll be able to get a car or something like that. See what he says.' 'Yeah,' I said, 'maybe we will.' Neither one of us had any idea. So when the cat came with $1,000, it was just like, 'Well, we were wrong.' I think little things like that will turn you against it."

Some guys learn to love the game long before they turn pro. Maddox wasn't one of them. He didn't grow up avidly following the game, spouting batting averages of his favorite players. "I guess everyone else, their love for the game was enough to keep them going," he said. "It wasn't for me. A lot of things I had to learn while I was in the big leagues and one of them was to love the game."

As far as Maddox was concerned, that first season in the minors was a disaster. "I couldn't stand those buses," he said. "Thirteen-hour bus trips! When I played in Salt Lake City, we'd go to Caldwell, Idaho."

A quiet, sensitive man, Garry must have done a lot of soul-searching during those long bus rides. He'd think about how the Giants screwed him, and he'd simmer, and by the time the bus deposited him and his higher-paid, if lower-round teammates in Caldwell, he'd be madder'n hell. It ate at him, and it ate at him some more until, finally, he decided to get out of baseball. He went in the service, wound up in Viet Nam for a year, and then decided to give baseball a second try.

"Service did something for me as far as helping me to grow up and helping me to realize there are people out there that are going to try to take advantage of you," Garry said. "When they do, if you think you can bury your head in the sand and run away from it, you're wrong. You've got to learn from these mistakes and be aware of these things. When I came out of the service I had matured to the point I wasn't going to run from anything any more. If somebody outsmarted me I was going to learn from it. I had a living to make and I had to do it in this world."

So he went out and did it. He went to Fresno for a year, hit .299 and was on his way. Fun year in Fresno, right Garry? Filled with lots of great memories and all that?

Not quite. If he had disliked playing in Salt Lake City, he loathed playing in Fresno. Or maybe it was the other way around. Maddox doesn't actually remember very much of what went on in those minor league seasons, before or after Viet Nam. "The year I played in Fresno," he said, "I can name maybe three guys off that team."

That's all. Three guys. And he'd have to think a while to remember them. That tells you a lot about what Garry Maddox thought about the minor leagues.

"I'm sure there were some good times," he said, "but I blocked them all out. I saw a thing on TV where they said people that were in Viet Nam, they block out the experiences they had while they were there."

Not that he was likening life in the minors to life in Viet Nam, mind you. But the fact is, Garry seems to recall as much about that year in Viet Nam as he does about those 120 games he played in Fresno in 1971, or the 68 games he played in Salt Lake City in 1968.

"In baseball," he said, "in life in general I guess, you've got to be able to enjoy things. The minor league experience was something else again. I didn't enjoy it. The only thing that got me to the big leagues was opportunity—the right place at the right time. I was in Triple A [in Phoenix] for 11 days. Eleven days isn't enough to tell whether you're going to be a good player, but the opportunity came. Gary Matthews was on the team. First or second game of that year, he hurt his ankle. Then, that's the year Willie McCovey broke his arm. I had to go [to the Giants]. I was all they had, all they could reach down and pull up. So I got up there."

He didn't really have that much of a feel for the game. He hated every minute of his minor league career, however brief it was. And he landed in the big leagues. Talent played a part, of course. So did luck. Never underestimate the importance of the latter in baseball.

Once he got to the big leagues and saw the players come and go, Garry Maddox came to truly understand what it was to play baseball for a living, and how difficult it was to establish relationships with people. A man loses something when a close friend suddenly leaves—as Jim Morrison did when Dane Iorg was traded, as Bob Forsch did when Jim Dwyer was traded—and so he builds that "wall". He toughs it out.

"Very seldom do baseball players say goodbye,'" Garry Maddox discovered. "We wear some kind of a mask. I guess in the back of your mind you know you're going to end up splitting up eventually. Very few guys keep in touch with one another. That's because you get close to somebody, then you 'lose' him and it's really tough. You have a friend and then he's gone. What we do is we block it out or we just turn off our emotions and never react to it. The game separates you."

In the minors, though, especially in the early years of a man's career, the game tends to bring players closer together. For a variety of reasons Garry Maddox missed out on that aspect of it. But then, minor league baseball can't be fun for everybody.

Larry Bowa found the fun in it—at least sometimes. There was the night in Eugene, Ore., when Frank Lucchesi, the Eugene manager, got the bright idea of entering Bowa, the scrawny, pitch-hitting shortstop, in a pre-game home run hitting contest. Eugene had some legitimate long-ball hitters on that team. Letting Bowa take his cuts with the likes of Joe Lis was virtually guaranteed to get a few laughs.

Bowa went along with the gag. He got up righthanded—that was the year he started switch-hitting—and, lo and behold, he sent a fly ball soaring over the left field fence. It was startling, astonishing and—what's more—nobody else could do it. Bowa won the contest. "They went nuts in Eugene," he said.

Garry Maddox may have been forced to learn to love baseball after he became a pro. Larry Bowa loved the game from the day he first played it. Along the way he had some rough times. His temper would explode—and when Bowa's temper exploded it registered on the Richter Scale. But watching Larry and his double play partner, Denny Doyle, come up through the minor leagues—through Spartanburg, S.C., and Reading, Pa., and Eugene, Ore.—was a treat. "We used to make people O-O-O-O and AHHHH in Spartanburg," Bowa said. "It was unbelievable."

They didn't exactly put the people to sleep in the other places, either. They turned "base hits" into double plays. They played with a flair, an exuberance that made them exciting to watch. Yet no two men could have been less alike. Bowa had that hair-trigger temper. He was liable to say anything at any time. Doyle was older and far more mature. He provided the steadying influence that Bowa needed.

"Denny was like a stabilizer," Bowa recalled. "He was very mature. He'd been to college. He had a family. He'd sit me down a lot of times and say, 'Man, you can't do this.' I was lucky to be able to play with somebody that mature. If I was playing with somebody as high strung as me, we'd have been tearing down walls."

Walls? Entire buildings probably. Maybe whole ball parks.

Bowa had a bad habit of getting tossed out of games. Bob Wellman, the Spartanburg manager, tried to convince him that he wasn't much help sitting in the clubhouse. Finally, Doyle came up with a plan designed to keep Bowa from getting ejected.

"He told Wellman, 'Next time he gets kicked out of a game why don't you take money from him?' " Bowa recalled. "Wellman calls me. 'Okay, Larry,' he says, 'from now on you pay the fine [to the league], then you pay me.' "

Bowa got the message and, with considerable effort, curbed his temper to a certain extent. Of course, he thought the idea was Wellman's. Little did he know his bosom buddy, his beloved pal at second base, had put the idea in the manager's head.

In those years, Bowa needed somebody to lean on, somebody who would give him a boost when necessary, or a boot when necessary. Larry was a worrier, and the first game he ever played in the minor leagues did nothing to ease those worries.

"My very first pro game," Bowa said, "and Nolan Ryan was pitching against us. I had four punchouts, man. You talk about a mismatch. I went back, I saw Wellman, and he knew I was disgusted. He came over and I said, 'Skip, if this is what it's like I'd better go home,' and he went, 'Lemme tell you something, this guy is going to be unbelievable. You're not going to face many pitchers like that.' "

Wellman was right. "Ryan was wild," Bowa said. "He struck out like 18 and walked nine. I look back on it, I think about those little 'candles' we were playing under and I say, 'How the hell did I get up there righthanded against that guy?' "

Between Doyle and Wellman, Bowa's sanity was maintained, his confidence restored. That Spartanburg team turned out to be something special. "We won 26 in a row," Bowa said. "We almost went a whole month without losing. Then we lost, 1–0, and won 13 more in a row."

The 1–0 loss, incidentally, was to the New York Mets' Greenville farm club. The winning pitcher? A guy named Ryan. "He was tall and lanky and had no idea where the ball was going," Bowa said. "None." All Nolan Ryan did that year [1966] was go 17–and–2 and strike out 272 batters [while walking 127] in 183 innings.

Larry Bowa will be the first to tell you that facing him that season wasn't any fun at all.

To a man in the minors, success means getting to the majors. That's the dream they all share, from the rookie leagues to Triple A. Making the big team—making the "show" used to be the popular terminology—was always cause for rejoicing, getting sent down cause for great sadness. Yet some far-sighted players have actually chosen the minors over the majors in certain circumstances. They wanted to play, not sit. They wanted to learn by doing, not watching.

In Jim Kaat's case, his father deserves the credit. "I could have signed for more money and gone right to the big leagues," said the lefthander, remembering back 25 years to the time he was 18. "My dad recommended I take less money and go to the minor leagues and learn to play the game right."

Jim took his father's advice, passed up a $25,000 bonus from the Chicago White Sox—"in those days that was a lot of dough," he said—and began his pro career in Superior, Neb. Under the rules in effect then, a player who received more than $4,000 when he signed had to spend two years with the big league club. Many kids opted for the big money and the quick trip to the majors, of course—and withered away there, trapped in a big league dugout when they should have been doing what Jim Kaat did.

"My dad used those players as examples," Kaat recalled. "the other example he always used was Jim Bunning. He said Bunning never had great stats in the minor leagues, but he went down and he pitched. He felt if you were going to make it, that was the way."

Learning the pro game from the ground up—from Superior and Missoula and Chattanooga—worked for Kaat. Last spring he attended his 25th major league camp as a member of the St. Louis Cardinals. "Every level I was at in the minor leagues I felt I benefited from," he said. "I was a young, simple kid away from home having a good time. I enjoyed it. I thought those 20-hour bus rides through Montana and Idaho were fun. I didn't know any better."

Kaat is, quite literally, a throwback to another era. Give the average kid today the choice that Jim had and there isn't much doubt he'd pick instant big league status. "I think the attitude then vs. now is the same in this game as it is in life in general," Kaat said. "Everything today is geared toward 'I want it now. I don't want to wait.' Those days, you used to say, 'Well, I'm going to give myself about five years in the minor leagues. If I don't make it, I'll go into something else.' Nowadays, if you have one pretty decent year in the minor leagues and you don't get a shot at the big leagues kids are disappointed."

And the big league clubs compound the problem by rushing kids to the majors before they're ready to handle it physically or mentally. More than a few careers have been ruined because of that.

What Jim Kaat—following the advice of his dad—did in 1957 was noteworthy. What John Stearns did on his own in 1976 was downright astonishing.

Stearns had been an outstanding football player at the University of Colorado, a defensive back who received national attention. And he played baseball the way he played football—all out all the time. It didn't matter to John if the score was close or one-sided, if his team was fighting for first or dead last. If there was a double play to break up, he'd do his damndest to break it up. If there was a catcher waiting to tag him at home plate, he'd smash into the guy and try to jar the ball loose.

He began his pro baseball career in the Phillies' organization and dreamed about a long career in Philadelphia. That dream ended in December, 1974, when the Phillies traded the young catcher to the New York Mets.

Stearns was a big leaguer in '75, but not the kind of big leaguer he wanted to be. He appeared in only 59 games for the Mets, only came to bat 169 times. The following year was more of the same. He did a lot of sitting, a lot of watching, a lot of squirming.

It would have been easy for a young man to shrug his shoulders, accept the big league meal money, the big league lifestyle and let the time pass. Stearns wanted more out of baseball than that.

"I wasn't getting any place," he said. "On May 18 we played the Reds in Cincinnati. I finally started a game on a Sunday. It was the fourth game I'd been in, and the season was five, six weeks old. I went 0–for–4. We had an off-day Monday. On the plane ride back to New York I decided I was going to go in and get my ass down to Tidewater [the Mets' Triple A club in the International League] so I could play. Here I was, second year in a row, doing nothing. I wasn't ready to come to the big leagues in the first place and now they were letting me sit on the bench."

Once John Stearns gets his mind made up, it's darn near impossible to change it. So the following day—Tuesday—he walked into general manager Joe McDonald's office before the game.

"I was very bitter," John recalled. "I said, 'What are you doing?

You get me from Philadelphia and this—*this*—happens. What's going on? What are you trying to do, ruin me? People are saying I can't play.' I said, 'If you can't trade me to another team, let me go down to Tidewater and I'll show you I can play.' "

It was an impassioned speech, one that not many major league general managers have heard. Here was a young man pleading to get sent down.

"He was amazed," Stearns said, "and very happy that I did that. It took a lot of pressure off him. Nobody wanted to tell me I was going down."

Stearns and McDonald went over to manager Joe Frazier's office and explained what had happened. "I told him [Frazier] that I could play the game and that I was the best catcher we had and that I wanted to go to Tidewater and play and then come back and be the regular catcher," Stearns said.

So Frazier and McDonald waved him a fond adieu. Down to the minors went John Stearns, eager to start playing baseball again.

"I drove down from New York," he said. "I got there in the evening, about 9 o'clock. We [Tidewater] were leaving the next day on a road trip. I went to the ball park and they were in the middle of a double header. Then, for the first time, I really felt despair—right there, for that one moment. The ball park was a minor league operation [although surely one of the better minor league parks]. I'd been in New York City. Tidewater was a nice place, but it was not the big leagues. I looked at the game and I was in shock. I went up in the press box. I met the general manager. When the [first] game was over, I went in the clubhouse. That was the hardest time I had. It was tough. It was a shock."

The realization had hit him. This wasn't New York. It wasn't the National League. It wasn't Shea Stadium. This was Triple A baseball, the thing players strive to escape. And he had talked himself into being a part of it.

"Next day when I woke up I got on that road trip—a plane ride to Charleston [W. Va.], which was real bush, a terrible ball park, terrible lights. I went 1–for–13 in the series. Then we went up to Toledo on a long bus trip and I didn't have any more problems. I loved it from that point on."

Stearns began hitting the ball in Toledo, began falling into a groove. The fact that he was playing every night meant more to him than the fact he was back in the minors. A determined young man, Stearns set out to prove to the people upstairs that he could do the job.

"At the end of the road trip we went to Richmond," he said.

"They had a pitcher named John (Blue Moon) Odom. He was acting like a big leaguer out there, pissing and moaning and getting on the umpire and acting like a big deal. So I screamed at him from the dugout. Next time I came up he threw at my head twice in a row. On the third pitch I swung through the ball and threw my bat at him. It went off to the side; it didn't hit him. So I walked out to get my bat and he was pissing and moaning at me, and I went after him. Both benches cleared and I had him in a head lock. And then everybody parted and we played ball, and he walked me. So I'm at first base and he tried to pick me off and I turned my ankle pretty bad. I had to call time out and he was calling me a 'pussy' from the mound."

They would have needed an army to get Stearns out of the game at that point. No way he was going to limp off with Odom laughing behind his back and making disparaging remarks.

"I stayed in," Stearns said. "We're down, 2–1, in the top of the eighth and Blue Moon Odom's still on the mound when I came up again."

There was a Tidewater runner on base. Stearns' competitive juices were boiling. "He'd thrown at me," John said, "and we'd had a scuffle and then he scoffed at me when I turned my ankle." Stearns wanted to drive one against Odom. To him, the game had become a personal war. And, lo and behold, he did drive one. Somehow keeping the anger he felt under control, he smashed a game-winning, two-run homer. "After that," he said, "the guys sort of knew I was there for serious business."

The rest of that minor league season was all that John Stearns had hoped it would be. He wound up hitting .310 and enjoyed himself immensely.

"It's different," he said. "Players get closer in the minor leagues. In the major leagues, you've got your stars and your established major leaguers. When they leave the park they go their separate ways. In the minors it's kind of like you're in school ball, in college all over again. Everybody's pulling together. You hang together on the road more. There aren't as many distractions. There aren't as many people after you for this and that."

Not an easy life, surely. John Stearns was well aware of that. "My brother [Bill] played seven years in the minors," he said. "He felt very disillusioned and bitter. He felt like he never got a shot when he was with the Yankees. It's sad. It happens to a lot of guys. A lot of people get their lives messed up."

John Stearns could have been one of them. "If I hadn't gone back to Tidewater I might have become a fringe catcher, got traded around, up and down," he said. "If that had happened, though, I would have been gone. I wouldn't have given it [baseball] that much of a shot."

But he forced the issue. He talked them into sending him down to the minors rather than let him waste away on the bench in the big leagues, and it turned out to be one of the best things he ever did. Stearns returned to New York as the Mets' No. 1 catcher. A year after going to Tidewater, he played in the major league All-Star game. He's an established big leaguer now . . . and a man who appreciates what the minor leagues did for him.

9

THEY EVEN DROVE THE BUSES

Major league managers get to feel like pretty important people. Some of them even have their own radio or TV shows, which in today's scheme of things, I suppose, is about as important as you can get.

But managing in the minor leagues is a horse of a different color. Down there, a guy really has to work for a living—and often not a very good living, at that. A minor league manager has to be a baby-sitter, a motivator, a cheerleader, sometimes even a bus driver. Often, they're underappreciated, underpaid and overworked. You've got to love the game to be a minor league manager. This is about some of the men who did love it enough to put up with all the nonsense that went on—all the bus rides, all the inconveniences—and kept coming back for more.

Let's start with Tommy Lasorda. He's a big name now. You never know when he's going to turn up on *The Tonight Show* or *The Today Show*. Frank Sinatra's his buddy. The world is his oyster. But who ever heard of Tommy Lasorda when he was managing in Ogden and Spokane and Albuquerque? Heck, half the people who wander in and out of his office at Dodger Stadium now probably can't even spell Albuquerque.

Lasorda came up the hard way, and he's never forgotten his roots. "I managed in the rookie league," he said. "I made $6,500 a year. Had a wife and two kids and I scouted and managed, and I was the happiest guy in the world. You give me a ball field with players and I'm happy. I don't give a damn how much I'm making. I'm doing what I love to do."

Lasorda, in case it's escaped your notice, is an advanced practitioner in the art of positive thinking. The man is a master motivator. It's hard to say no to Tommy Lasorda. He could probably talk Ralph Nader into buying a used car.

"They moved me to Triple A," he was saying, "and I started there at $9,000 a year. I managed there for four years and I was the happiest son of a bitch in the world because I was on the threshhold of putting guys in the major leagues. Here they were, one step away. What a great feeling it was to call a guy in and tell him he was going to the big leagues. I enjoyed it very, very much. I never asked them to move me up to the big leagues as a coach. You got to be happy in your work. But until the time I managed the Dodgers I never made anything. I never made no money, at all. I struggled."

Success, and all that goes with it, hasn't spoiled Tommy Lasorda. He still tells funny stories, sometimes the same funny stories he told in Ogden and Spokane and Albuquerque. And he still loves what he's doing.

"I still live in the same house I did when I moved to California 20 years ago," he said. "I have the same friends. I do the same things that I did when I managed in Ogden. I still got the same guy that filled out my income tax. I don't do anything different. I still drive the same kind of cars. I even go to the same wholesale places that I went to 20 years ago. Here's the thing about it. I know where I came from and I know how happy I was where I came from and if the day comes I've got to go back to it, I won't regret it. I could've gone out and bought a big home and elaborate cars but I get to the same places with the car I drive.

"I went out to California [two decades ago] and my wife said, 'They're building a Montgomery Ward two blocks from our house. You know, I think it'd be nice if we got a credit card from Montgomery Ward.' She filled out this application and Montgomery Ward turns us down. I didn't have no credit. So I said, 'Fuck 'em. Who wants a credit card at that place?' You know what, a couple of years later they wrote me asking me (to use one of their credit cards). I wouldn't do it. I wouldn't go into a Montgomery Ward if you gave me a thousand dollars to make an appearance there. I met the vice-president of Sears and I told him the story. Two days later there was a Sears credit card at my home. I told the chairman of the board of Union Oil the same story and two days later there was a credit card from Union Oil."

Okay, so remember that, will you? Don't invite the president of Montgomery Ward and Tommy Lasorda to the same department store. And let that be a lesson to you, Montgomery Ward. The minor leaguer you turn down for credit in the '60s may be a friend of Frank Sinatra's in the '70s and '80s.

Lasorda was a winner in the minor leagues, too. Seven seasons, five first-place finishes. Not bad. Of course the Dodgers supplied him with some exceptional players. Steve Garvey, for instance.

"Tom and I have always been very, very close," Garvey said. "He's always been like a second father to me. Tom is more of a psychologist than anything. What he tries to do, he tries to find out what motivates each player. It may take a pat on the back with one, some harsh words with another. We're all basically different. He finds out. Like I'm the type of guy he doesn't have to yell at. I just naturally get down on myself [when things are going badly]. So he's got to come over and say, 'Hey, Garv, we'll get 'em tomorrow.' "

Lasorda started saying that to Garvey in Ogden, Utah, in 1968, Steve's first pro season. More often, though, he must have said, "That's the way to go, Garv." Steve hit .338 that year under Tommy's fatherly command.

"Fond memories," Garvey said. "Great times. Tom always made a bus ride [seem] half as long with his stories, his humor, his kidding around. The game of baseball is very demanding, much more than the public realizes, but Tom makes it that much more fun because of the way he is. He's able to extract fun out of it, which is a nice virtue."

Lasorda didn't change his ways when he finally got his chance to manage in the big leagues. Come to think of it, that took a lot of guts. People were standing in line waiting for him to fall on his face. They snickered at his cornball humor, at his sayings, at his super-positive approach. But he kept winning, and they stopped snickering.

"You know what happens?" said Lasorda. "A guy manages one way in the minor leagues. Now when he comes to the big leagues and everything is right there in front of people he says, 'I can't do that,' and now he's changed from the way he got there, or the reason he was brought there. He does it different because it's magnified. I make a mistake in Spokane, who knows it? Or I make a mistake in Albuquerque, who knows it? I make a mistake up here [in Los Angeles] and nine million people talk about it. So I said, 'Hey, when I come up here I'm going to do it the way I did it down there. If it's not good enough, then that's the way I've got to go down the tubes. But I'm not going to go down the tubes trying to do it somebody else's way. That's like you trying to copy from this guy's test. How do you know he's right?"

So Lasorda kept doing it his way—the way that kept them smiling and winning in the sticks. Always the showman, Tommy was quick to jump on any scheme to make people laugh and add a little

Bill Schlesinger (*top*) is shown being congratulated by his Eugene, Oregon, manager Frank Lucchesi (*back to camera and in lower left photo*) after hitting a home run. A few days later Schlesinger was beaned in a game in Tucson and his promising career came to an end. Lucchesi spent years in the minors before making it to the big leagues as manager of the Phillies and, later, the Rangers. Pat Bayless (*lower right*), the can't-miss pitcher with the big smile and the big league fastball, blazed through the minor leagues at the start of his pro career.

Pat Bayless today, his dream shattered, looks out from behind a backstop at the playing fields he never wanted to leave and, baseball in hand and an old trophy at his side, sits in the living room of his parents' home in California.

The inimitable Max Patkin, seen (*top left*) as a young coach for Bill Veeck's Cleveland Indians and in various stages of his present act as the Clown Prince of Baseball.

A young Mike Schmidt (*top left*) provides a hint of the greatness to come as he crosses home plate after hitting an Eastern League homer. Two-time National League MVP Schmidt is one of the game's most feared hitters (and one of the most sought-after autograph givers—seen here at an exhibition game at Reading) and a thoughtful, sensitive man who handles himself as well off the field as he does on.

Greg Luzinski left a trail of tape-measure home runs through the minor leagues, from A ball through Triple A, on his way to becoming one of the top producers in the majors with the Phillies and White Sox. Photo at right shows present-day bull and baby bull.

Much of the excitement in minor league ball comes from the fields and stadiums themselves. Pictured here are examples from Canada: Three Rivers Stadium (*top*) and Thetford Mines (*below*).

John Poff (*top left*), a lefthanded-hitting first baseman-outfielder with a degree from Duke, never really got a full shot at making it with a major league club and finally quit baseball. Keith Moreland (*top right*), once a football teammate of Earl Campbell's at the University of Texas, played minor league baseball in the Phillies organization. Dickie Noles (*below left*) was a wild righthander—on and off the field—in his minor league days. In 1982, he started regularly with the Chicago Cubs. Garry Maddox' minor league experience in the San Francisco organization was short and not at all sweet.

Hall of Famer Warren Spahn waves from the home dugout of the Reading Phillies during a visit, as Ron Clark, then manager of the team, looks on. Jim Bunning (*right*) returned to the game he loved after retiring his pitching arm, only to be fired by the Phillies organization before beating the bushes as a manager.

spice to a ball game. Larry Bowa remembers when Lasorda's Spokane team was playing Frank Lucchesi's Eugene team in 1969, and the two managers cooked up an act for the fans. "It was our last game against them," Bowa said, "and Frank and Lasorda decided to give the fans a kick. They were both going to get thrown out in the ninth inning."

It seemed like a jazzy idea, designed to add spice to a meaningless game. But the best laid plans of mice and managers sometimes go astray. Meaningless game or not, an umpire made a call in the second inning that sent Tommy into a rage. Out of the dugout he zoomed to dispute the call. Things got heated; Lasorda had quite a temper in those days. Lucchesi watched from the top step of the Eugene dugout for a moment or so, then rushed out, too.

Frank figured there'd been a foulup in signals. Lasorda was supposed to wait until the ninth inning to go into a rage. "Frank was pushing him away [from the umpire]," Bowa recalled, "but Lasorda wasn't acting. He was really mad."

And having the rival manager on top of him, trying to shove him away did very little to soothe Tommy's wounded feelings. It didn't take Lucchesi very long to realize that Lasorda was genuinely angry, and that this second-inning rhubarb had absolutely nothing to do with their pre-game plotting.

"Lasorda got thrown out," Bowa said. "Frank came back to the dugout and, boy, was he laughing."

Lucchesi didn't always get the last laugh on Lasorda, though. "Spokane was going to play a seven-game series in Hawaii [Eugene's top challenger at the time for the division title in the Pacific Coast League]," Bowa said, "and Frank told Lasorda, 'Win four from them and I'll buy you a steak.' They won five and the next time we played Spokane Frank put a raw steak in Lasorda's locker."

Ver-r-r-y funny. But Lasorda's no dummy. He did what any red-blooded American would do. He broiled the steak, put the bones and the fat in a gift wrapped package and sent it back to Lucchesi.

In case you haven't figured it out by now, Frank Lucchesi was quite a card, too. He spent a quarter of a century in the minor leagues—as player and manager—before making it to the big leagues as manager of the Phillies, and later manager of the Texas Rangers. Spend that many years in the minors and a man needs a sense of humor. Frank had one. One night in Hawaii a Eugene batter smashed a vicious foul that hit Lucchesi in the third base coaches' box. The manager collapsed in a heap and remained motionless for several seconds. It was a frightening scene. The crowd grew suddenly silent. The rival manager came out. The umpires dashed over.

Players ran out of the bullpen. Interestingly enough, though, one man who didn't budge was the Eugene trainer.

"He knew me too well," explained Lucchesi, who waited for the crowd to gather around his limp form, then jumped up and began shadow boxing.

Lucchesi's also the guy who, after getting thrown out of a game, climbed a water tower in center field to see what was happening. All part of the Lucchesi minor league saga. Listen to the men who played for him tell stories and it sounds like one big laugh after another. But there were lots of very serious moments, too.

One of the most serious occurred in Pine Bluff, Ark., in 1954. Frank was player-manager for the team owned by the old St. Louis Browns. Batting practice was nearly over. Frank asked the pitcher who was throwing it how he felt. "I'm getting a little tired," the young man told him. "Okay," replied Lucchesi, "I'll come out and finish."

It would only be for a few minutes, Frank figured. No reason not to help the guy out.

"My shortstop stepped in to hit," Lucchesi said. "His name was Gene Oden. He was from Shreveport. How can I ever forget this guy? I threw one pitch. He hit it to left field. I threw the next pitch. He hit a line drive."

Normally, there's a protective screen set up in front of the mound during batting practice. But this wasn't the big leagues, or even the high minors. This was Pine Bluff, Ark., and there was no screen. The ball went shooting back at Lucchesi. He turned his head at the last moment and the line drive hit him in the left temple.

Frank and Cathy Lucchesi had been married two months when that happened. "I guess I was in pretty bad shape," Frank said, "because they called a priest."

"I was getting ready to go to the game," Cathy remembered. "They called me. There were two blood clots. . . ."

Frank had to undergo surgery. He was in the hospital four weeks. But he pulled through it. For years after that he lived the nomadic life of a minor league baseball manager. "Two years of 'D'," he said, "four years of 'C' in a row, then two years of 'B', three years of 'A', one year of Double A, then back to 'A' because the Southern League folded, then Triple A for three years, then back to Double A, then Triple A again."

In 1981, when Cleveland's Triple A team in Charleston, W. Va., was struggling, special assignments scout Lucchesi tried his hand at managing in the minors again. "The first meeting I had," said

Frank, "I told them, 'Fellas, remember one thing. This is not new to me. I've been here before."

It was one of the great understatements of our time.

Lucchesi can spend hours talking about his minor league experiences. "They were struggling years," he said. "I remember, I went from Pocatello to Salt Lake. I was making $3,700 as a player-manager at Pocatello and I got this big raise. They gave me $5,000 as a player-manager for the whole year. One year we had to borrow about 500 bucks because we barely could make it. I was really struggling. I never made any money, and I made a lot of sacrifices. But I wouldn't trade it for nothing."

Lucchesi is a man filled with warmth and compassion and humor. He likes people. He and Lasorda are similar in many ways. Like Lasorda, he was an ideal manager for kids trying to climb the minor league ladder.

"I have some great memories," Frank said. "It was tough—especially for the family. She [his wife, Cathy] went through it all. I think the baseball wives are really the unsung heroes. That's why in my office [in his home in Arlington, Tex.] you'll see on a wall a wire dedicated to her. I sent it before my first big league game. After all those years in the minor leagues, I wanted her to know how much I appreciated what she went through."

"There was no pressure [in the minor leagues]," Cathy Lucchesi said. "We didn't worry about next year or next month. It was fun. You did a good job," she told Frank. "You were proud of it. There were no problems."

The problems, the pressures came later—in the big leagues, under that powerful magnifying glass.

"The things that happened all my years in the minor leagues, you can write a book about," Lucchesi said.

All right, if you insist. There was Frank's first bus-driving stint in Bisbee, Ariz. "I was a player then," he said. "Charlie Metro was the manager. We had to go from Bisbee to Tucson, a few hundred miles. The regular bus driver was sick. Charlie says, 'Who can drive a bus?' I guess I was a little flaky when I was younger. I never drove a bus in my life. But I raised my hand.

" 'Lucchesi?'

" 'Yeah.'

" 'Where'd you ever drive a bus?'

" 'I'm from San Francisco, you know,' I told him.

" 'All right,' he said. 'Frank, you start it. . . .' "

Eager to please, bus driver Lucchesi jumped behind the wheel, revved up the motor and prepared to embark on his perilous journey. "First mistake I made," he said, "I put it in reverse instead of low, almost went through a garage behind me. He looked at me. 'I'm just checking the gears out, Charlie,' I said."

In no time at all Lucchesi had the Bisbee team purring smoothly along the open road. Things were going so well that Frank burst into song, doing his ever-popular Vaughn Monroe imitation.

"I'm singing, 'Racing With the Moon,'" Lucchesi said. "Everything's going fine. But in those days they didn't have the freeways. They had two-lane highways and they had little dips in them. There'd be mirages on the highway. . . ."

You'd look off in the distance and you'd see water—or what appeared to be water in the middle of the highway. "You'd get there, and it would disappear," Frank said. "So I'm driving along imitating Vaughn Monroe and someone says something to me and I turn around and a guy hollers, 'Look out for the water, Frank!' 'Aw,' I said, 'that's a mirage.'"

Next thing he knew, he hit the mirage. It was the wettest, deepest mirage he had ever seen. "Evidently," said Lucchesi, "they have flash floods in Arizona."

And he had just driven the Bisbee baseball team into the middle of one. "We got stuck in the mud," Frank recalled.

No more racing for the moon for Lucchesi on that trip. It was time to go looking for a tow truck instead.

By the time he became a manager, Lucchesi could handle just about any challenge. He could even play center field and manage at the same time. "I'd come running in [to make a pitching change]," he said. "I did this in Medford [Ore.], Pocatello [Idaho], Thomasville [Ga.], Pine Bluff [Ark.]."

Back and forth he'd sprint. Some fun. The worse shape his pitching staff was in, the better shape Lucchesi would have to be in.

"Talk about the challenge," he said. "When I was at Medford, I was the manager, the center fielder, the bus driver and the trainer. Oh yeah, and traveling secretary. All that for $575 a month. Looking back at it now you say, 'Man, how did you do it? How'd you ever put up with all that—the traveling, the hotels, the meal money, the bus rides?' But then you were tickled to death to be there."

Life was a constant battle of wits. Player-manager Lucchesi was in center field one night in Thomasville. It was the top of the ninth. His team had a one-run lead. The enemy had a runner on first with two out.

"The batter hits a smash to the fence," Lucchesi said. "Ordinarily the tying run would've scored, but there was a drainpipe sticking out of the center field fence . . .''

Thinking fast, Frank sprinted to the fence and in one, fluid motion grabbed the ball and rammed it into the drainpipe. Then he whirled and began screaming at the umpire that it should be a ground rule double, and that the runner shouldn't be allowed to score.

"I showed him the ball stuck in the drainpipe," said Lucchesi. "He made the runner return to third, and we wound up winning by a run."

What Lucchesi didn't show him was his mangled right index finger, which he ripped open when he shoved the ball into the drainpipe. "I've still got the scar," Frank said in a voice filled with pride.

One of his best managerial moves was coming up with a pinch-hitter for a center fielder named Lucchesi. "That was in Pocatello," said Frank. "The pitcher was throwing the ball right by me. This guy was throwing a 94-mile-an-hour fast ball. I couldn't handle it. so I called time. I looked at Tony Cannizzo [who was to become the godfather of Frank's son, Brian] and I said, 'C'mere. Get a helmet' or an insert or whatever it was then. 'Hit for me.'

" 'You're the manager,' he said. It was the last of the eighth. He went up to hit and I went out to coach third. He hit a double off the boards and won the game."

It should be emphasized, however, that driver Lucchesi wasn't as successful as` manager Lucchesi. Frank not only had his difficult moments behind the wheel of a bus, but he apparently hit one bump too many while driving with his wife from Florida to High Point, N.C., at the end of spring training.

"We put all our things—my summer clothes, the baby's clothes, everything—in a carrier and tied it on top of the car," Cathy Lucchesi recalled. "We stopped for gas and, you know Frank, he's always joking. He says, 'The suitcase, where's the suitcase?' I said, 'Oh, it's there.' He said, 'Where is it? It's not there.' I said, 'Frank, c'mon, I'm tired.' 'I'm not kidding,' he said. 'It's gone.' So I get out and look and there's nothing up there. We didn't see it fall. We didn't hear anything."

They drove back about 10 miles, searching along the road for that missing suitcase, but finally had to give it up for lost.

The insurance didn't cover it. It was a total loss. And for a family trying to live on a minor league manager's salary, that was no small matter. Now, though, it just provides another story Frank and Cathy Lucchesi can tell about their years in the minor leagues.

"I have a soft spot in my heart for the minor leagues," Frank said recently. "Really, I do."

I believe him.

Dave Bristol was another who served a full apprenticeship in the minor leagues, as player and manager, before making it to the majors as manager and coach.

Dave spent nine years managing for the Cincinnati organization in the minor leagues, and one of the promising, young players he helped bring along was a gung-ho kid named Pete Rose.

Joe Carroll was the trainer in Macon, Ga., 20 years ago, when Bristol and Rose were there. It's a season he'll never forget.

"Pete was sort of a new gimmick to the game," Joe said. "People had never seen the likes of him—the way he got a base on balls and ran down to first base. Everybody went, 'Oh-h-h, what's this?' Of course, the opposing team thought he was putting it on, but that's the way he was. He captured the fans no matter where he went. Pete was always dreaming ahead, thinking all the time that he was going to make it. There was no question in his mind that he was going to make it. He'd say, 'I'm going to be up there.' He was always at the ball park early, always had his bat in his hand, always ready. The fans in Macon loved him. Pete thought he owned the town. He had a car there and he kept speeding around and the cops would stop him and he'd say, 'I'm Pete Rose of the Macon Georgians' and the cops would say, 'I don't give a damn who you are.' We had to have a meeting one time about it, and he stopped it."

But he never stopped swinging that bat, smashing those base hits. With Rose and Tommy Helms leading the way on the field, and Bristol directing things, Macon wound up on top that year.

"We went around in station wagons," Joe Carroll remembered, "and we had a lot of fun. We'd travel all night. We had a car one time that got a flat tire with Dave Bristol, myself, Tommy Helms and Pete Rose in it. We're in no man's land sleeping in the damn car with the flat tire and we're laughing like hell and we've got to be in some town to play ball. I remember, we got there at nine o'clock in the morning. The longest drive was from Macon to Knoxville [Tenn.]. Oh Boy, that was a terrible drive. We'd leave about 11:30, right after the ball game, and we wouldn't get there until about nine or 10 the next morning. But it was a lot of fun. They never complained. We'd stop at some place—some gas station that had soda and candy—and we'd all get there like four o'clock in the morning and we'd all be eating and drinking soda and laughing like hell, telling stories."

Bristol, who would go on to become the manager of big league teams in Cincinnati, Milwaukee, Atlanta and San Francisco, remembers those days with great fondness. "It was always a challenge to me," he said, "and I loved it. I just loved working with young players and trying to see if I couldn't send them to a higher classification the next year as better players."

Hard times? Sure. But also fun times to a man who was as immersed in baseball as Dave Bristol was. Hardships were simply a part of the game that he knew, and grew up with.

"My first professional game was in 1951, the Appalachian League," Dave said. "I signed and I went to join the Welch [W. Va.] club. I met them in Elizabethton [Tenn]. A damn tornado came through there about two weeks before and lifted the top off the dressing room and nobody bothered to replace it. So you just had nails up there, and poison oak was growing up the walls where you hang your stuff."

Bristol's first managerial job was in Hornell [N.Y.]. "The Reds had sent an extra player or two to Bradford [Pa.]," he said. "Well, Bradford folded and they called and asked the Reds what they wanted to do with the young players they had there."

The Reds decided to put a team in Hornell to take care of those surplus players, and they needed somebody to manage them.

"I get a call in Wausau [Wisc.]," said Bristol, who was playing second base there at the time. "The manager tells me, 'Dave, we're going to release you.' I started to cry and he said, 'No, we're going to release you as a player and make you a manager."

Dave dried his tears and headed for upstate New York.

"We only had enough players to field a team," he said. "We played Olean the first night. Paul Owens [who went on to become general manager of the Phillies] was player-manager over there. I only had three pitchers, and all of them went nine innings [against Olean]."

They had no choice, actually. "The only thing we had in the bullpen was a bench," Bristol said. "There weren't any bodies down there. I was so nervous . . . I was playing second base and somebody singled to left field and the guy tried to stretch it into a double. They threw the ball in, a perfect, one-hop throw. I went down to tag the guy, and I didn't have the ball. The ball hit me right in the face."

Merely filling out that first lineup card was an adventure. Dave had never filled one of them out before. He wasn't exactly sure what to do. "Paul Owens showed me how to do it, where to put the extra men and all," he said.

Considering that Bristol's team didn't have any extra men, it probably wasn't that difficult to figure out.

The Hornell club, a member of the New York-Penn League, trained in Laredo, Tex., in '57, Bristol's second year at the helm. Laredo, all you geography experts will realize, isn't particularly close to Geneva, N.Y., where Hornell was scheduled to open the season. Transporting the team from Laredo to Geneva was no easy undertaking. But where there's a will there's a way. At least, where there's a bus there's a way.

"We rode a city bus," Bristol reminisced, "a straight-back city bus from Laredo Tex., to Geneva, N.Y., and they gave us enough meal money to last."

That is, enough meal money to last if the players got in the habit of skipping meals. "We spent the third night in Indianapolis," Bristol said, "and then we had to keep going because we ran out of money."

Ah, but who cared? "What did you have to judge by?" Dave asked. "They were all happy to be there. I was 23 years old and I just started managing. Shoot, you got to get there and that was the only way to do it."

The Hornell park was, well, peculiar. "The center field fence was about 290 feet," Bristol said. Still, that park was better than the one in West Virginia, where Dave broke in as a professional player. "It had a sidewalk running through left field where the people came in," he recalled. "Yeah, it was in fair territory. And you ran downhill to second base and uphill from third to home."

Naturally. Didn't everybody?

"And then, when I managed in Palatka, [Fla.], in the Florida State League," said Dave, "I told the infielders, 'Here's the water hose and the rake. You go fix your position anyway you want it. If you want it soft, that's good. If you like it hard, make it hard.' "

Bristol didn't have time to be groundskeeper, too, in those minor league days. "In Macon," he said, "we wouldn't have a lot of new balls all the time. So I'd go to the ball park early in the afternoon. I used to take some Pet Milk and a towel and I'd wash those balls and they'd stay white. We had good players and I wanted them to be the best and have the best. We hit white balls as long as I could keep 'em white."

One of the biggest problems in Macon, Bristol said, was deciding who was going to "ride shotgun"—sit in the right front seat in the station wagon on road trips. The front seat was roomy. The righthand seat was the place to be. The thought of getting jammed in the back on a long trip was enough to make a large man want to fight for his rights. "One time," said Dave, "I let Mel Queen and John Flavin fight to see who would get the seat. That's two guys who got over $100,000 [to sign]. Gabe Paul [then the general manager of the Reds] would've fainted in Cincinnati if he knew I let that happen. But it got everything right. They fought, got up, dusted themselves off and shook hands, and the winner got the seat."

See how simple things could be when a manager used his head?

The road trips in the Northern League took the cake. Charley Fox, now a super scout for the Montreal Expos, spent 16 years in the minor leagues as player and manager. He particularly remembers the bus ride from St. Cloud, Minn., to Winnipeg, Canada.

"They didn't play on Sunday in Winnipeg," Charley said. "So you'd play a double header in St. Cloud on Sunday afternoon and on Monday you'd play a 10 o'clock [morning] game and an 8 o'clock [night] game in Winnipeg."

Four games in two days with a king-sized bus trip in between. You wonder how the human body could stand it.

"You'd finish the Sunday double header in St. Cloud," Fox said, "and you'd get on the bus and start riding. You'd get there [Winnipeg] about 4:30, 5 o'clock in the morning. The rooms wouldn't be ready then. People weren't out of them yet. So you slept in the lobby or maybe you slept in the bus."

First time Charley's team had to do that, the boys went out and played a heckuva game. "They were so mean getting off the bus they destroyed the other club," he said.

The morning game wrapped up, they checked into the hotel, finally got some decent rest—and got clobbered in the night game. That was enough for Charley. If his athletes played better tired than rested, he would see to it that they remained tired the next time they bused into Winnipeg.

"I said, 'Nobody sleeps,' " Fox recalled. "I took them all out. I bought them their lunch. I took them to the quarter horse races. I kicked the hell out of them."

They felt so absolutely rotten by the time game time approached that they went out and won. Who says managers don't win ball games?

One of the most inspiring stories of all, though, involving a man who went on to manage in the minors—and eventually in the majors —concerns (who else?) Tommy Lasorda. This was in 1956, when

Tommy, a lefthanded pitcher, opened the season with Kansas City in the American League. He didn't close it there, however, handicapped by a 0–4 record and a 6.20 earned run average. The inevitable happened. Kansas City shipped him back to the minors. Lasorda was told to report to Denver, where Ralph Houk was managing.

The average guy gets sent down, he takes his sweet time reporting to the minor league club. Lasorda, as has been well documented by now, isn't your average guy. As gung-ho as ever, he jumped in his car and started driving from Kansas City to Denver.

"I'm 40 miles from Denver," Lasorda recalled. "It's two o'clock in the afternoon and I buy a Denver paper. I read where Ralph Houk is having trouble with sore arms. So I say to my wife, 'C'mon, let's go. I'm going to pitch this game tonight.' 'You're crazy,' she says. 'We've got to get a place to live.' 'C'mon,' I tell her, 'let's go.'

"So we drive right into Denver. We get a motel. I go to the ball park and I'm there about 3:30. Nobody there yet but the trainer. Then Ralph comes in. I didn't know him at all. I said, 'Ralph, I read in the paper that you've got pitching problems. I'll pitch this ball game tonight.' He looks at me and he says, and I'll never forget these words, he says, 'I've seen 'em go from Triple A to the big leagues in one day but you're the first I ever saw go from the big leagues to Triple A in one day.'

"I said, 'I want to pitch.' 'Hold it,' he said. 'You got to get used to this place, the light air. . . .' I said, 'Get used to what? They got a mound, don't they? They got home plate, don't they? Who gives a damn about the air.' 'I'll tell you what I'll do," he says. 'I'll put you in relief.'

"Second inning, I'm warming up. I'm thinking, 'Wait'll these guys see this curve ball.' "

They wouldn't have long to wait. Houk's starter was getting battered. Lasorda to the rescue.

Bubbling over with confidence, the ex-big leaguer marched to the mound—this was long before Tommy's walk became a waddle—and started pitching. Hmmm. The air *was* different.

"I can't breathe," Lasorda said. "I can't get the curve ball to turn over. I feel like home plate is so far away, like I'm in a big barn. The first hitter's Bill Taylor. I said, 'I know this guy is a horseshit breaking ball hitter.' I threw him a curve ball. He hit it off the wall. Ozzie Virgil got a base hit. After that they got doubles, triples, home runs. I got 'em out after about six runs. I go back out for my second inning, and they did a job on me again. Houk comes out. He takes the ball away from me and he says—I'll never forget this, either—he says, 'Hang in there. I like what I saw.' I told my wife. I said, 'This guy's crazy.' "

Just goes to show you what managing in the minor leagues can do to a person.

10

THE WINTER GAME

Baseball is called "the summer game." But for many, it's also the winter game. For a minor leaguer, the winter game—in the Dominican Republic or Venezuela or Puerto Rico—represents an opportunity to hone skills against good competition and to make some badly needed money. Winter baseball can be an exhilarating experience. And it can be a frightening one.

For a kid scrambling to make it to the major leagues, the winter game provides a taste of big crowds, big pressure and—judged by minor league standards—big money. A young man can make a few thousand dollars a month playing the winter game, and if he does well it can turn into one of the great adventures of a lifetime. If he doesn't do well, however, the adventure can have an ugly side.

For a look at both the positive and negative sides of winter baseball let's examine the Venezuelan adventures of a young, hard-throwing righthander named Derek Botelho. Once one of the top prospects in the Phillies organization, Botelho was traded to the Cubs, in the Manny Trillo deal, released after coming down with a sore arm, then picked up by the Kansas City Royals minor league organization. He was at the peak of his game the winter the Cubs got him in February, 1979, but something happened in Venezuela. In fact, a lot of things happened in Venezuela.

"I started feeling something in my shoulder the last two weeks in January," Botelho said. "At the time it was just a stiffness, not an excruciating pain. Once I started throwing it'd loosen up and everything would be fine."

But as the winter season neared an end—and playoff time loomed—warming up became more and more of a chore. "I hated to warm up," he said. "The first five minutes were tough. Then, all of a sudden, I'd go into the game and it was gone."

The adrenalin must have had something to do with that. A young man accustomed to pitching in front of crowds numbered in the hundreds in the Eastern League, where Botelho had worked the previous summer, had to get revved up by the size, the noise, the excitement of a Venezuelan playoff crowd.

Botelho had pitched for his team, managed by Tony Taylor, in the final game of the regular season. "We had to win for home field advantage in the playoffs," he said, and they did win, 2–1.

But the pitching staff was hurting. "A lot of guys were coming up saying their arms were tender," Botelho recalled. "It was time to go home. I wanted to go home as bad as everybody else, but it was my turn to pitch and I couldn't tell Tony, 'I can't pitch.' I'm not that kind of guy."

So Derek got caught up in the playoff atmosphere. "I came back on four days' rest," he said. "We were down two games to one. I started off shaky. They had three or four (early) hits. But I ended up pitching a five-hitter. Then we went back to Maracaibo [the home field], and I pitched on three days' rest. I pitched a complete game there, a four-hitter in the seventh game of the playoffs and won, 6–1. It was awesome. There were over 30,000 people there that night. They were chanting my last name, every pitch practically. They were going, 'Bo-tel-ho . . . Bo-tel-ho.' "

Pretty heady stuff for a kid who had been doing most of his professional pitching in the semi-privacy of the low minors.

There might have been apathy in some of those minor league towns, but there was no apathy here. The people cared. Oh boy, did they care.

"After the game I had to get people away from me," Botelho recalled. "There were so many people around me I could hardly breathe. I came inside the clubhouse and everybody's just going crazy. The owner's around, too. Then all of a sudden I hear this chanting outside. They wanted me to come out again. I go outside the dugout and all the people are giving me a standing ovation, just going nuts. These people picked me up on their shoulder and paraded me around the stadium. That's how it is down there."

It was an unforgettable night in Derek Botelho's young life. He felt so caught up in the excitement that he could have gone out and pitched nine more innings. Or at least tried. As it was, he pitched once more that winter—in the fourth game of the next playoff round with his team down, three games to none. "This time," he said, "there were probably about 400, 500 people in the stands. They had already given up. I took the ball and I went out there. I said [to the pitching coach], 'My shoulder is sore.' He said, 'Just try it. If it's sore we'll get you out of there.' I threw an inning, two innings, all of a sudden the pain went away. I pitched a four-hitter against Willie Horton's team."

But from that day until he went out a year later and underwent surgery at his own expense, there was pain in Derek Botelho's right shoulder. That's what can happen to a kid pitcher. He can try to do too much, and his most precious possession—a healthy throwing arm—can get damaged in the process. In all probability, that's what happened to Pat Bayless. And it happened to Derek Botelho. He has some great memories of that winter in Venezuela. But if not for all the pitching he did there, on top of a full season in the minor leagues —who knows? Maybe he'd have made it to the big leagues the following summer.

The world of winter baseball is a wacky one, unlike anything in this country.

"I went down to the Dominican one winter," Garry Maddox recalled. "I just couldn't make the adjustment. Sometimes there were no showers after the games. Sometimes the lights didn't get turned on. There were mosquitoes in the locker rooms."

If you are looking for things not to like, the winter game provides you with a long list.

If you aren't ready to accept life in a strange society—a culture vastly different from anything Americans have grown to know—the best advice is: stay home.

If the minor leagues are another world, then the winter leagues are another galaxy. You have to see it to believe it. And even then . . .

Outfielder Rick Bosetti found out in a hurry how different it was when he headed for Santo Domingo in the winter of '76–'77 to play for Jim Bunning's Escogido team.

Bosetti's flight out of Miami, Fla., was scheduled to leave at 2:30 in the afternoon. It said so right on his Dominican Airways ticket. But Dominican Airways, Bosetti discovered, was not at all like, say, Delta Airlines. They were not ready when Rick was.

"I go to the desk at 12 to check in," Bosetti said. " 'No flight,' they say. I go, 'What d'ya mean, no flight?' "

The young lady behind the counter was only too happy to explain. They had been doing some work on the runway, she said, and one of the cement trucks ran over the wing of the Dominican Airways jet.

Bosetti finally got to the Dominican Republic aboard a Spanish airline that stopped in Santo Domingo on the way to Madrid. "My first taste of baseball in the Dominican," Bosetti said, "and before I even got there I knew what it was going to be like."

Nothing unusual about that, it developed. I went down later that same winter, and sat in that same Miami airport waiting for that same Dominican Airways flight, in all probability that same banged-up jet. It was a long wait. An hour passed. Two hours. The girl behind the counter couldn't have been nicer. She explained that the plane would not be available for another few hours. It was being used by the president of the country to take his wife to the dentist.

Oh well, that was all right. As long as it was something important. Anyway, it seemed fitting. Trying to get a firm departure time on a Dominican Airways flight, I learned, was like pulling teeth.

Eventually the plane showed up, barely five hours late and with both wings intact. Oddly enough, hearing the reason for the delay did much to restore my confidence in that Dominican jet. It seemed reasonable to assume that the president would have the plane checked out carefully before sending his wife to the dentist on it.

Anyhow, two hours later, there it was: Santo Domingo. If you think U.S. fans tend to get a bit rowdy at Yankee Stadium or Comiskey Park or Veterans Stadium, you ought to spend some time watching *beisbol* in Santo Domingo's government-owned Estadio Quisqueya, where two of the four Dominican teams play. The first thing you're likely to notice is the seemingly endless parade of vendors that walk through the stands peddling bottles of rum and scotch and various other liquid refreshments designed to get the spectators "up" for the game.

Some players love it in the Dominican. "I made a lot of great, great relationships in Santo Domingo," said Bill White, who played there nearly a quarter of a century ago.

Others hate it. Bosetti ranked high on that list.

He was playing right field for Escogido one night and made a throw to the plate that didn't please some of the home fans. And when these home fans get displeased, look out. Between the alcohol and the gambling, it's not quite the kind of crowd you'd find at your neighborhood tennis club.

The inning ended, Bosetti ran in toward the dugout and a fan—turned out, he was a local politician—screamed nasty things at Bosetti from a box seat near the dugout.

Rick whirled and made a beeline for the leather-lunged critic, trying to leap over the railing to get to the man. Let us all be thankful that his teammates prevented him from getting to the guy, hauling Rick back onto the playing field. But the incident didn't die there.

The man in the stands had a gun, a fact that did little to soothe Bosetti's ruffled feelings. And that night, allegedly, Rick received a phone call in his room at the Jaragua Hotel in downtown Santo Domingo. Precisely who made that call is open to considerable question. Bosetti claimed at the time that his "friend" in the stands made it, and that he threatened the player's life. It's entirely possible, though, that (1) Rick overdramatized the call because he was so anxious to get out of the country and go home or (2) that one of his teammates, pretending to be the gun-toting local politician, faked the call.

"There was a phone call," Bosetti said recently. "I don't know who it was. It might have been one of the players, just a joke. That's what Jim [Bunning] thought. He said, 'Well, was it a joke?' I said, 'All I know is, it's my ticket out of here. I'm gone.' "

Bosetti meant it. "Hell," he said after debating the validity of the threatening phone call, "it happened to Eddie Ott two weeks before in Santiago [where another Dominican team is located]. He punched out with a man on third and one out twice in one game. After the game he's walking out and a guy stuck a gun in his belly and said, 'No more punchy-punchy or I keel you.' Eddie Ott didn't figure he could go the rest of the season without striking out, so next day he was on the plane."

Bosetti stayed around a while—just long enough to get beaned in his very next game and land in a Dominican hospital, where he spent a night he described as a horror show. Phoning teammate Jim Morrison to rescue him, Bosetti fled the hospital early the next morning and left Santo Domingo shortly thereafter, leaving a trail of jet vapor behind him. He and his buddies had gotten themselves into too much trouble, gotten close-up looks at too many guns. One night Morrison tried to climb over a high, iron fence. Bosetti was there, watching him. "Mo was up on top, balancing," Rick said. "And then he slipped and fell right on one of those spikes—hit it with his chest. Quency [pitcher Quency Hill] was at the bottom of the fence when Mo fell back. There was a lot of blood. Quency's going, 'EAGHH!' "

Quency, a Texan, always did have a way with words. Undaunted, Morrison tried to climb that high, iron fence again. "This time," said Bosetti, "he fell over on the ground on the other side."

Somehow, Morrison walked away from all that. "Didn't he ever show you the scar?" Bosetti wondered.

Before they all got away from there that night, a security cop arrived on the scene. And pulled a gun on them. It was all kind of scary.

Then there was the time Bosetti, Morrison, catcher Gary Alexander, and pitcher Wayne Simpson were sitting in the bar at the Jaragua Hotel, having a few too many. There was a pretty, stained-glass partition near their table, separating the bar from the dining room. "Mo stands up and says, 'I'm going to the bathroom,' " Bosetti recalled. "I got up and said, 'Yeah, I'm going, too.' Simpson goes, 'Sit down, you'll get him [Morrison] into more trouble,' and he pushed me back."

It wasn't *that* hard a push, but considering the condition they were in, it was hard enough. "I stumbled," Bosetti said, "and I went through that glass. Wayne and Mo left. It was just me and Gary Alexander sitting there. This guy comes around and starts hollering at me in Spanish, and he pulls a gun. . . ."

Always, it seemed, somebody down there would wind up pulling a gun on one of our heroes. Life in the Dominican—really a very beautiful place, in spots—could be dangerous. On the other hand, it could be most rewarding. The trick is to get yourself in the frame of mind to appreciate it.

"The people in Santiago are so crazy none of the umpires will ever make a call against the home club there," Bosetti claimed. "Those guys are scared to death."

Rick's Escogido team was leading Santiago by three runs there one night. Two men were on base for the home team. There was a long fly ball. Bosetti faded back for it, drifted back a few steps more until he was at the bleacher wall. "I know I've got it," he said, "but I'm going to have to jump."

Bosetti jumped, but the ball never got to him. Fans reaching over the railing got their hands on it first. It was, according to Bosetti, a clear case of fan interference.

Hmmm. How'd you like to be the umpire who calls that one?

"This little umpire, he's nowhere near the play," Bosetti said. "He starts saying, 'Home run, home run.' Jim [Bunning] gets thrown out. It was just a big mess."

For some, winter baseball was just a succession of big messes. To hear Bosetti tell it, he spent most of his waking hours trying to stay out of jail. One day pitcher Pat Darcy and Bosetti inadvertently went through a stop signal and were flagged down by a policeman who commandeered a private car to catch them. Things looked grim. The cop was saying something that sounded very much like "prison". And then he said something else that sounded exactly like "20 dollars".

"We ended up bartering with this policeman over how much we were going to give him," Bosetti said. "Finally, we got it down to 10. We gave it to him. He smiled, said 'Gracias' and we took off."

Another time Bosetti faced possible arrest for driving without a shirt on. "I couldn't believe it," Rick said. "Half the people down there didn't even have money to own a shirt."

Again, it cost a few bucks, but Bosetti bought his way out. Don't get the idea that Rick was the only American who had problems with the long arm—and outstretched palm—of the Dominican law. Bob (Buck) Rodgers, who was managing Licey at the time, was nailed for going 10 miles over the speed limit and spent 45 very harrowing minutes in a jail cell before Manny Mota—"a friend of the president," Rodgers explained—got him out. In most cases, though, a bribe would do the trick.

Of course, the language barrier could be a problem, too. "Pat Darcy ordered two cheeseburgers and french fries from room service one night," Bosetti said. "They brought him a plate of bananas. He said, 'That's it. I can't take it any more.' He picked up a chair, slammed it against the floor and broke off a leg. Then he picked up a bat and beat it against the bed. And Pat's a quiet guy. After a while it gets to you.' "

Maybe so, but the Dominican could be a great experience, if you'd let it. Quency Hill and his wife, Susy, had a great time there. "We just fell in love with it," the pitcher said.

Above all, they fell in love with a cute, little native boy named Willie, who was always hanging around the hotel, where most of the players lived, running errands for them. Just before they left the Dominican, the Hills and the Jim Morrisons bought presents for Willie—mostly clothes and other useful, badly needed items. The look on the kid's face when they gave him the gifts was something to treasure. As much as they—and all the Americans—wanted to return home at the end of the playoffs, leaving Willie behind wasn't easy.

"He wrote us a letter," Quency Hill said. "We had a lady translate it. One of the lines—I'll never forget it—was, 'After you left my heart felt like it was run over by a truck.' "

One of those who found baseball life in the Dominican Republic a positive experience was pitcher George Frazier. "I was down there making the most money I'd ever made," he said. "My first year [in the minor leagues with the Milwaukee Brewers organization] I was 9–and–3 with seven saves in two months of work in 'A' ball. I got promoted to Double A and I was making $675 a month [up from $500]. I went to the Dominican, I was making $2,000 a month. I thought I was a millionaire. Plus they gave me a new car and a three-bedroom house to live in."

Frazier played in Santiago and had a wonderful time. Mondays and Thursdays were "beach days," he said. It was an idyllic existence compared to life in the low minors.

George's biggest problem involved long-time major leaguer Rico Carty, a native of the Dominican Republic. Frazier got the hard-hitting, slow-footed Carty to rap into a key double play in one game, and afterwards a reporter asked George what he had thrown Carty. "I told him, 'Sinker, slider,' " Frazier recalled. "I said, 'He can't run as well as he used to. Hell, the guy's 38, 39 years old now.' So this guy prints it in headlines: 'Frazier says Carty can't hit, can't run, can't throw, should get out of the game of baseball.' I didn't know. It was all in Spanish. I couldn't read it."

But Carty could. "Next time I was warming up against them Carty started yelling at me from first base," Frazier said.

The pitcher asked a Spanish-speaking teammate what it was all about. "He told me what I had [allegedly] said," recalled George. "I said, 'I never said that.' "

It made no difference. The only thing that mattered to Carty was that the slur had appeared in print. His friends, his countrymen had read it.

"About a week later I was around the batting cage," said Frazier, "and I told Carty which reporter had written it. Still, every time he came up against me he was trying to hit the ball out of the Dominican. He said, 'You made me look bad in front of my countrymen. I got to make you look bad.' "

As usually happens when a man tries to hit the ball out of sight on every swing, Carty couldn't do a thing. "He went 0–for–15 against me the rest of the year," Frazier said. "He never did pay me back yet. Maybe he will some time."

Getting misquoted in inflammatory headlines wasn't enough to turn George Frazier against the winter game, Dominican style. "It's fun playing down there," he said. "I was pitching one night and the lights went out. It was only for maybe five minutes. They had flashlights they kept in the dugout for those situations, so I ran straight for the dugout. They turn the lights on five minutes later and every base, home plate and the pitcher's rubber was gone. I mean dug up and gone. Nothing left. It was like a big cow pasture. Everything was gone."

Eric Gregg, the National League umpire, spent three and a half winters working in the Dominican. "That's where I met my wife," he said. "She's Dominican."

That's also where Gregg really learned to umpire. If a man can umpire down there, he can umpire just about anywhere.

"The players go berserk," Eric said. "They act like real assholes. And the fans get so involved . . . I got hit in the head with a couple of oranges one time. They threaten you. They look at you and they go like this: 'Hey ump [making a throat-cutting gesture].' Then they get a starter's gun and they shoot it up in the air. You hear it. You don't know they're shooting blanks. You just start trembling. It's a trip. It really is a trip. You just try to get out alive. You threaten to forfeit the game. I had a big 'shithouse' [a heated dispute] with Tom Lasorda. I called Bobby Valentine out on a checked swing in a close game. He threw the bat at me. It landed right on the first base bag. I said, 'That's it.' I ejected him from the game right there. The next day I called the league president. I said, 'This guy's got to be suspended. He can't throw a bat at an umpire.' 'Well,' he said, 'We'll look into it.' "

Eric placed a phone call to the United States. He was told that he'd have to work for a couple of days while the thing was being ironed out. No soap, said Gregg. The umpires went on strike to protest the non-action and, about a week later, they were fired en masse. "All the guys went home," Gregg said. "I stayed there because my wife lived there. I was watching a few games on TV. They had all kinds of 'shithouses' [with the substitute umpires] and finally they brought one American umpire down to help everything out and they finished the season. But it was complete chaos. Every year for the last seven years umpires have either quit or got fired."

Despite that argument with Lasorda over the checked swing, Tommy proved to be a most valuable ally in Gregg's battle to get his wife out of the country. "Tom Lasorda is 'bad' [i.e., big] down there," Eric said. "without him I couldn't have got my wife out. He got her a visa in one day. It usually takes 60 days."

With all those headaches, Gregg still has some pleasant memories of umpiring in the Dominican. He'd especially get a kick out of standing at home plate during the playing of the National Anthem. "You've got to stand at attention," he said. "The guards, they can't move for nothing."

And while they stood there, unable to so much as twitch a muscle, kids would scale the outfield walls, jump down and mix with the crowd in the stands. "Once the National Anthem's over," they're gone," Eric said. "It was so funny watching them."

Wild incidents were a dime a dozen in the Dominican. When Lonnie Smith played there he saw Jose Moreno intentionally drop a pop fly as the winning run scored in a game that eliminated the losing team from the playoffs. "It was very obvious," Lonnie said. "Two outs, everybody was moving. He had it, and he dropped it."

The motivation, Lonnie claimed, was simply that Moreno, and several others, couldn't wait to go home. It was not an unlikely scenario. But the fans who had wagered money on the team weren't about to accept that muffed pop fly—intentional or not—sitting down. "They started throwing things," Lonnie Smith said, "and they knocked down the clubhouse door."

Fortunately, there were two clubhouse doors—an outer one and an inner one. Only the outer one went crashing down. "They kept Jose in the clubhouse," Lonnie said. "Then, when all the Latin players left, they took him across the field and smuggled him to the other side. All the Americans waited in the office. I don't think anybody was willing to take a chance on going out. Everybody was happy, though, because they knew they were going home. Everybody had reservations to leave the next day, just in case. It was scary that day. Before that, though, it was nice."

Two decades before that, it wasn't so nice. Santo Domingo was known as Ciudad Trujillo then, but "the winter game" still flourished. Bill White was on the Escogido team, which was playing Licey for the Dominican championship. The Trujillo clan, White came to realize, took its baseball seriously.

"One of Trujillo's brothers was a Licey fan," the announcer said. "They got us down, two games to one, and we came back to tie the series."

In game four, Andre Rodgers, who was staying with Bill in a private home, got knocked down by the Licey pitcher. Rodgers got up and headed for the mound. He took a swing at the Licey pitcher, and the dugouts emptied. In a twinkling of an eye, there was a mob scene in the middle of the diamond, players milling around. "All of a sudden," White said, "everybody moves apart. Here comes Trujillo—one of the brothers—with a gun, and he walks up and he slaps Andre and he says, 'Americano, go home.' Andre's British, so he's got the wrong guy. Anyway, Andre started for him, but he's got all these bodyguards and they've got guns."

Wisely, Rodgers held his ground. Trujillo and his armed bodyguards left the playing field and the ball game resumed.

"We decided we were going to go home," Bill White recalled.

But first he and Rodgers had to get through the night. A person can get paranoid in that atmosphere. All sorts of crazy—or were they crazy?—thoughts flashed through their heads. Maybe Trujillo's men would come after Rodgers in the apartment he shared with White. Thinking about it now, nearly a quarter of a century later, it sounded a little far-fetched. But that night, almost anything seemed possible.

"You should have seen us blockading those doors," Bill White said. "We barricaded all the doors, just in case."

They made it safely through the night. Came morning, and they—and several of their teammates—stuck by their decision not to play the rest of the series. Salty Parker, their manager, got on a plane to fly back to the States. "They [the Dominican soldiers] go on the plane," Bill said, "and they took him off." Now some of the players, White and Rodgers among them, tried to get out of the country. They, too, were stopped. The series went on, as scheduled. Not at all surprisingly, Escogido lost.

The Trujillo era was long gone by the time Bunning, Morrison, Bosetti, Simpson and the rest put on Escogido uniforms, but baseball remained a most serious business. The night the '77 Escogido team lost the final game of the playoffs, a crowd of at least 50 angry fans surrounded the limousine that was to take them back to the hotel. They shouted "Yankee go home," and worse. A few of them shook the car after the players had climbed into it. The police had to come and clear a path through the mob. But clear it, they did, and everybody got out of there with nothing worse than a small scare. Actually, after a few weeks there, the players seemed to grow accustomed to such incidents. Many of them genuinely grew to like the place.

If things occasionally got to be on the wild side in the Dominican, it would be stretching the truth to say that sanity was always the order of the day in the other strongholds of the winter game.

Jim Bunning managed in Puerto Rico in '75. His team was in the final game of the playoffs when the situation nearly got out of hand. "We're trailing, 2–1," Bunning recalled. "The situation is this: two out, Sergio Ferrer on first base. Felix Millan is the hitter. Base hit to right field. Ferrer goes to third. . . ."

Potential tying run on third, potential go-ahead run on first. Ah, but wait . . .

"The hit didn't count," Bunning said. "The left field umpire had called time just as the pitcher released the ball. Nobody heard him. Nobody had seen him."

Bunning went out to argue with the left field umpire, Greg Kosc.

Just as I'm ready to leave Steve Palermo—he's the third base umpire—comes up and says, 'Let's go.' I lost my complete cool. I cursed him and all the rest of them. He threw me out of the game. I said, 'I'm not leaving. Go ahead and forfeit the game. There are 18,000 people here. They're all stirred up because of the situation.' "

Bunning walked back to the dugout and refused to leave. "I stood there," he recalled. "I said, 'You can't throw me out. It's the last game of the playoffs. You can't do it.' "

Opinions seemed to vary on that score. Bunning kept standing there—"so everybody in the park could see me"—and the umpires kept waiting for him to leave. "Now all six umpires come over," he said. "They're going to make me move. I said, 'Go ahead, forfeit the game. I want to see if you have any guts. Forfeit the game, and then I want to see you get off the field alive.' "

"Palermo threatened me. He said, 'I'll have your job in the States.' " Still, Bunning held his ground.

"Now Durwood Merrill comes over," he said. "They're throwing beer and everything and he's standing there. A big thing of beer comes down and hits him. It goes all over his face."

Merrill managed to keep calm. "He says, 'Please Jim, will you leave. We don't want to have a problem here. We want to get out of here alive,' " Bunning recalled. "I said, 'There's no way he can throw me out of this ball game. Not in this situation.' He says, 'Maybe he was a little hasty.' I said, 'Then let him change his mind. Let me stay.' "

Another impasse. Another uncomfortable wait while more objects came hurtling out of the stands. "Finally," said Bunning, "the army came. I figured, 'Hey, it's time for me to go.' They were going to take me off the bench bodily, anyway. This guy, the general, said, 'I don't know anything about baseball, but I think you'd better leave.' So I left.

"Now they bring Millan back to home plate and put Ferrer back on first base. The very next pitch, Millan doubles down the right field line. If he hadn't gotten that hit I hate to think what would've happened to those umpires."

The double put runners on second and third, but Sixto Lezcano bounced back to the pitcher and Bunning's team lost, anyway.

For the real winter fun, though, the place to go is Venezuela.

"I went there in 1970," National League umpire Frank Pulli said. "The fans there—phwew! But I had a good time."

Some good time. "One day I got an off day," Pulli remembered. "I'm sitting off to the side of the plate. The native umpire has a play at first base. The next thing, the player and the umpire, they're going at one another. Before you know it, the player swings at the umpire. The umpire swings back. I'm saying, 'What the hell is going on?'

"I go down to the locker room after the game. The president of the league is there. The secretary-treasurer is there, too. They're talking in Spanish. I said, 'Will you tell me what's going on?' He said, 'They want to fine the umpire.' I said, 'Fine the *umpire*? What about the ball player?' "

The unwillingness to back the umpire so upset Pulli that he told the league officials, "If you're going to fine and suspend the umpire, I'm going home. That's open warfare on us guys. I'm looking for protection for myself, too."

They debated the subject for a while. Then Pulli said, "I'll tell you what. Put the guy with me."

Native umpires, he knew, were working for the whopping sum of $11 a game. "Hey," said Pulli, "$11 to that guy was a lot of money."

The league officials relented. Pulli, and the native umpire, were allowed to work as a team. Another winter baseball crisis had been averted.

Len Matuszek, his wife, Karen, and their two young children went to Venezuela in the winter of '81–'82. Matuszek, a powerfully built, lefthanded-hitting first baseman (and occasional third baseman), was coming off a fine Triple A season in the Phillies' farm system and was on his way to the big leagues. He'd heard a lot about the winter game in Venezuela and he thought he was reasonably well prepared for it.

"But until you go down there and you really experience it—I'm talking about the first two, three weeks when you go through a culture shock—things are just different than they are in this country," he discovered. "It takes a while to get acclimated to the lifestyle. For us personally, our toughest adjustment was our living conditions. We were living in a very small efficiency apartment with one bedroom. It made it kind of tough. You don't have the opportunity to go to a beach or go to a park. Transportation is a problem. It's so hot, if you go out for any length of time your energy just gets sapped."

But they managed to get through it quite well, all things considered. The road trips could be hard to handle, however.

"The longest was five days," Len said, "but a five-day road trip seemed like a two-week road trip. You're traveling so much. You just don't fly into a main airport and go 10 minutes to the hotel. You may fly to an airport an hour and a half away, then get on a bus—and any time you're driving down there it's a harrowing experience. They don't drive the same way we do here."

Pitcher Kelly Downs, one of Matuszek's teammates on that Maracaibo team, recalled an early-morning bus ride in the rain on the way back to Maracaibo. There was a large lake to cross. Downs awoke just as they were going over the bridge. He took a quick look, then dozed off again. Next thing he knew one of the coaches was yelling, "Watch out!" Kelly opened his eyes in time to see a frightening sight. "There was a stalled car [actually two or three cars] in the passing lane," Kelly said. "It was pouring. The driver put on the brakes, but it didn't do any good. He smashed into the car and threw it off to the right."

The bus careened along. "In my mind," said Kelly, "I'm thinking, 'We're going off the bridge.' I thought we were still over the water."

They weren't, though. "All I remember," said the pitcher, "is seeing a great big cement thing coming up on us quick."

They hit it at an angle. The bus wound up on the wrong side of the road. But everybody was able to walk away from the accident.

That, in itself, was a minor miracle. "I got off that bus," said Kelly Downs, "and I said, 'I'll never take another bus in Venezuela. I'm going home. If I'm going to get killed, I'm going to get killed in the States.' "

"It's like they don't have any speed limit over there," said pitcher Jerry Reed. "Well, they have a speed limit, but nobody enforces it. I remember just before the accident people [coming from the other direction] were blowing their horns, blinking their lights. . . ."

Apparently, they were trying to warn the bus driver that there was an accident ahead, that one or more cars were blocking his side of the road. The driver, however, misinterpreted their signals. "He acted like he was in the Fourth of July parade," Jerry Reed said. "He was waving back at them, blowing his own horn. It was like we were coming back from the war or something. Next thing I knew—boy, we were in trouble."

Reed was just waking up when it happened. The long bus trip from Valencia was almost over. "You could see the lights of Maracaibo," said pitcher Jim Rasmussen.

Jerry Reed was sitting next to Kelly Downs, about halfway back in the bus. Rasmussen was two seats from the back, directly in front of Maracaibo's star second baseman, Manny Trillo. Manager Ron Clark and coach Rollie DeArmas were in the front, where managers and coaches usually are.

"It was foggy and raining," Rasmussen said. "The slow lane had maybe half a mile of cars that were just stopped, so we swung over into the fast lane and started passing those cars."

By the time they saw the accident, it was too late. "We were going fast," said Rasmussen, "maybe 70 or 75. We were just flying. The bus driver hit the brakes and he locked them. We just started skidding, like hydroplaning, and Clarkie yelled, 'Heads up!' and I kinda yelled, too, because I saw what was going on."

"Kelly [Downs] sat there and he just watched it," Jerry Reed said. "He told me the front windows popped out like contact lenses. I was down in the seat, braced against the seat in front of me."

"We smashed through the wreck," recalled Rasmussen. "The bus ran right through the accident [sending the stalled cars flying]. That's when we started going sideways. I thought we were going to roll."

"We hit three times," said Reed. "It seemed like a long time when it was happening. Actually, it might've lasted three seconds."

"We kind of came out of the skid," said Rasmussen, and then we started going sideways again and we jumped up over the median."

They were lucky. At that moment nothing was coming the other way. Minutes before, and minutes later, there was a steady stream of traffic on that side of the road.

Jim Rasmussen, staring out the window through the fog and the drizzle, saw a cement support for a bridge; the bus seemed to be heading for it. "I just ducked down," he said. "My arms were up against the seats in front of me. Manny Trillo wasn't awake at all in the seat behind me. The first thing I did [after the impact] was fall foward because the seats ahead of me just broke. They went down flat. Trillo's body must have hit the seats behind me because he landed on top of me."

For a moment or two, they feared the worst. "I raised up," said Jerry Reed, "and I just knew that Rollie DeArmas and Ron Clark were out the front windows. I didn't think there was any way they could have survived it. But I looked and they were both there, kinda looking back to see if anyone was hurt. Ron had a little cooler of orange juice sitting next to him in the front seat. They never did find that. It just went flying out. He lost a pair of glasses, too. Seats were broken where the players flew over the front of them. We were just extremely lucky nobody was hurt worse than we were."

There were some bumps and bruises. Nothing serious. A local radio station reported that a couple of players had been killed in the crash. A newspaper mentioned severe injuries. The reports were erroneous. But there wasn't a man on that bus who didn't realize how fortunate he was to be able to walk off that bus in one piece.

Memories of that early-morning crash remain etched in the minds of those who survived those moments of sheer terror. But even at its best traveling in Venezuela left a lot to be desired.

"Believe me," said Len Matuszek, "the road trips from a mental standpoint were probably the toughest thing to go through. You were really forced to get out, to go eat in restaurants, to kind of live the way the people live. If you don't have the right attitude down there, if you're not willing to adjust and adapt you're going to be in trouble. I felt we adjusted real well. Besides the fact we had cramped living conditions, we felt like it was home after a while. We were happy to be coming home [at the end of the playoffs], but it was kind of sad leaving some of the people because they had great people down there—especially the ones who ran the club. They really tried to make you feel as comfortable as possible. When either of our two children were sick there'd be three, four doctors coming over immediately if we wanted them. You felt like they were taking an honest concern over your situation."

The fans demanded a lot from their ball players, but the good players don't really mind that. "They just asked you to play hard and play enthusiastically and give them a little bit of your time," Matuszek said. "I tried to do that, and they responded favorably."

As a result, Matuszek didn't feel any undue pressure. He just went along, did what he was supposed to do, and had a pretty good time—until the playoffs. "That was an experience I've never, ever experienced before," he said.

The baseball playoffs down there are like the pro basketball and hockey playoffs up here. The regular season is mostly for laughs. The post-season is deadly serious. "Once the playoffs start it's like the regular season's nothing," Matuszek found out.

The best-of-seven series with Caracas opened in Maracaibo, where the teams split two games, then moved to Caracas for the next three. It was wild in Caracas.

"The stadium seats 35,000," Matuszek said. "the first two games there was a policemen's strike going on. There might have been 12 cops trying to police 35,000 really unruly fans that were just out of control. They were throwing things at you. I mean, bottles or firecrackers or what have you."

The bottles were dangerous. The firecrackers were scary. And the what-have-yous were enough to make you want to run for cover.

"By the last game of that series I had reached a point—I think our whole club had—where winning and losing didn't matter," Matuszek said. "It was just survival, get off the field alive. One of our reserve players got hit in the head with a rum bottle. What makes it bad is that the umpires are so intimidated by all this—and maybe rightfully so—that they only cleared the field one time. I felt there was one game when things got so bad they should have stopped the game halfway through and we should have left. There was nobody there to control the fans. They don't listen [to warnings over the loudspeaker]. They feel they've come to the game, they've paid their money and anything goes. They have no respect for the players' safety out there."

He was talking primarily about the safety of the visiting players. "Believe me," said Matuszek, "they help their home club."

Caracas swept the three home games against its intimidated opponents, who were just grateful to escape in one piece. The final game was the only close one.

"We ended up losing on an umpire's call," Matuszek said. "I really believe he was afraid to make the call [against the home team] and one of the reasons was, an umpire got shot and killed down there this past winter a day after he made two controversial calls against the Caracas team. He was in a bar the next night and somebody shot him."

The last game turned around on a smash down the third base line hit by Caracas catcher Bo Diaz. "We were winning, 2–1," recalled Matuszek. "I was playing third base. The ball was a good foot foul, if not more. The umpire hesitated and then he punched his arm inside to call it fair. I couldn't believe it."

That call enabled Caracas to tie the score, and the home team went on to wrap up the game, and the series, in the bottom of the ninth.

"I had a couple of pop ups that were close to the stands," Matuszek said. "I guess because I was concentrating on the ball I didn't realize it, but I was later told they were throwing cups full of beer and sand or whatever. I guess one went right by my ear."

Caracas fans, it seems, are noted for their strong throwing arms. Alan Clark, now an American League umpire, worked the winter game in Caracas during his minor league days. He particularly remembers a Sunday morning game. "It was Rubber Ball Day," Clark said. Hey, it could have been worse. It could have been Bat Day or Hand Grenade Day.

"Everything was fine," Alan said, "until I made a call at home plate against the home club. Thirty-five thousand rubber balls came down."

Clark did what any sensible umpire would do. He ran to second base on the theory he'd be a little safer out there. At least, it would require a longer throw for the fans.

In Valencia, Venezuela, Clark was working a game with three

native umpires. Dave Parker was on third base. A ball was hit in the air to center field. The center fielder got his glove on it, juggled it, and finally caught it. Parker tagged the instant the ball was touched by the center fielder and raced home. One of the native umpires called him out, ruling—incorrectly—that he couldn't tag up until the ball was actually caught.

"Steve Demeter [the manager of Parker's team] came out to argue," Clark said. "All of a sudden out of the corner of my eye I saw something hurtling towards us. It was a bomb, some sort of big cherry bomb. It hit Demeter, put a four-inch gash in his arm, bounced off him and hit the native umpire in the leg."

Clark promptly forfeited the game to the visiting team. Now the crowd *really* got upset. "When those people yell, 'Kill the ump,' they aren't kidding," Alan said.

It took Clark two and a half hours to get out of the stadium. Without police protection he might never have made it. And he wasn't too sure of the police protection. What if the cops were betting on the home team that day?

There was Alan, trapped in the umpires' dressing room while the crowd milled outside. Finally, a paddy wagon worked its way through the angry mob and backed up to the dressing room door. Alan jumped in, and away they went to a predetermined spot where Clark's regular driver was to pick him up.

The fearless Mr. Clark even returned to the same ball park to umpire another game, and lived to tell about it.

"It was a very valuable experience down there," he insisted. "You certainly learn how to handle every situation. It definitely does get scary at times—scary in an eerie way. You don't know what they're going to do. But when push comes to shove, the ball players will help. When a situation would break out and people would start throwing things at you, some of the big-name ball players—Manny Trillo, Bo Diaz, Steve Braun—would walk over and stand next to you."

It couldn't have been much fun standing there, getting bombarded by missiles thrown from the stands, or waiting for two and a half hours in a tiny dressing room while, on the other side of the door, a mob gathered, intent on putting you out of your misery. Why would a man keep coming back for more?

"You think about leaving," Alan Clark said. "But as a minor league umpire you don't want to quit and go home. You tough it out."

Such is the raw courage that a man must have to make it through the Winter Game.

11

THE DREAM ENDS, THE NIGHTMARE BEGINS

"Failing in minor league baseball is not failing," Tug McGraw once said. "It's just a chase after a dream that didn't come true."

That's a very nice way of putting it. A man is liable to put up with almost anything in pursuit of that dream. Occasionally, though, the dream turns into a nightmare—or ends in tragedy.

The kid's name was Alfredo Edmead. He was 18 when the Pirates signed him, and the fleet outfielder from the Dominican Republic was considered one of Pittsburgh's finest prospects.

In 1974, Edmead was a member of the Salem Pirates of the Carolina League. The second baseman on that Class A team was Pablo Cruz, Edmead's closest friend who had played a major role in the young man's decision to sign with Pittsburgh. Today, Cruz is the Pirates' scouting supervisor for Latin America.

The Salem Pirates were loaded with hot prospects that year. One of their pitchers was a lefthander named John Candelaria, who won 11 games as a second-year pro. The catcher was Steve Nicosia, who hit .305. The center fielder was Miguel Dilone, who hit .331 and stole 84 bases. Edmead, the right fielder, hit .314 with seven home runs and 61 stolen bases in 119 games.

On an August night, the Salem Pirates were hosting the Rocky Mount Phillies. It was an exciting occasion for Edmead; some of his relatives had come to see him play. Early in the game a Rocky Mount batter blooped one into short right field. Second baseman Cruz went back. Right fielder Edmead charged in. At the last instant, Edmead went into a slide and caught the ball as his friend jumped over him.

A couple of innings later there was another short, high fly to right field. Again Cruz dashed out. Again Edmead rushed in. This time they collided.

It was a terrible crash. Pablo Cruz was wearing a brace on his knee—"a heavy, plastic and metal brace," recalled Eddie Molush, who was a member of the Rocky Mount team. Edmead's head caught the full weight of it. His skull was crushed.

"I knelt over him," said Molush. "He was bleeding very slowly and thickly from his ears and mouth and nose. He was having trouble breathing . . . Then he stopped breathing."

There was a volunteer fireman on the Rocky Mount team and he began pounding on Edmead's chest in an attempt to get his heart beating again.

"I could see his left eye socket," Molush said. "It was all crushed in."

The call went out for an ambulance. "It took about eight or 10 minutes for it to get there," recalled Molush. "There was a gate in right field. I ran out there as soon as he stopped breathing, went through the gate and ran up this street. I remember, there was a real long hill."

The hill, perhaps 500 yards long, led to the town's main street. Molush heard the siren wailing in the distance. "I stood there, waving my jacket," he said. "The ambulance stopped. The guy said, 'How do you get in there?' I told him, 'You have to go to right field.' "

The driver took off. Molush, running, followed him. It was too late. Alfredo Edmead died. Apparently, he passed away before they got him to the hospital.

The players didn't know it at the time, but they had a pretty good idea. "Nobody wanted to play," said Molush, "but they kept going with the game. I think the reason we kept playing, nobody wanted to admit he might die."

Eddie Molush had to pitch the last two innings of that game. "I pitched harder than I ever did in my life," he said. "I just wanted to get out of there."

Later, Rocky Mount coach Scott Reid told the players that Edmead was dead. "It's amazing how many of the details I remember," said Molush, eight years later. "I remember the whole ride home in the bus, close to six hours. It was funeral in that bus. All you heard was the drone of the engine and little whispers. Then, about 3:30 or 4 in the morning we made a stop. I think that allowed everybody to have a release from it. Anyhow, it seemed like the fresh air helped."

Something like that happens and suddenly the game doesn't seem all that important. You watch a young man lose his life and the winning or losing of a ball game becomes virtually meaningless. "I think it made me see sport in a different light," Eddie Molush said. "It's just a game, not what people try to make it into."

Bill Schlesinger is 40 now, although he looks younger. He owns a neighborhood hardware store in Cincinnati that he inherited from his father. It's hard work. You can almost always find Bill at that hardware store—at 9:30 in the morning or 9:30 at night, on Saturdays as well as weekdays.

Thirteen years ago Schlesinger was a long-ball-hitting outfielder with the Phillies' Triple A Eugene (Ore.) team in the Pacific Coast League. Originally, he'd been Boston Red Sox property. In 1964, his first year as a pro, he met Ted Williams in spring training—a meeting that Schlesinger still remembers vividly. Williams, after all, was one of the game's greatest all-time hitters. Apparently the tall, slender kid with the raw power caught Williams' eye.

"He walked up to me," Bill recalled, "and he said, 'So you're Schlesinger, huh?' I said, 'Yeah.' He said, 'You know who I am?' I said, 'Yeah, you're Ted Williams.' He said, 'You think I was a good hitter?' I said, 'Yeah, you were a real good hitter.' He said, 'A real good hitter? I was the best God damn hitter who ever lived and don't you forget it.' "

Schlesinger never has. Nor did he forget what Ted Williams said after that. "You've got a pretty good chance," he told the young man. "I like your swing."

Schlesinger, a righthanded hitter, never got the opportunity to take aim at that left field wall in Fenway Park, except in batting practice. He spent six weeks with the Red Sox, but got to the plate only once—in a game against the Angels at Dodger Stadium. "I was just sitting there, about the eighth inning," he said, "and [manager] Billy Herman says, 'Pinch hit.' I got so nervous I couldn't find my helmet. And I couldn't find my bat. The clubhouse guy had to find them."

The California pitcher was Marcelino Lopez. Bill chopped a ball off the plate. The catcher gunned him down at first base. End of big league career.

It shouldn't have been, though. Getting traded to the Phillies organization looked like the break of a lifetime. The Phillies were weak then. A righthanded hitter with power figured to have a good shot at making their ball club. When Eugene manager Frank Lucchesi told Schlesinger in August that the big club was going to call him up for the final month of the major league season Bill was esctatic.

Three days later, disaster struck in Tuscon, Ariz. Or, to be more precise, a Larry Sherry fast ball struck.

"It was my fault," Schlesinger insisted. "He was just brushing me back. I should have gotten out of the way. It was a fast ball, but it wasn't that hard. He didn't throw that hard. It was just like I froze, I guess. It just seemed like forever for that ball to get there, too. I just couldn't get out of the way."

Lucchesi came running out of the dugout. "I almost lost my life getting hit by a baseball," Frank said. "When anybody gets hit in the head I get kind of panicky about it."

The ball hit Schlesinger around the left eye. He didn't lose consciousness. He kept telling Lucchesi he was all right. But the manager wasn't taking any chances. He had Bill carried to the clubhouse on a stretcher.

Bill stayed in the Eugene clubhouse until the game ended. There was a ringing sensation in his left ear. "My ear still rings today," he said. But he didn't feel dizzy. He was able to get up, walk around, take a shower. When the game ended Lucchesi buzzed around him like a mother hen.

"He was so concerned," Schlesinger said, "you'd have thought I was his kid or something. 'Where are you going to go right now?' he asked me. I said, 'Well, I'm going to eat.' He said, 'Eat a good dinner, then call me when you get back.'

"I went out and had a big dinner and got back at two o'clock [in the morning]. I sat down and wrote a letter, went down to the lobby and mailed it. I'm feeling great. I called Frank, told him I felt fine. He said, 'I don't want you to play tomorrow. Sit out tomorrow.'

"So I go to sleep. Next morning I wake up about seven o'clock and I'm sick. I'm really sick, throwing up."

He wound up stretched out on the floor in the bathroom, which is where he was when Lucchesi called. Later that night, when Lucchesi checked on him after the game, Schlesinger still felt nauseous. "Well," the manager told him, "we'd better get you to the hospital."

The following morning had to be one of the scariest in Bill Schlesinger's life. When he woke up he couldn't see. He was totally blind. "I thought they'd put something over my eyes," he said. "I felt there with my hand, but there was nothing there. The nurse came in. 'Good morning,' she says, 'how are you doing today?' 'I can't see anything,' I told her. 'Don't worry about it,' she says. 'That's normal. We expected that to happen. Your brain has expanded. It'll be okay.'

"It was like that for about a day," Bill said. "Then, the next day, I could see. It was a little fuzzy, but I could see."

He remained in the hospital for two weeks, the fuzziness gradually disappearing. During his stay there he lost about 30 pounds. The Pacific Coast League season was nearly over. Lucchesi suggested he fly straight home from Tuscon and call it a year, but Bill wanted to return to Eugene for the last few games.

The Emeralds were playing Tacoma. Schlesinger took batting practice. No way he was ready to face a pitcher under game conditions. The trip to Eugene appeared to be for nothing, but Lucchesi saved the day.

"He gave me the lineup card to take out to home plate," Bill said. "The place was pretty crowded. I went out and they gave me a standing ovation."

For Bill Schlesinger, it was to be the last hurrah. The doctor in Tuscon had told him he'd be all right—as good as new—in six weeks. The doctor was wrong.

Bill had exceptionally good eyesight—20–15 in each eye. He still has 20–15 in each eye, but there are blind spots. "If I'm looking right there," he said, turning his head to the right, "I don't know you're sitting there in front of me. It's just a big blind spot and it hasn't changed one bit."

An eye specialist in Philadelphia told him it wouldn't change, that his days of hitting a baseball for a living were over. Schlesinger didn't give up without a struggle. He tried to come back the following season. No use.

A lot of years have passed, but he still thinks about his playing days, about what might have been if he'd been able to duck that Larry Sherry fast ball, and about the good times he had playing the game. Mention Larry Bowa's name to him and he brightens up in a flash. He and Bowa roomed together on the road for part of the ' 69 season. Schlesinger loves to tell about the night Bowa had a big game. "He'd always get up at eight or nine o'clock every morning," said Bill, "especially when he had a good game. He had to go out and buy the papers."

So that night Schlesinger and friends went to the guy who ran the newsstand in the hotel lobby and made a deal. "We bought up all his morning papers in advance—about 75 of them, I think—and we told him to put them outside the door to our room. The next morning Bo wakes me up.'I'll be back in a minute,' he says. He's rushing around, getting dressed. Then he opens the door and there are 75 papers out there. He closes it, looks at me and says, 'You're not going to believe what's on the other side of this door.' "

Those memories remain. So do the pictures of a lean, powerful righthanded slugger named Bill Schlesinger that adorn his office wall. "I should take them down," he said. "People come in and they want to know all about it. They ask me how long I played and why I'm not playing anymore. I don't tell them anything about getting beaned. I tell them I got released or something, that I couldn't hit a curve ball. I don't tell them I got hurt, although I still think about it. That was the big thing I didn't want to happen. I wanted to find out if I was good enough to play in the big leagues. After I had that big year in Triple A I really thought I had everything together. That's what makes me sick."

As shattering as that disappointment was—"I still haven't completely gotten over it," he said—Schlesinger doesn't regret spending all that time in baseball, building himself up for that awful letdown in Tuscon. "I wouldn't give up anything I went through in baseball," he said. "There was just one bad thing, but there were about 200 great things. That's the best part of your life. It's probably the best living anybody could have—besides being a sportswriter."

A pitcher never knows when it's going to end. One minute he's firing 90-plus mile an hour fast balls across the plate, challenging hitters, getting them out. Next minute something goes haywire. There's a pain in the shoulder, or maybe in the elbow. It happens to so many of them.

It would be hard to imagine a more painful scene than the one that unfolded at Jack Russell Stadium in Clearwater, Fla., on a March morning in 1979. It was just a "B" game between the Cardinals and the Phillies. No admission charged, virtually nobody in the stands.

To Jim Wright, though, it was an important outing. The tall, good-looking righthander had been one of the gems in the Phillies farm system, another of those "can't-miss kids".

"He reminds me so much of Robin Roberts," Phillies general manager Paul Owens said. "He comes at you and comes at you. It's just a matter of being sound."

Wright had always been sound—never even thought about arm trouble—until the middle of the 1977 season in Oklahoma City. He was burning up the American Association when the pain started in his right forearm. It grew progressively worse, and prolonged rest wasn't the answer. The pain was still there in the spring of '78. Finally, a West Coast doctor found out what was wrong. A growth had formed on the bone; remove the growth and the pain would vanish.

The operation done, Wright showed in the spring of '79 with high hopes. Then, on a spring training trip with the Phillies to the Dominican, he felt the pain again. Not quite the same pain, but a pain nonetheless. Maybe, he thought, it was a normal part of the rehabilitation. Maybe he could "pitch through it". So that morning, there he was, pitching against the Cardinals' "B" team at Jack Russell Stadium. He felt he had to impress the brass, convince Paul Owens and Dallas Green that he was ready to pitch in the big leagues.

Watching him, you could see something was wrong. By the third inning he was throwing nothing but fast balls. It hurt too much to snap off a breaking ball.

The Cardinals had two runners on base when he tried to put a little extra on a fast ball to Tom Grieve, who bounced a single into right field. The lead runner, Roger Freed, rounded third, was trapped and finally tagged out. Then, and only then, all eyes refocused on Jim Wright. He was standing on the mound, his right arm bent in front of his body in a peculiar way. "Straighten it," Jose Cardenal, the Phillies first baseman, told him. "Straighten it."

"I can't," the pitcher replied.

Ray Rippelmeyer, the former Phillies pitching coach, was in the dugout as an invited observer. He went to the mound to see what was wrong.

"Think you should come out?" he asked Wright.

"I'd better," Jim replied. "It's broken."

He'd heard the crack. He'd felt the pain. He knew. The bone had snapped in two as he released that final fast ball.

There are few young men you'd rather see make it than Jim Wright. He loved the game. He worked hard at it. He went out of his way to be nice to people. And something like that had to happen.

To his everlasting credit, the young man battled back. "It's easy to feel sorry for yourself," he said. "I think everybody does for a while when you go through something like that. But it depends on how you believe. You've got to keep your faith in God."

The following spring, Wright was pitching again. The dream of making it to the big leagues was still alive. "I don't know how it's going to feel when I stand out there [on the mound in his first major league game]," he said. "I'm going to have goose bumps, I think, in every pore. I'm going to be thinking of a lot of different people. I'll be thinking of my dad and my mom and, God, I'll be thinking about everybody. It'll be a dream come true. It'll be everything all at once, a family dream, my dream, the dream of a lot of people. I just wish my dad could see it. He lived baseball. He knew I was going to play it ever since I was a little kid, when I was eight, nine, ten. He asked me what I was going to be then. I said, 'A big league ball player.' "

Jim Wright became a big league ball player in 1981, winning a couple of ball games for the Kansas City Royals. He still faced a long, hard, uphill climb to become the kind of big league player he wanted to be—and almost surely would have been by now if not for those injuries. But after what he'd gone through, merely making it to the mound in a big league game was a huge accomplishment.

"The hardest thing in baseball is watching a dream slip away that at one time you had a full grasp of and control of and now you can do nothing about," relief pitcher Ed Farmer said recently. "That's the most saddening part of the game. You're watching something die that's a part of you that you can no longer do."

Farmer was a hard-throwing 18-year-old when he began his professional baseball career. He didn't always know where the ball was going, but he knew it was going to get there fast. Farmer's career, like Jim Wright's, nearly came to a sudden, sickening climax. In Ed's case the excruciating pain was in the shoulder. "If it wasn't for my wife and her strong will, pushing me to come back, I wouldn't be here," he said on a July evening in 1980 when he was in Los Angeles as a member of the American League All-Star team. "I remember saying to Barbara, 'I can't go out there and pitch with this kind of pain. I just can't do it. If it takes that, then I don't want to play this game anymore.' She said, 'Well, I think you ought to have surgery. You ought to do what you can.' "

So he had it in 1976, and then he embarked on a second baseball career that far surpassed the first. There aren't many athletes in any sport who earned the big money that goes with success more than Ed Farmer. Nor are there many who appreciate it more.

He hurt his shoulder in Sacramento in 1975. "The worst place I played," Farmer said. He meant the ball park, not the town. It was a terrible ball park, a joke of a ball park. In reality, it was a high school football stadium. The left field fence was so close a batter could almost spit over it.

"That was the roughest time I've ever spent playing baseball," Ed said. "It was a carnival, a joke, a sideshow."

Before the shoulder injury, he'd spent time in the big leagues with Cleveland, Detroit and Philadelphia. Following the operation, it was back to the minors, which was a rough thing to go through, too.

"I'll tell you what it's like," he said. "It's like going back to the place you grew up in after an absence of, say, five or six years. All of a sudden the trees you used to walk by before, now they jump out at you. You say, 'Whooo, look at that tree,' or, 'Look at that railroad crossing; I never noticed that before.' Everything is magnified. You see it in a different perspective. Before, you were on your way up and you hadn't known anything better than that. Now you're on your way down and you've known everything better. It takes you about two or three weeks to get back, to fit right into the flow. Each week you spend there the big leagues become a little bit further away."

But Eddie Farmer made it back to the big leagues. What's more, he bounced back from what could have been a career-ending injury to become a major league all-star. "I'm in my second career," he said. "Somebody asked me, 'What are you going to do when you retire?' I said, 'I retired once and I didn't like it, so I came back to play baseball.' I'm fortunate. God, I'm fortunate."

The country is full of guys who weren't so fortunate, whose promising baseball careers ended almost before they got started. There's Wayne Simpson, a flame-throwing righthander who had a brilliant half season with the Cincinnati Reds before his arm went bad. A tough competitor, Simpson worked his way back through the minor leagues, made it briefly to the majors, but he was never the same and it was a shame because he could have been great.

You could fill a book with the stories of big league arms that turned to dust. So let's settle for just one more—the story of a young man named Dave Downs, who made the jump from Double A to the big leagues in 1972 and shut out the Braves in Atlanta in his very first big league start. Then, halfway through his next start for the Phillies, he felt a pain in his shoulder.

That was the end for big leaguer Dave Downs. He underwent surgery; he returned to the low minors, but it was no use. Add him to the long list of super prospects who got rushed to the big leagues by impatient management—and had their careers ruined.

Downs did find time, however, to help some others become major leaguers. Dickie Noles, for one, can thank his lucky stars that Dave Downs, his shoulder surgery completed, was attempting a comeback with Spartanburg in the Western Carolinas League when Dickie was there in '76.

Noles had a terrible time of it that year. He finished with a 4-and-16 record and a 5.91 earned run average. If not for Downs, it might have been worse.

Despite all his own problems, Downs took Noles under his wing.

"He was throwing good pitches and next thing you know, they were flying out of the park," Dave said. "There were some games he didn't get out of the first inning. He had the best stuff of anybody I'd ever seen. He threw so natural. His velocity was incredible. He had a real sharp breaking pitch. And he couldn't get anybody out."

Downs roomed with Noles on road trips. At a time when his own career was in its death throes, Dave did his best to keep Dickie from packing it in. "He went through hell," Downs said. "Three, four, five times he was ready to go home. He was in tears."

Dave kept talking him out of it, kept telling him that better days were coming. " 'Mark my words,' I told him, 'in two or three years you'll be in the big leagues.' "

Then Noles would go out and get clobbered again. "I remember he got his third or fourth beating in a row," Downs said. "He was ready to go [home]. I had to physically grab him and hold on to him. I was scared doing it. He was so mad and so frustrated I didn't know what he might do. The big thing was to keep him from hurting himself. He would've put his fist through a brick wall, he was so frustrated."

It says a lot for Dave Downs that, while going through his own private hell, he found time to help somebody else. Downs' baseball career ended at age 23. It was a bitter blow, one that threatened to leave permanent scars.

"I could have ended up the way Pat Bayless did very easily," Downs told me several years later, after he'd successfully fought back the disappointment and started a new career in business. It was two years before Dave could bear to watch another baseball game. He wouldn't even look at the baseball results in the paper.

What made it worse was the feeling that the shoulder problems could have been averted with a little more care, a little more patience. "I didn't do it myself," Dave Downs said. "I threw 269 innings in 1972 and I don't think I had more than 100 innings in a year before that. I think they should be watching that kind of stuff. They won't look at it that way because all I was, was a horse and I went lame and that was the end of me. They might as well have put a bullet in my head."

To Dave, it's almost as if that brief major league experience never happened. It seems so unreal, so long ago that it might as well have been a dream—the one Tug McGraw talked about that didn't come true.

12

THE PROFESSIONALS

It's easy to tell the professionals from the amateurs in baseball, the minor leagues from the colleges. The pros are the ones who run their games like amateurs. The amateurs are the ones who tend to run their games like pros.

Okay, that's an exaggeration. Some minor league operations are first class. There's a trainer who knows what he's doing. The lights are bright. The park is clean. The infield doesn't look like a rockpile. But too often things that we take for granted in decent college programs—some high school progams, too—are missing when a kid gets to the pros. That's sad. And it's also dangerous. An athlete shouldn't have to wait until he's in the big leagues, making big money, to play under safe conditions. I've never been able to understand how baseball people can permit their players to face what can only be described as unreasonable risks.

In June of '78 I had the dubious privilege of watching an Eastern League game at Quigley Stadium in West Haven, Conn. A young man named Len Matuszek was on first base for the Reading Phillies with two out in the top of the sixth. Don McCormack lined a double to left and Matuszek, who scored standing up, was accidentally tripped up by the West Haven catcher and went flying through the air, landing some four or five yards from the plate. It was immediately evident that Matuszek was hurt. The Reading trainer rushed out, took a look at him and called for a stretcher. Nothing happened. Matuszek remained on the ground in obvious distress. Again the Reading trainer called for a stretcher. Again nothing happened. There was no stretcher available in Quigley Stadium that night. Imagine that, if you will: a professional baseball game between two teams of highly skilled athletes, and no stretcher. Matuszek's teammates had to carry him bodily to the visiting clubhouse—a damp, filthy place—and then, when the game was over, pick him up again and put him in a station wagon. Only then did Matuszek, his feet sticking out the window, go to the hospital for treatment.

I can still remember Reading relief pitcher Pete Manos commenting on that grotesque scene as Matuszek waited—for more than three full innings—in the clubhouse, stretched out on a table. "Can you believe that?" he asked. "They don't have a stretcher. They don't have anything. The guy could be dying here and they still don't have anything."

Matuszek was fortunate. The injury wasn't serious. But it could have been. What then?

Remember the Pittsburgh farmhand who was killed when he collided with a teammate in a race for a short fly ball in Salem, Va.? Dallas Green was the Phillies' farm director at the time and he pulled no punches in giving his opinion of the incident and the way it was handled. "They were playing our farm club," Green said. "The game was on their field, but they had no trainer. Our trainer kept that kid alive long enough for him to be put in an ambulance."

His charges represented a shocking indictment of professional baseball.

"Baseball's wrong," Green said. "We're economizing where you can't economize."

It's been getting better in the last few years. More qualified trainers. More decent facilities. But it's nowhere near good enough. And that's inexcusable.

I told Tug McGraw the Matuszek story and he didn't seem the least bit surprised. "Can you imagine how many horror stories like that are around?" he said. "They invest big money in these draft choices, and yet it's like throwing them into the jungle. You take your best prospects and you just throw them to the wolves."

McGraw was speaking from experience. He'd been in the minor leagues. So had his brother, Hank.

"My brother's life was in Pete Cera's hands once," Tug said, "and he almost lost it."

Cera, it should be pointed out, is one of the most dedicated lifetime baseball men you'll ever meet. Currently, he's the Phillies' assistant clubhouse manager and equipment man. He's got friends throughout the game. But in the period Tug was talking about, Pete was one of many less-than-fully-qualified trainers in the minor leagues.

"It was in Reading," Tug said. "Hank was in a collision with another player going from first to second. He tried to avoid a tag or something and dive over the second baseman. Hank landed on the back of his neck and rolled over and got up."

Hank, playing center field that night, stayed in the game. "As each inning went by," said Tug, "he started getting increasingly worse abdominal pains to the point where they had to carry him off the field. During the time the pain was getting worse and worse, Pete was giving him Pepto Bismol and stuff. He thought it was the typical minor league pizza and beer upset stomach. By chance, Dr. [Patrick] Mazza was at the game that night."

The doctor saw them carry Hank McGraw off the field and went to the clubhouse to see how he was. "He said, 'You know this sounds like more than just an upset stomach,' " Tug said. " 'Let's get to the hospital,' he told Hank, 'and test your blood.' "

"They got to the hosptal. They took blood tests. Dr. Mazza said, 'You know, Hank, I'm fairly sure you have some damage in your appendix. I'd like to go in and take it out. We can do it tomorrow morning or we can do it tonight.' Hank said, 'Let's get it over with.' "

There was nothing wrong with Hank McGraw's appendix. He had, in fact, ruptured a blood vessel in his abdomen. "He was internally bleeding to death," Tug said. "If he hadn't decided to go do it then, he'd have gone into shock and possibly died within the next hour. He lost the maximum amount of blood you can lose. If Dr. Mazza hadn't been at that game just by chance and decided to come down and check, my brother's a dead duck. You can't have that. The [major league] ball clubs have to make a commitment to the minor league system. They have to clean it up and streamline it and make it better. The major league level used to be just as trouble-ridden as the minor leagues are. Then, the minor league problems didn't stand out. But now that the major league level is really a sophisticated machine, that's got to filter down to the minor leagues.

"Baseball," Tug said, "is going to have to have some sort of revolution in the game to correct all that minor league shit. They see what happened on the major league level where players united. They brought in a powerful guy, Marvin Miller, to get things done, things that should've been done a long time ago by management. They should be able to see that same potential at the minor league level. There are guys that have been in the minor leagues a long time. There's going to be some way to organize those guys."

Frankly, I doubt it. Minor league players don't have the

leverage—or the dollars—to fight the establishment. It seems inconceivable that minor leaguers could threaten to strike for higher pay, improved playing conditions and all the rest.

"All right," said Tug, "maybe a strike isn't what's going to bring it about. Maybe it's going to be a lawsuit. Read that minor league contract. It's all the responsibility of the players. There's nothing where the club is committed to conditions . . . One of these players is going to be a top draft pick. He's going to have a sharp lawyer. He's going to ask for some special covenants in his contract. The guy's going to go to the minor leagues. He's going to see what goes on. He's going to become a victim somehow. He's going to say, 'Look right here in my contract, under special covenant seven. It says I'm supposed to play on quality fields. I'm supposed to have a trainer or doctor that's qualified. I didn't have it. I lost my leg because of gangrene and it's going to cost you $10 million.' You can see it coming. It doesn't have to be a strike. You don't have to have leverage."

It should never come to that, of course. The people who run baseball should recognize the commitment they have to the young men playing their game on a professional level.

They should make sure they are treated like professionals.

13

THE AXEMAN COMETH

Cutdown day is the cruelest day of all. Spring training is just about over. Bags are packed. Plans are made. In many cases wives and children have headed for the city in which they think—or at least hope—they'll be spending the summer. There's one problem, though. The big league roster contains 26 names. By opening day, under the rules, it cannot contain more than 25. Somebody's got to go.

There might be three fringe guys, or four fringe guys, or only two fringe guys who aren't sure where they stand. When that plane leaves late in the afternoon for the trip north, will they be on it? Will they be going to New York or Columbus, Ohio? To Baltimore or Rochester, N.Y.? To Chicago or Edmonton, Canada? To St. Louis or Louisville? To the big leagues or the minors?

In the next few hours one of those three or four fringe guys will get the terrible news. A coach will walk over to him in the clubhouse, or on the field, and say, "The Skip wants to see you," or something to that effect. Those words have the ring of death about them. There isn't a man in camp on that day who doesn't know what they mean.

There aren't many things worse in sports than finding out, on the last day of spring training, that you're the 26th man on a 25-man team. Finishing fourth in the Olympic Trials is worse because only three go to the Olympic Games and an athlete has to wait four years for the next chance. But at least in the Olympic Trials it normally comes down to a person's performance on a given day; in that sense, the athlete controls his or her own fate. In baseball, the decision will be made behind closed doors in a meeting room. It doesn't always matter if you hit .300 in spring training or had an earned run average under 2.00. Anything is liable to happen behind those closed doors. Maybe the manager doesn't like you. Or the general manager doesn't like you. Or the top scout doesn't think you can hack it in the big leagues. Maybe you have an option left, and the guy fighting you for that 25th spot doesn't and so, rather than risk losing him, the club decides to send you out. On cutdown day, the world is filled with maybes.

So you show up at the ball park, the way you've been showing up all spring, and you try to act unconcerned. You make small talk in the clubhouse. You put on your uniform. You do your work. And you sweat bullets. A coach approaches and you die a thousand deaths. Is he coming over to say hello, or is he coming over to say goodbye? Is he coming over to say, "You're playing the first three innings at third base today," or is he coming over to say, "The Skip wants to see you?"

Occasionally, of course, a man headed for the minors doesn't get the news in the customary manner. Mike Fremuth, a righthanded pitcher, nearly made the Phillies' pitching staff in the early '70s. Came the final day of spring training and 11 pitchers remained in the big league camp. One had to go. Fremuth turned out to be the one, but at least he got the word in a rather novel way. Before a coach had the opportunity to track him down and tell him the manager wanted to see him, a sportswriter walked up, extended a hand and said, "Good luck, Mike. I'm sorry to see you go." It was only when he asked Fremuth when he had found out about it and the pitcher replied, "Just now, from you," that the writer, Bus Saidt of *The Trenton Times*, realized that his well-intentioned words had let the cat out of the bag. Happily, Fremuth had that rare ability to laugh at the bizarre happenings that he recognized as being part of life in a baseball uniform. If anything, the news was probably less painful coming from a friendly writer than it would have been coming from a considerably less friendly manager. Anyhow, Fremuth survived the jolt quite well, thank you. After getting released later that season, he went to Stanford Law School. He is now an attorney in Washington, D.C.

For most, though, getting sent down at the very end of spring training is an exceptionally difficult experience, one that can produce a lingering feeling of anger and frustration.

Take the case of Don McCormack. A highly-regarded catcher, he came up through the Phillies' organization. Called up by the big club in September of '80, he was behind the plate in the final innings of the dramatic, division-title-clinching game in Montreal on the next-to-last day of the regular season. He had worked hard for that opportunity, spending seven years in the minor leagues, and he handled himself well that day at Olympic Stadium. McCormack felt like a million dollars when he went home at the end of the '80 season. He couldn't wait for spring training to start. Finally, he was on the verge of earning a big league job.

There were many who thought he earned it in the spring of '81, too. "I really had my mind made up that I was going to give it everything I had and do everything as well as possible to try to make the team," McCormack said. "I had heard through people that I had a chance. First [spring training] game against Kansas City, boom, I catch nine innings. Every game I caught, I caught eight or nine innings. I was really playing well."

But as so often happens, there was a number of problems. And McCormack had an option left, which meant the Phillies could send him out without risk of losing him. As spring training wound down, the uncertainties mounted. Sure, McCormack had done well. Sure, he had earned a place on the team as a backup catcher. But still, that was no guarantee.

"The last three days were really tough," he said. "There were 26 people and that even made it tougher. I heard both sides. I heard people saying, 'Yeah, you're going to make it,' and I heard others saying, 'Ah, they don't want to carry three catchers.' "

The Phillies had Bob Boone and Keith Moreland. They could get along without McCormack. The waiting grew progressively harder.

A camera crew from a cable TV outfit had been following Don McCormack since early in spring training, preparing a piece on a rookie's struggle to make it to the big leagues. It had been fun for a while, but by the final day of spring training—with the camp count still at 26—nothing was fun any more.

"That last day—phwew!" Don McCormack said. "My wife drove me to the park and the film crew was waiting for me outside. They were going to interview me after the decision was made."

McCormack said hello and walked inside the clubhouse. "Everybody was sitting there," he said. "I took my time getting dressed. No use me getting dressed if they're going to cut me. Here I am in a cold sweat and these guys with a camera are standing right there in front of my locker, and that didn't help, either. And then Dallas [Dallas Green, who was managing the Phillies then] comes out, points a finger at me, and I knew it was all over. I just kind of—my whole mental outlook completely dropped. Boy, there were so many things went through my mind in those 10, 15 steps into his little room back there. In fact, my whole life just flashed right in front of me."

Devastated by the news, Don McCormack walked out of Green's office and found the camera crew waiting for him. Under the circumstances, he might have told them to get lost, to come back another time, anything to save himself from having to answer questions at a time like this. But he didn't, which tells you a lot about Don McCormack. "That was really tough," he said about that TV interview. "We went out there in the bullpen. I didn't know what to do, what to say. All I knew was, I had to go out and talk to them."

The following spring, McCormack went through it again. No TV crew this time, but what happened was even worse. Since he was now out of options, the Phillies gave him his unconditional release. Eight years in the organization and suddenly he was gone. But baseball gets in a man's blood. As hard a blow as it was, as seriously as he thought about getting out of the game and embarking on a new career, McCormack eventually chose to return to the minor leagues with another organization.

If you want to talk to an expert on late-spring axings, try Yankee pitcher George Frazier. Starting in '78, it happened to him three times in four years when he belonged to the St. Louis Cardinals.

"The craziest thing," said George, "you're getting sent out the last day and your wife's headed for the town you think you're playing in because they haven't told you anything. The truck's gone with all your belongings on it. The only thing you've got is a suitcase with two pairs of jeans in it."

Frazier's worst experience came in the spring of '81. The day before the Cardinals were scheduled to leave St. Petersburg, Fla., and head north George told manager Whitey Herzog that he wanted to take his car over to the garage to have some work done on it before his wife drove home. "He said, 'Okay, go ahead. You can miss batting practice,' " Frazier said. "So I rushed out. I got the car fixed. After the game Whitey asked me, 'You get the car fixed? Everything set for your wife?' I said, 'Yeah, fine.' Next morning I get dropped off at the ball park at 7:30 in the morning and as soon as I walked in the door Whitey calls me in and tells me I've been sent down."

Frazier was stunned. He had just flown his mother in so she could be with his wife and kids on the long drive back to St. Louis. And to compound matters, they were already on their way. "I mean," said George, "they're five minutes up the highway. I could call the police and get them to find them for me and stop them. But what sense is there for me to flag them down? There's no room for me to ride in the car, anyway. That kind of stuff can drive you up a wall."

A lot of baseball players have made a trip up that wall. "I've seen so many guys," said Frazier. "They've rented houses because they've been told, 'You're on the ball club,' and then, boom, they're gone. They've got you. There's nothing you can do about it. If you want to play the game you better keep playing (wherever they tell you to play the game you better keep playing [wherever they tell you to play]. Six years in the game and I'm in my 23rd city now. One year— Milwaukee organization], and I lived there for six weeks. Then I went to Holyoke [Mass.], Spokane, back to Phoenix, and then to the Dominican Republic in six months. Each time the wife moved."

"You don't have to tell Joe Kerrigan about it. He knows. He's been through it, too.

A righthanded relief pitcher, Kerrigan has appeared in 131 big league games. Five years ago, he saved 11 and won three for a Montreal team that finished in fifth place in the National League East. But that winter he was traded to the Baltimore Orioles—"the worst thing that probably happened to me in my life," he said.

At the time, though, it looked like a great thing. He was going from an also-ran to a contender. Then Joe Kerrigan found out that in baseball the way things look isn't necessarily the way things are.

He made it through the '78 season in Baltimore, winning three and saving three in 26 appearances. He had no reason to think his place on the team was in jeopardy in the spring of '79. "I was doing promos for the team—for bat day and ball night, that kind of thing," he said.

They don't ask guys who aren't going to be on the team to make TV and radio commercials. Besides, Joe had a good spring on the mound, pitching 12 scoreless innings.

"It came out of the clear blue sky," Kerrigan said. "The last day, as we were getting ready to go on the plane, I get called into his [manager Earl Weaver's] office. Tippy Martinez says to me, 'You lucky dog. You've been traded.' I said, 'All right, maybe I'll go to a place where I can pitch more.'

"I'll never forget walking into the room, sitting down on that chair. I had my suit on, ready to get on that plane. He [Weaver] says, 'I got some bad news, Joe. We've got to send you down because [Tim] Stoddard and [Sammy] Stewart, we found out, are out of options.' I mean, that was something. Phwew! That was the hardest moment of my life."

Kerrigan went to Rochester, winning 10 and saving 11 for a bad ball club, and didn't even get called up in September. Oh yeah, that's the year the Orioles won the American League pennant.

It's a weird feeling, getting cut like that. "Jim Bouton writes about it in his book, *Ball Four*," Joe Kerrigan said. "Somebody gets sent down, they [the other players] say, 'There was a death in the family today. Somebody died.' Bouton said when it happened to him all of a sudden he was on the outside; he stopped being one of the family, one of the guys. He's no longer taking part in the jokes, the small talk, yet he's over on another field a couple of hundred yards away. It's like he doesn't exist anymore. And that's how it is. When the manager closes the door or when the pitching coach comes over and says, 'The Skipper wants to see you in the office,' your heart beat 's up, you've got sweaty palms. That day I got sent down to Rochester I was rock bottom. I was stunned. I couldn't move for about 24 hours. I said, 'What about my family?' [Joe's wife and two children had left for Baltimore by car two days before.] Earl Weaver said, 'Well, I'm sure Hank [general manager Hank Peters] will take care of you.'

"My wife was already up in Baltimore. She got in the apartment, got everything turned on. Joey, my boy, was three at the time, and Kelly was two or three weeks old; she was born in spring training. I lost the electricity deposit. I lost a rental deposit. I lost the telephone deposit. I hit them for about $900 in expenses, but I was out about $1,200."

Also, there was the cost of the telegram Joe Kerrigan sent to his wife in Baltimore, the one that let her know they were moving to Rochester.

The first time around, the minor leagues don't look that bad. It's the second time around—after a man's been in the big leagues—that the negative side of the minor leagues experience stands out in bold, bitter relief.

"You go down a second time," said Kerrigan, "and all of a sudden the lights are darker than they used to be and the fields aren't as good. The first time you didn't know the difference. You didn't know if the lights were good or bad. You didn't mind the bus trips. But going down the ladder, it's not quite as sweet."

And when the financial pinch hits home, it can get downright sour.

A pro baseball career for a man who goes through what a Joe Kerrigan or a Don McCormack goes through is a constant struggle. Common sense says, "Get out." But there's something inside you that won't let you break away, even if the price you're paying in dollars and cents and heartache is absurdly high.

"It's like a total war between your heart and your mind," Joe Kerrigan said on the spring day in 1982 when the Phillies sent him to their Oklahoma City farm club.

More often than not, it seems, the heart wins. Surely, it did in Kerrigan's case. A few years ago, when he thought his big league status was secure, Joe and his wife bought a house in Bucks County, Pa. "You think you're going to stay in the big leagues for a while," he said. "Then the bottom drops out."

It's a long, hard fall.

"We're down to our last $500 in the bank," Joe Kerrigan said last spring. "We've got a $700-a-month mortgage, and we've got the house up for sale. You've got to have a good family to stick in this game. There were times my wife said to me, 'Why don't you get out? You're crazy for staying in this business.' That's the realistic side of it. But you're always chasing that dream."

That dream again. Always, it's that dream of making it some day, making it big. A few of them do. Most of them don't.

The Kerrigans had to sell some of their furniture just to keep their house going. Joe's wife had to get a job. Joe's mother had to baby-sit for them. Joe had to get a second job. "If you want to stay in the game, that's the price you've got to pay," he said. "Eddie Farmer will tell you that."

Damn right, he will. A year ago, during the baseball strike, Farmer read a quote from pro golfer Tom Watson, who was critical of the players. "He said something like, 'I don't even know half their names and they're making X amount of dollars,'" Farmer said. 'Well, Tom Watson is a guy who was probably wined and dined as a kid and taken to a country club. While he was hitting golf balls I was in the minor leagues, playing under adversity, away from my family."

Farmer is in the big-money class now. A year ago, even figuring the losses from the strike, he grossed $355,000 for playing baseball. But that was more money, by far, than he made in the previous 13 years.

Farmer, like so many others, has felt the sharp edge of the ax on cutdown day. And he knows the feeling of being out of the game, if only temporarily. He worked in a warehouse the year he was hurt, and he has never forgotten it.

"I never lose sight of picking up a box of nuts and bolts and putting it on a shelf for $3.25 an hour," he said. "I never have and I never will . . . I'll tell you what, this [pitching] beats the shit out of working in a warehouse."

Most of the time, it does. But sometimes—say, when you're the 26th man on a 25-man team on the last day of spring training and a coach walks over and says, "Uh, the Skip wants to see you"—it doesn't really beat it by all that much.

14

LOOK FOR THE
UNION LABEL

There are those who say if a baseball player has the ability to play in the big leagues, he'll get there. That's nonsense. I wish I had a dollar for every player who got buried in the minor leagues because he was in the "wrong organization," or because a manager didn't like him or a scout for the big club didn't like him. The big leagues are loaded with fringe players who got a break and, yes, made the most of it. The high minors are loaded with players who have comparable talent, but didn't get the opportunity.

John Poff is a case in point. No less an observer of baseball talent than Dallas Green went on record as saying that Poff, a lefthanded-hitting first baseman-outfielder, had the ability to be an everyday player in the big leagues. But Poff was stuck in an organization—the Phillies—that was overstocked with first basemen and outfielders at the major league level. As a result, he spent three and a half seasons in Triple A. In his three full ones, from 1978 through 1980, Poff averaged .292, 18 homers, 85 runs batted in and a .519 slugging average. Finally, the Phillies did him a favor. They sold him to the Milwaukee Brewers in September of '80. John did decently in his first real big league shot, hitting .250 (17 for 68) with a double, two triples, a homer and seven runs batted in for the Brewers in the final month of the season. With men on base, his average jumped to .292. Poff's chances of making the Brewers in '81 seemed reasonably good, and they soared when he had an excellent spring training, hitting better than .300 in the major league exhibitions. Then, a week before the season began, Poff got traded to the White Sox. His chances of making it to the big leagues hit a sudden, very solid road block.

The White Sox promptly shipped Poff to their Triple A team in

Edmonton. John's career went downhill from there. Discouraged and downright disgusted, he was forced to go through yet another minor league season. When it was over, the White Sox didn't call him up to finish out the year in Chicago. They sent him a minor league contract for '82 that represented a whopping cut—well over 20 percent—from the big league contract he had signed in '81. Since it seemed evident the White Sox had no plans for him on the big league level, Poff asked to be traded. The answer was typical: we'll try, but we aren't going to give you away.

John and his wife, Patti, spent the '81–'82 winter in the state of Washington, awaiting word, trying to decide what to do. It seemed ridiculous to return to Edmonton. John was 29. He had a B.A. degree in English from Duke University. Even so, Poff very nearly gave pro baseball one more year. He made plane reservations to fly to Florida spring training. He called a friend there and told him he was coming; plans were made to meet him at the airport. The next day John Poff got in his car and started driving to the airport in Spokane. He was nearly there when the absurdity of the whole thing hit him. He stopped the car, phoned his friend in Florida and told him that he'd changed his mind. He'd spent enough years pounding the minor league trails, enough years getting sent to places he didn't want to go. He was quitting.

I've seen John Poff play a lot of baseball games. I have no doubt that, in the right place at the right time, he could have had a big league career. And believe me, the bushes are well stocked with John Poffs.

Men signed to minor league contracts are at the mercy of their employers. It's as simple, and as sad, as that. They're professional baseball players in a society that perceives professional baseball players as being filthy rich—spoiled millionaires who get paid hundreds of thousands of dollars a year for hitting .250. But the 650 big leaguers are merely the tip of the iceberg. Hidden beneath the surface—and in some cases beneath the poverty line—are five or six times that many professional ball players wearing minor league uniforms. The big leaguers have lots of protection. The minor leaguers have virtually none.

Nobody is more acutely aware of that than Marvin Miller, for 16 years the executive director of the Major League Players Association. In effect, Miller is baseball commissioner for the players, Bowie Kuhn the baseball commissioner for the owners. Under Miller's guidance, big league players have never had it so good. The mere mention of his name to some old-line owners, who fondly remember an era when they held the hammer, is enough to make them turn more colors than a Houston Astros uniform.

"I was Genghis Kahn [to the old-line owners]," Miller said. Some of those owners—still living in the past—hated him so passionately they literally refused to look at him. Ruly Carpenter, who sold the Phillies after the 1981 season, was a classic example.

"I've come into a reentry draft at the Plaza Hotel [in New York City]," Miller said, "and Carpenter was sitting at this table and Steinbrenner at this table, and Steinbrenner would get up and shake hands. . . ."

Ruly? He would look the other way. That's how deep the feeling ran.

Marvin Miller has waged his war against the medieval practices of baseball owners. He's preparing to turn over the Major League Players Association to a younger man, probably some time in 1983. Which means somebody else will have to wage the war for the minor leaguers if, indeed, it's ever going to be waged.

Miller, however, has hit repeatedly on the plight of baseball's minor leaguers. "I've never left it out of any of my testimony [before Congressional committees]," he said. "I can't tell you how many times I've testified now. 'All right,' I tell them, 'major league players have made progress, but stop focusing on that. We've got this outrageous condition affecting so many people in the minor leagues . . .' I'm astounded by one thing. I watch the faces of some of those Congressmen, and some of them are baseball fans. I say something like, 'The number of minor league players outnumbers the major league players by four or five or six to one.' It's like somebody turned on a light."

Like most Americans, the Congressmen never stopped to think that the overwhelming majority of professional baseball players are minor leaguers, not major leaguers. We can snicker when we hear big leaguers talk about being "slaves." Sure, we say, I'd like to be a slave, too, at those prices. But how about those two or three thousand minor leaguers out there? Now *that's* slavery.

In 1976, during one of his appearances before a Congressional committee, Miller attempted to explain just how one-sided minor league player contracts were.

"I want to call the committee's attention to two facts," Miller said. "In baseball, minor league players outnumber major league players by about six to one. Minor leaguers have no collective bargaining, and no representation of any kind. Given these circumstances, I think it is instructive to examine their conditions in light of the commissioner's claim that baseball operates at a high level of responsibility."

At that point Miller introduced for the record a copy of the old standard minor league contract, as it existed until 1976, and a copy of the new standard contract "unilaterally changed by the owners."

"I would ask," said Miller, "that you keep in mind that the typical signer of a first contract is a draftee out of high school. When selected he may deal with only the club that has drafted him. His one choice, other than signing, is to fail to sign and be thrown into the next draft six months later, where he will be picked by one other club, and then be forced to deal only with that club.

"Now, the contract such youngsters were forced to sign prior to 1976 was unconscionable enough. I think the new one is a good example of overkill. I would like to just call your attention to a few points.

"First of all, it is a standard contract. It may not be changed by the player at all. He is handed the document, period. It's unilaterally drawn up by the owners and their attorneys and cannot be altered. . . . The new contract changes the employment year. Formerly, it was a one-year period. This new agreement drawn up by the owners and their attorneys provides for one year and the players must give the club six successive, separate annual renewal options. [Thus] when he puts his name to this, he is subject to seven years. . . .

"The contract provides that if a player is disabled, he is entitled to two weeks pay, or to the date of release, whichever is longer. So if they keep him under contract, and he is hurt on the field, they must continue to pay him. But if they release him they can get by with just two weeks pay for a serious disability. And the club can refuse to release him, and not even pay him the two weeks pay, if the injury was not incurred during the course of his employment. . . .

"On termination, the club can terminate the contract at will—no pay, no termination pay."

Marvin Miller sat behind the desk in his 26th floor office on the Avenue of the Americas, pulled out a copy of the new standard minor league players' contract, and shook his head. He didn't know where to start, he said. The whole thing was outrageous. "Imagine," he complained, "in the 20th century, a contract like that. The prior minor league contract was bad enough. It was terrible, as you might guess."

Then came the Andy Messersmith decision that shook the very foundations of the game. The old minor league contract had language regarding the reserve clause similar to the language interpreted in the Messersmith case, where it was ruled that a player, by playing unsigned for one year, could become a free agent. So the owners had their lawyers write a new minor league contract to block that potential escape route.

"After the Messersmith decision they revised their minor league contract to try to cover the situation," said Miller, "and then they apparently decided to go over all of it. And when they got finished, what I thought had been the world's lousiest contract no longer was. The new one was. It's unbelievable."

He turned to the section on "termination" and began reading aloud. " 'This uniform players contract may be terminated as follows: if the club is in arrears to the player for any payments due the player under this contract for more than 15 days or if the club fails for more than 15 days to perform any other obligation agreed or required, player shall be entitled to apply to the president of the National Association'—appointed by the club owners, Miller hastily pointed out— 'to terminate this uniform player contract.' "

"That's after they're in breach and not paying you at all." Miller laughed. "Isn't that nice?"

In the event of an injury incurred on the field, the club will pay medical expenses. But even there, the player could be left holding the bag—or at least holding the bill. "If you had a really serious injury and it runs past six months, forget it," Miller said. "That's it. Expenses are yours. And the club has the right to select the physician or dentist and the hospital. If they assign a quack to you and you don't want him, you waive all of this."

It's as one-sided as a pennant race between the Minnesota Twins and the big league team of your choice.

A first-year man, sent to either a rookie league or a "high A" league, gets a *maximum* salary of $600 a month. Take it or leave it. In some cases, of course, he'll get a signing bonus to help him through the early pro years. Let's hope it's a big one. It's easier to hit .400 than live on $600 a month.

And what if our first-year pro is assigned to a higher classification—Double A or even Triple A? His *maximum* salary takes a gigantic leap—all the way up to $750 a month for Triple A. Lots of luck, fella.

"Even that's not enough," Jim Baumer, the farm director of the Phillies, readily admitted. "But the major league clubs set it. Every time a situation comes up that costs a little extra, they vote it down."

The meal money has been increased in recent years—to $15 per day in Triple A, $12.50 in Double A, $10 in A. "It was obvious," said Baumer, "you couldn't eat on $5 or $7.50 a day." But if a man wants a good meal in any number of Triple A towns—say, Denver or Omaha or Richmond or Phoenix—even $15 isn't going to be enough.

Okay, so what can be done about it? Here we have a large number of professional athletes with no representation, no protection, no leverage. Minor leaguers with big league contracts are all right; all the benefits of that contract remain in effect. But the vast majority of minor league players are working under minor league contracts. What about them?

"We had a case this year involving a kid named Combe," Marvin Miller said, referring to Geoff Combe, who pitched briefly for the Cincinnati Reds. "They sent him a split contract* and by our calculations they violated the maximum cut rule. We filed a grievance. While our grievance was pending, they quickly outrighted his contract [to a minor league team]. We filed a separate grievance alleging that the outright assignment was intended to discriminate because he had filed a grievance. That's a fairly typical case, a player who hasn't established himself and who, if he works for Cincinnati or the Yankees or Detroit, will soon find the hammer of authority hitting him over the head when all he's doing is really exercising the right that he has under his contract. A Steinbrenner doesn't give a damn if you're an established major league player and you exercise your right to go to salary arbitration. It doesn't matter if your name is Rick Cerone or Ron Davis or whatever. What do you expect them to do with a rookie?'"

You expect them to screw them. And you aren't too often disappointed.

"There are two basic answers," Marvin Miller suggested. "They've got to be organized, and I think that coverage [of baseball] under the antitrust laws would make a tremendous change. One without the other may not be that effective. The two together I think would be tremendously effective."

Talk of a Minor League Players Association has popped up periodically, and then faded away. The problems in forming such an organization are enormous, if not quite insurmountable.

"Realistically," Miller said, "it probably has to be done by an existing organization. Professionals have to do the organizing. Unfortunately, that doesn't mean that there won't be some casualties. In

---

*A player signing a split contract gets a specified amount if he makes the big league team, a lesser amount if he plays in the minors. Under the terms of the 1980 basic agreement, split-contract minimums have been established for players signing their second major league contracts and for players with a least one day of major league service. For 1982, that minimum is $14,000 a season. For 1983, it's $16,000, and for 1984, $17,500. Of course, if the player is in the big leagues he must be paid at the big league minimum— $33,500 for 1982.

any organizing campaign you've got to have some people from the inside who are willing to speak up or are at least willing to work sub rosa. First, you have a difficulty in finding such people. Mostly, minor league players are young kids. They've got stars in their eyes. They just want to play, want to get to the major leagues. Those who are a little more sophisticated than that have the further handicap of realistically appraising the danger of doing it. You can't take the cynical attitude of saying, 'Well, what we're going to do is to tell these people we'll protect them.' It's a lie. . . . It may be like anything else when you try to make a very great change. It may be that you have to have a number of martyrs out there."

An 18-year-old kid with a major league dream isn't likely to be too thrilled at the prospect of being a martyr for the minor league cause, and you can hardly blame him.

"The problem is monumental," said Marvin Miller, who has learned to always "see the difficulties first."

"Now," he said, "I'll give you the plus side. I don't think that given the record of the Major League Players Association it would be all that difficult to organize a sizeable majority of all the minor league players. The problem then would be how would you service them? How would you do more than just say, 'Okay, I've got a majority of the members'? I suppose practically what you ought to do—and if I were a lot younger I might really put it up to the players—would be to start one level at a time. Go to Triple A, then to Double A. . . . I don't think we've got the resources or the capabilities of suddenly saying, 'Well, we'll organize this vast group, which is so scattered and has such a tremendous turnover.' "

At first glance, it would seem simple for the Players Association to send out letters to Triple A players (in the Pacific Coast League, American Association and International League) outlining the substandard conditions that exist and asking the players to return the enclosed card if they're in favor of being represented by the union.

Uh-oh, better look again. Under the labor laws, the Association would then have to demand that the owners recognize the union's right to represent minor leaguers. If the owners challenge the union—and it would be hard to think of a surer bet than that—then the Association would have to present some of those signed cards to the clubs and to the National Labor Relations Board. Thus, any player returning a signed card must be warned that his name could wind up on management's desk, and that, in itself, could result in the end of what had been a promising career.

If you think that statement is extreme, you simply haven't been around baseball owners. Let's turn the calendar back a decade. It was April, '72, the spring that produced major league baseball's first strike. Emotions ran high. Baseball management types made no effort to conceal their hatred—and fear—of Marvin Miller, and of labor unions. The nation's sports pages were filled with strike stories. In general, public sentiment seemed to be running rather strongly against the players. We didn't like to see our baseball heroes go out on strike in 1972 any more than we did in 1981. At any rate, that was the climate as the big league strike began and it prompted me to skip the big league mess for a day and write about the minor leaguers, who were still conducting business as usual.

I spent a day at the Phillies' minor league complex in Clearwater, Fla., observing how the other half lived. In particular, I had a lengthy interview with a pitcher who was beginning his 11th year in the Phillies' minor league organization. His name was Jerry Messerly. He was 29 at the time, married, and the father of a five-year-old son. This was to be his seventh season at the Triple A level. If ever there was a man who appeared well equipped to present the minor league side of things, it was Jerry Messerly.

The result of that interview was a column that appeared in *The Philadelphia Inquirer* under the headline: "Minor Leaguers Need a Union." In it, I wrote about the managers, coaches and players who had spent years in the minors and yet, if they were fired tomorrow, would have nothing of substance to show for it. Minor leaguers, after all, had no pensions.

And then I zeroed in on Jerry Messerly.

"What's Jerry Messerly got to show for it," I wrote, "except a $5,000 insurance policy that terminates 31 days after he quits playing? No pension. No big bank account. Nothing but dreams of what might have been."

Messerly had a lot to say on the subject. He wasn't a bitter man. Hell, he loved the game. He was simply being truthful when he talked about the minor league condition.

"It's hard to give up something like baseball," he told me that day when practice was over. "I probably could have gotten better jobs, jobs with a future, but I wouldn't have been happy in them. Now I'm just going to be forced to get out of the game."

We were sitting in my room in the old Fort Harrison Hotel in Clearwater. A tape-recorder was propped on the table next to Messerly, but he held nothing back. He'd be forced to get out, he explained, because he couldn't afford to stay in. Take spring training, he said. It cost a man money to attend a minor league spring training camp—unless he actually attempted to eat on the five-dollar meal money he received in those days.

"You know what irritates me?" Messerly asked. "We get four

ounces of Gatorade. No more. And I see some guy reach in and get three packs of crackers [to eat with the soup at lunch break] and they tell him to put two back. That just irritates me to death.

"I don't think it'll ever come where big league ball players go on strike for minor league ball players," he went on. "And maybe I don't expect that. Only thing I'd like to see are a few more guys like Terry Harmon [a utility infielder with the Phillies] and Jim Bunning. They're the only ones I've ever heard mention getting help for minor leaguers. It would make me feel a lot better if others spoke up. It would make me feel like, 'Go ahead, fellas. Fight for everything you can get even if I'm still down here trying to make it on five dollars a day.

"Of course, guys like myself who've played longer are more concerned with the problems than the kids out there making five bucks a day, three to a room. They really don't give a damn half the time. They don't know any better right now. Two, three years from now they'll get tired bringing down two or three hundred dollars to get through spring training.

"I've often thought about it. I was looking at the kids standing out there [at the minor league complex] and I was thinking, 'For every bright moment in baseball there must be four, five real dim ones.' Take a guy like Scotty [Reid] or John Vukovich or Joe Lis. I can think of 100 names. Think what they've gone through, the agony of sitting on the bench, the frustration of being sent down. Yet they've got enough love for the game to hang in there with that dream, thinking, 'Maybe next month . . . next year.' "

We talked about a lot of things that evening, among them the hospitality room the Phillies had for the press, and the management types, etc. It annoyed Messerly that, on one hand, it was fine to spend money on cold cuts and liquor for the press, but on the other hand all a minor league player was allowed to drink during lunch break was one small cup of Gatorade and a cup of soup.

"I feel like they blow a lot of money on booze," he told me. "They're trying to impress people by inviting them into press rooms, things like that. Really, it's all for one thing—to get what they want in the paper. I'd like to see the bill for that. It's one of my pet peeves. . . . Look, I'm not knocking it, but if they want to do that should they tell a kid he can't have something as important as a decent place to live or decent meal money?

"It all boils down to one thing: do the owners want to give it to you? I don't think they're ever going to really come across with any nice benefits for the minor leaguer . . . unless you've got that union, that power."

There was nothing outrageous in what Jerry Messerly said. He'd been in the minor leagues a long time. He had a right to speak his peace. And he spoke it. I didn't expect the Phillies' front office to give him a $100 bonus for getting all that newspaper space. On the other hand, I was totally unprepared—blame it on naivete, I guess—for management's reaction.

The day the column appeared I got a phone call from Messerly late in the afternoon, immediately after he had finished practice. A copy of that column had been transmitted by telecopier from the Phillies' offices at Veterans Stadium to Clearwater. Apparently, there were orders to send any stories or columns that might be construed as less than favorable.

When Messerly arrived at the minor league complex that morning, the brass was waiting for him. He was called on the carpet, given what amounted to a third degree. Had he really said all those things that Dolson put in the paper? If the quotes had been made up, was he prepared to say so? Etcetera, etcetera, etcetera. It was sickening.

Jerry Messerly was a fine young man. He didn't think he had done anything bad enough to bring about that extreme reaction. He knew he'd been quoted accurately, and he wasn't about to tell the front-office Gestapo otherwise. But he was an obviously upset, worried man when he got me on the telephone. I told him I'd try to smooth things over as much as possible, and got hold of Ruly Carpenter. He was outraged at the Messerly quotes and the column in general. It damaged the organization's image. It was tearing down everything they were trying to build up. How could I write such awful things about the Phillies' minor league system?

I remember telling Ruly that the Messerly column was merely one of several I had written about Phillie minor leaguers in the last couple of years, and that if he stacked up the ones he would consider positive in one pile and the ones he would consider negative in another pile, the positive pile would tower over the negative pile. Turned out, Ruly hadn't seen the positive ones. The hired hands, apparently, were only instructed to bring the negative ones to his attention.

The violent front-office reaction to Jerry Messerly's comments—however accurate those comments happened to be—tells you all you need to know about the attitude of baseball ownership, and the helplessness of the men who play in the minor leagues. Needless to say, Jerry Messerly's career in the Phillies' organization did not have much longer to run.

When you try to pin down major league executives on the yawning disparity between the major league lifestyle and the minor league lifestyle, their argument frequently is: "We don't want players to be too comfortable in the minors. It would destroy their incentive to reach the majors."

Marvin Miller also talked about incentives—but from a different point of view. "If, for the sake of argument," he said, "you outlawed the whole system whereby you draft somebody, I would be hopeful that the natural forces of competition would be a lever to improve conditions. In other words, one, two, three or four enlightened club owners creating decent conditions in order to hold on to players could work miracles. The way it is now, there's no incentive to do that. What incentive is there, if you own the player, to improve anything? You own him, period. Reserve rules, as they used to work in the major leagues, still work in that fashion in the minors. It admits you to have abuses that you otherwise couldn't get away with because the players have no other place to go. If they [the owners] want to talk about incentives, they ought to have some built-in incentives for themselves."

It's Miller's feeling that the failure to improve the minor league situation is potentially harmful to both sides. "I think in a way it's shortsighted on everybody's part—management and the Players Association alike—to let the problem just fester indefinitely," he said. "I think it can boomerang on everybody. At some point you're going to get an even better educated, a more streetwise group playing in the minors than you have now, and I think they're going to be saying to themselves, 'We need help and we need it badly and this [the Players Association] is the place to get it and if we don't get it, by God, that's terrible.' And some of those people will come into the major leagues with a certain hostility to the Players Association. It's possible."

There can be no doubt that a substantial number of professional baseball players come into the major leagues with hostility to management as a result of their minor league treatment.

Marvin Miller has an interesting theory on that subject, one that explains the major difference in the attitude of the major league baseball players and the National Football League players. When the strike talk began in baseball, the players voiced overwhelming, virtually unanimous support of the Players Association. When the possibility of a pro football strike came up, no such unanimity was in evidence.

"Our guys," said Miller, "with rare exceptions, have been through the mill when they get here. They know what the employer-employee relationship is like. A football player—again with certain exceptions—goes from big man on campus to the National Football

League. That's my theoretical answer to the people who say, 'Account for the differences in the behavior of the NFL players and the major league baseball players in a crisis. I really think my theory is sound."

The more you think about it, the more sense it makes. Baseball players have learned, the hard way, what it is to deal with ownership from a position of weakness. It's true that major league baseball players have never had it so good. But it's equally true that the majority of professional baseball players remain trapped in a system that hasn't begun to catch up with the times.

For some, the trap seems more like a torture chamber designed to push players and their families to the limit, and occasionally beyond. Under baseball rules it is possible for a big league team to spend an entire season calling up a player from the minors, sending him down, calling him up again, sending him down again. By the time August rolls around, the player feels more like a human yo-yo than an athlete. The problem is that no matter how many times a club sends down a player in the same season, it uses up only a single option, thus retaining its hold on the player. Bobby Brown was caught in the trap during his time as an outfielder in the New York Yankees organization. He spent that portion of his career commuting between Columbus, Ohio, and The Bronx. Dave LaRoche, a lefthander relief pitcher, went through a similar experience in 1982, making four trips to Yankee Stadium and three trips back to the Yankees' International League farm club, the Columbus Clippers. Joe DiMaggio may have been the original "Yankee Clipper," but in 1982 Dave LaRoche qualified as the ultimate Yankee Clipper.

"The rule should be changed," Marvin Miller said. "We had a proposal on the table two years ago that everything past a second time a player is sent down (in the same season) would use another option. There's no question in my mind it's unfair and inequitable the way it is. It's a callous disregard of a player as a person."

Financially, it isn't all that bad. Major league clubs pay the traveling expenses for a player and his family when he's shipped from one team to another. But there's more to it than money. The problem of relocating an entire family, time and time again, and the strain it puts on a player, his wife and their children cannot be solved by money alone.

Len Matuszek, a lefthanded-hitting first baseman owned by the Phillies, experienced the ordeal in '82. A level-headed young man, Matuszek seemed capable of handling it better than most. Yet even his head began spinning after a full season of going from Philadelphia to Oklahoma City and back.

"I guess you get a little immune to it after [getting sent down] the third time," he said in late July after getting the word that he was Oklahoma City-bound once again. "But there's still that thing about the way they can manipulate you. I think it's wrong. That rule needs to be changed. It's not hurting them any to send me down three, four times. They just use up one option. That's a joke. How can they have power like that over somebody? And it's usually a young guy. I'll tell you what," he added, looking around the Phillies' clubhouse at Veterans Stadium, "a few people in this room wouldn't be able to handle it. There are some guys here who would go off the deep end. Does that concern them [the ball club]? I guess not. The way I feel, why should it happen to somebody else if it can be prevented? I don't want to stir anything up, but the Players Association should be aware it's happening."

The Association is acutely aware that it's happening. Perhaps it will succeed in having the option rule modified in the next basic agreement.*

Matuszek is a classic example of a fine prospect trapped by the system. At 27, he was in an organization that had a guy named Pete Rose playing his position and showing no signs of giving it up in 1982. By late summer the Philadelphia-to-Oklahoma City-to-Philadelphia-to-Oklahoma City routine had begun to get to Len, his wife, Karen, and their two children. "It's been a tremendous strain on the family as well as myself," Matuszek said. "She [Karen] has probably done better than I have. I posed the question to her one time. I said, 'Why are you still here?' I think if I was in your shoes, I'd have been gone a long time ago.' But obviously she's in it to the end like I am."

It should be pointed out that the Phillies went out of their way to treat the Matuszeks fairly each time Len got shipped to Oklahoma City. But that still didn't make up for all those moving days, all that turmoil.

"Money is one thing," said Danny Boitano, a veteran of nine pro seasons who knows what it is to be jerked around, from the minors to the majors and back, "but the real pain is going back and forth, back and forth, driving your family all over the place. I hate it. I loathe it. Susan and I figured out that since we were married in 1975 we have moved 23 times."

Boitano opened the 1982 season with the Denver Bears, the No. 1 farm club of the Texas Rangers. He had been sent down despite an

---

*When a player is optioned by the big league club to a minor league team, the big league club retains the right to recall him. Such assignments are permitted for not more than three seasons. However, while the number of seasons in which a player may be optioned is limited, there is no limit on the number of times a player can be optioned in any one season.

outstanding spring training, and he stayed down until mid-summer despite getting off to a great start in Denver. Danny and his wife had two children with a third on the way. It wasn't easy to keep living the baseball life, but they did.

"I want to keep going to prove to myself that I'm a big league pitcher," Boitano said. "A lot of times I've wanted to hang it up; I came very close to that this year. But I just had this feeling that I'm reaching my prime. I'd hate to go out right now [at 29] and look back and say, 'Man, I was at my prime and I got out.' I'm lucky. I've got a great wife. She loves the game. She doesn't ever want to get out. She says, 'Don't quit because of us.' She's a super woman. But it's just a pain in the ass going up and down, up and down and dragging them all over the country. A couple of years ago I wouldn't have been able to handle it, but I handle it now. I just kind of look through it. I don't let it mentally affect me because I guess I've matured to the point where I expect anything. You either accept it or get the hell out and get yourself a 9-to-5 job—and most of the people I've seen that get out and get the 9-to-5 jobs, two years later they're begging to get back in the game."

It's strange but true. For all the inequities, all the injustices it isn't easy for most young men to tear themselves away from the game. And the longer they're in it, the more they've put into it, the harder it usually becomes.

Boitano was called up from Denver just before the 1982 major league All-Star break. He was advised by the Texas organization to bring his family with him. So, during the All-Star break, Danny flew home to get Susan and the kids and drive them from Denver to Arlington, Tex. The flight to Denver and the drive back to Arlington were at his expense, of course, but he didn't mind under the circumstances. At least they'd be together the rest of the summer. No more moving. No more uncertainty.

But wait. Things change fast in baseball. Don Zimmer, who was manager of the Texas Rangers, got fired. Suddenly, Boitano's place on the team wasn't so secure.

The Rangers' front office received considerable criticism for the way the Zimmer firing was handled—and deservedly so. Zimmer, informed he was being fired, was asked to stay on and manage the club for three more days. It would have been laughable, if it wasn't so sad. And what happened to Boitano was just about as bad. Shortly after Zimmer's firing Danny was informed by Paul Richards, the club's acting general manager, that he was going to be shipped back to Denver to make room on the big league roster for a player coming off the disabled list.

"But first," said Boitano, "they wanted me to stay there [in

Texas] another three days and pitch [in a series against the Yankees]. I couldn't handle it. I was a basket case for three days. It's like they cut your throat and they don't want you to bleed."

The Rangers were going to send him to Denver, then recall him in September when the minor league season was over—until they found out they couldn't do it. Danny pointed out to them that he was out of options. If they sent him down, he'd be "frozen" under the rules. "Nobody in the front office knew what the hell was going on," the pitcher said.

So the Rangers didn't send him down after the Yankee series. Danny Boitano and his family were able to remain in Texas a while longer. Such is life for a fringe big leaguer—crisis after crisis, uncertainty heaped upon uncertainty. Maybe the big-name players have it made today. Indeed, maybe they're too well off. But, as Marvin Miller keeps trying to explain to those congressmen, there are more Danny Boitanos and Len Matuszeks playing professional baseball than Dave Winfields and Mike Schmidts.

15

THE HARDEST JOB
OF ALL

If you think playing in the minor leagues can be tough, try umpiring there. "In A and Double A you're driving from town to town," said Alan Clark, now an American League umpire, "and you're splitting hotel rooms [with your partner] because you can't afford your own room, and you still stay in dives. You know what a 'tube steak' is? Yeah, a hot dog. Well, I promised myself that I'd never eat one again. And I'll never eat in Sambo's or Denny's again. I used to eat there 15 meals a week. It's amazing how guys can do it. But if you want something bad enough you tough it out—if you can see the light at the end of the tunnel."

Sometimes you have to have exceptionally good eyesight to see that light. "You've got to realize," said Harry Wendelstedt, a veteran of 17 National League seasons, "there are only 58 jobs really worth having in the profession."

A player, at least, has 650 jobs to shoot for.

Why does a guy subject himself to the life of a minor league umpire when the odds are stacked so high against him? For the same reason that a player or a manager or a coach or a trainer or a clubhouse man keeps going back for more: that light, way off in the distance.

Frank Pulli, a National League umpire for the last decade, was 32 when he started working in the minors. "I'd worked in a factory 10 years," he said, "and I'd done some umpiring locally. One day some guy said, 'Did you ever think about taking a shot?' I said, 'No, not really.' Then all of a sudden I got this urge to try something different. . . ."

It was no easy decision. "I had three kids," he said. "It was difficult. Very, very difficult."

His first year, 1968, Pulli cleared $475 a month.* "I sent $200 of that home," he recalled. "I was living on $275."

Pulli's first shot at professional umpiring came in the Class A Midwest League. "We've driving [from city to city] in cars," he said. "This kid I worked with, he had a brand new Mustang. We made six-hour trips, eight-hour trips. I mean it's just tough. Up here [in the big leagues] sometimes guys are saying, 'Oh boy, we've been on the road 10 days.' Big deal. I was on the road one time 58 straight days. Hey, I'll tell you, it takes a very, very dedicated guy. The money isn't there. It's just not there. Guys with families. . . . I don't know how the hell I did it. Well, my wife went to work, that's how I did it. Here I am, stuck in the Midwest League. My grandmother died at the end of May. If she doesn't die, I never get home until the season's over. And the conditions . . . I remember Waterloo, Iowa, dressing underneath the stands. You put your head down so you wouldn't hit the pipes. Dubuque, Iowa, they had railroad ties out by the ball park. There was mud laying around the railroad ties and that's what we used to rub up the balls. It's funny now, but it sure as hell wasn't funny then."

Clark, Pulli and Wendelstedt spent only four years apiece in the minors. Eric Gregg made it to the National League after just five and a half years. They were the fortunate ones. "You've got guys like Paul Runge [a National League staffer since 1974] who worked 14 years in the minor leagues," said Gregg. "You just never know."

Which is why the major league umpires' strike of April, 1979, confronted some minor leaguers with the most difficult decision of their careers.

Steve Fields had been a minor league umpire for 11 years. He began in the Midwest League in '68, moved on to the Western Carolinas League, the Carolina League, the Southern Association, and finally the International League, where he remained for seven years. "I was the oldest minor league umpire in the country," he said.

And then came the strike. And the phone call. It was Blake Cullen of the National League office. "He says, 'Steve, we need eight umpires—four in the National League, four in the American League,' " Fields said. "He says, 'We've chosen you for the National League. We want to know if you accept.' I say, 'How long do I have to think about it?' He says, 'We have to find bodies fast.' "

---

* Today's salaries for minor league umpires range from $1,100 in rookie leagues to approximately $1,700 in Triple A plus per diem allowances, according to the National Association.

There he was, stuck in the minor leagues, making $700 a month plus $33 per diem—and suddenly he had a chance to work in the big leagues. The working conditions, he knew, wouldn't be very pleasant. The striking umpires would call him a scab and worse. But still, it was a once-in-a-lifetime opportunity. Put yourself in Steve Fields' shoes. No umpire ever had to make a more difficult decision.

Fields called his father and asked for advice. "Steve," his dad said, "you get the opportunity, you better take it because you'll probably never get another one."

So he took it. "What was I supposed to do, live like a bum the rest of my life?" he asked.

Randy Marsh's phone rang in April of '79, too. He's started umpiring in the minor leagues as an 18-year-old. "You know," Harry Wendelstedt told him, "a kid like you, they tend to think, 'He's really young,' and they put a label on you. It's going to be tough. You're going to have to spend 12, 13 years in the minor leagues.' "

Wendelstedt was right. Randy Marsh was approaching the 12-year mark when Blake Cullen phoned.

"Imagine how difficult the decision had to be for him," Wendelstedt said. "Here, he's being offered a chance to go to the big leagues."

"It started out as a one-year guaranteed contract," Marsh recalled. "Then it was a two-year, then a three-year."

He had a wife and a small daughter. The temptation had to be tremendous. Somehow, Randy Marsh kept saying no.

"Eddie Montague and I were partners two years in the Pacific Coast League," Randy said. "I've been associated with Harry Wendelstedt's school. Guys like Lee Weyer and Bruce Froemming and Dick Stello, they did nothing but try to help me all through my career. How could I go against those people?"

Besides that, Randy Marsh was confident that he would make it to the big leagues one day. Steve Fields obviously wasn't. Still, for all Marsh knew, saying no to Blake Cullen could have meant slamming the big league door shut.

"The next couple of years were my toughest financially," Marsh said. "It wasn't a fun thing to do. I didn't like going back to open up in Phoenix when I could have opened up somewhere else, but that was what I had to do. I wasn't a wise guy when I said no. I told them where my heart was and that I couldn't go to the big leagues in that situation."

And, to their credit, they understood. Two years later, Randy Marsh got another telephone call, and this time he was able to say yes. In '82 he was the junior member of a crew that included Lee Weyer, Harry Wendelstedt and Ed Montague.

Steve Fields? He was fired by the National League prior to the

'82 season. According to the people who had hired him during the strike, he simply hadn't graded out as a good enough umpire.

The difference between umpiring in the minors and in the majors is night and day, as Steve Fields lasted long enough to discover. "In the minor leagues," he said, "nobody knows who you are. You get to the big leagues, everybody's your friend." Well, almost everybody. Fields and the other so-called "scabs" were treated as outcasts by the other big league umpires. Still are, for that matter.

Obviously, though, life in the big leagues—even when your partners won't talk to you—beats life in the minors.

"It's nice to be able to take care of a family," Harry Wendelstedt said. "Now, if you make it to the big leagues you can look forward to an outstanding salary and a retirement program that's second to none. In my case, if I retire under the existing contract I'll get $55,000 a year right now."

Not bad for a guy who broke into pro ball making $300 a month in the old Georgia-Florida League. "The next year" he said, "I moved up—to Double A in the Texas League—and I had to take a $50 cut."

There are those, however—and Wendelstedt is one—who think back to those toughest of times as the good, old days.

"I had more fun in four years in the minors than I had all the time in the big leagues," Wendelstedt said. "The thing is, it's a great adventure. You get to see the whole country as you move up. I treasure those days. . . . The difference in the big leagues is the money."

Well, it goes a little beyond that, but Harry's point is well taken. Even Randy Marsh, who wound up spending 13½ years in the minors, talks about the fun he had there and the nice people he met. And the unforgettable situations that arose.

"You have some situations in the minors," Harry Wendelstedt said, "that you wouldn't believe. I remember one time we were in a little town, a place called Moultree [Ga.]."

That was Wendelstedt's first pro year, and he was lucky it wasn't his last. The Georgia-Florida League had a first-half winner and a second-half winner that season, and the two teams met in a best-of-three series for the championship. Harry worked the rubber game behind the plate.

"The home team [Moultree] is trailing by two runs in the bottom of the ninth," Wendelstedt recalled. "They get two runners on and a guy hits a home run. When he comes around third base, he misses it. He goes in the dugout and they're celebrating, but the other team sees it. They asked for another ball to be put in play, and they appeal. I call him out. You never saw anything like it."

Instead of a dramatic, one-run victory for the home team, the game went into extra innings. Sure enough, the visitors won in the 11th. There isn't an insurance company in America that would have taken out a policy on Harry Wendelstedt's life when that go-ahead run scored. But somehow this bravest of mortals survived to tell the story.

"We had to have a police escort from that town 100 miles up the road," Harry said. "I thought, 'Holy cow!' I mean, when you walk out of the ball park and you see these old farmers standing there with their shotguns laying across their arms and they're just looking at you, you know something's going to happen on up the road. And then, as you pull out, all of a sudden there are a dozen trucks and stuff following behind you. I'll tell you what. I didn't go back to visit Moultree for about 15 years because I think they'd still be laying for me."

They loved him in Brunswick, Ga., though. The mere mention of the Wendelstedt name was enough to make the natives smile in those days. Harry's very first pro game was in Brunswick, you see. But let him tell it.

"I had a mail order uniform come in. It was there the day of my first game. I put on the pants and they fit me like leotards. I got out there and I'm scared to death. You know, my first play in pro ball. I squatted down for the first pitch and the tailend of my britches split. The crowd just howled. A photographer came down behind the screen and took a picture when I was squatting down with this big patch of white showing through and the next day on the *front* page of the Brunswick newspaper they had a half-page shot of me and there was an arrow pointing down to the split in my pants and the headline said, 'Official Opener.' "

Which just goes to show you how tough it is for minor league umpires to make ends meet.

If it's hard for the Harrys and the Franks and the Erics, think what it must be like for the Bernices and the Christines and the Pamelas.

We've got women sportswriters, women wrestlers, women jockeys. Why not women umpires?

Bernice Gera was the first to try, although the evidence indicates she didn't try very hard once the game began. "She wanted to be the first woman umpire," said Barney Deary, who's in charge of umpires for the National Association. "We said she wasn't qualified. She took us to court and won. So she got her wish, and she proved our point in the end."

Bernice Gera made history of a sort in the first game of a Saturday night doubleheader in Geneva, N.Y., in June of '72. It was a great media event. Unfortunately, Bernice Gera was not a great—or even an adequate—baseball umpire.

"Look at her and 'umpire' would be the furthest thing from your mind," said Noley Campbell, manager of the Auburn, N.Y., team that played Geneva that night in the Rookie League game. "She was such a small woman. . . . It was the first time in 15 years I was able to look down on an umpire."

Mrs. Gera was scheduled to work the bases in the first game, call balls and strikes in the second. She never made it past the first.

For a couple of innings there were no problems as the television crews and the visiting writers waited impatiently for one to develop. In the top of the third it happened. Auburn had a runner on second with one out. The batter ripped a line drive to the Geneva second baseman. "Back! Get back!" screamed Noley Campbell from the third base coaching box.

The runner did his best, diving back to the bag. Bernice Gera gave the safe sign. "I turn my back," said Campbell. "Next thing I know the [Geneva] team's running off the field. My kid's standing on the base, dusting his pants off, and they're running off the field. I ran out. I said, 'What the hell's going on?' "

It was a helluva way to begin a conversation with a lady. But Noley Campbell, the male chauvinist pig, didn't give a hoot. "When she walked on that field she ceased being a woman," he said. "She became an umpire."

And so, to the delight of the fans and the media, for the first time in the history of professional baseball a male manager confronted a female umpire.

"Why'd you change the call?" Campbell asked her.

"I made a mistake," she replied.

"That's the second mistake you made," the Auburn manager countered. "The first one was putting on that uniform."

Let the record show that Bernice Gera threw Noley Campbell out of the ball game. Some women have no sense of humor at all.

Campbell, who swore later that he didn't swear, wasn't about to leave quietly. He went after the little lady, who sought refuge in the outfield. "I said, 'Why are you running me?' " Noley recalled. "She didn't say anything. She ran off, so I ran alongside her. I said, 'You've got to give me a reason,' but she wouldn't say a word."

For Noley Campbell, it was a unique experience. Never before, in all probability, had he gotten into an argument with a woman who turned and ran and refused to answer back. At any rate, he apparently decided the ump was weakening because, instead of leaving the field as ordered he returned to the dugout. "I was going to make her come and throw me out," he explained.

Noley didn't get his wish. Doug Hartmayer, a 24-year-old male-type umpire working his first pro game as Mrs. Gera's partner, took charge. Campbell left peacefully.

The game continued. So did the lady ump's problems. When Sterling Coward, Auburn's acting manager in Campbell's absence, decided to make a pitching change the base umpire didn't realize she was expected to walk to the bullpen to get the reliever.

"Finally, she goes to the bullpen," Campbell said. "They tell me we only had one guy warming up, but Tief [pitching coach Bob Tiefenauer] decided to have some fun. He says to her, 'Which relief pitcher do you want?' She comes all the way back and asks Sterling Coward. He says, 'The righthander.' She signals with her left hand."

"It was utter confusion," confirmed Doug Hartmayer.

What happened moments after the first game ended was also somewhat confusing. "She walked over to me and told me, 'Inform the people I resign, Doug,' " Hartmayer said. "I was dumbfounded. I stood there in amazement."

"I saw her outside," remembered Barney Deary, who was on hand for the history-making event. "She didn't bother to pick up her pay. She had a car waiting."

All of which led observers to believe that she had planned the whole thing that way from the beginning. "She didn't even have gear she would have needed to work [the second game] behind the plate," said Deary.

Poor Noley Campbell, of course, was afraid that he'd be blamed for the lady's sudden departure. "I sure as hell don't want to be made the scapegoat," he said the next day.

It seemed like a reasonable request under the circumstances. Let it be known that the first professional baseball manager in the history of the game to be ejected by a lady umpire was an innocent victim of circumstances, the hard-luck "loser" in the Great Experiment in Geneva, N.Y. You might say that Noley Campbell was nothing more than a helpless, male chauvinist guinea pig.

Bernice Gera simply may have been trying to win a point. The next lady ump, Christine Wren, made a serious attempt to work her way up in the minor leagues. "She worked four or five years," said Deary, "and did fairly well."

Christine was a pleasant, young lady with a pony tail hanging out from underneath her umpire's cap and a nice sense of humor. God knows, she needed it.

Her first year in the Class A Northwest League her partner was a guy named Lieberman and a heckler in Eugene, Ore., kept referring to him as "Lieberperson." Christine laughed it off. "I can't say I enjoy that part of it," she said, "but if it draws fans, more power to them. Maybe I should ask for a cut off the top."

By opening night of the '76 Northwest League season, her second year, much of the novelty had worn off. Still, the hecklers were out in force at the Eugene ball park, starting on her the moment she appeared for the pre-game conference at home plate. "Quit stalling, sweetie-pie," one leather-lung shouted. "What's the matter, can't you make up your mind? Over there, that's called right field." Etcetera, etcetera, etcetera. The guy must have had Henny Youngman writing his material.

Christine Wren didn't bat a false eyelash. She handled the game well, and when it was over walked quickly to the umpires' room under the stands with her partner, a 26-year-old first-year ump named Terry Luhr. You couldn't blame them for walking quickly. The route to the umpires' room took them past two overflowing garbage cans. After that came a sharp left down three wooden steps into a long, narrow corridor illuminated by bare, cobweb-covered bulbs. Finally, they reached the room where Arrow, Christine's dog, was waiting. It was a happy reunion. Every umpire should have an Arrow to wag its tail and lick his/her hand after a hard game. I think the next time I see Doug Harvey I'll suggest it.

Of course, for a lady umpire who traveled alone, by van, all through her first season, the dog—"a cocker-poodle with a little Irish setter"—was especially valuable.

Christine and Arrow had some rugged road trips in her rookie season. As the first serious lady ump Christine attracted almost as much attention as Bernice Gera. "I was followed all over," Christine said. "Lots of reporters waiting for something to happen. Nothing did."

The worst day, she said, was the first game she ever worked behind the plate. It began with a 12-hour drive from Seattle, Wash., to Boise, Ida. She arrived in time for an 8 A.M. press conference. With that out of the way she had to fly to Walla Walla, Wash. "It was a bad flight," she said. "I got awful sick." Then there was the game to umpire. Naturally, it was one of those wild, high-scoring affairs with a rain delay thrown in for bad measure. "The game lasted four hours and 20 minutes," Christine said. "But I was proud of myself. I didn't throw up on the field."

She felt like throwing up, though, when she saw her paycheck. "My income form says I made $750 [for the entire first year]," she said. "You don't call it pay. You call it peanuts."

So it came as no great surprise when Christine Wren, the second lady umpire—and the first to give it an all-out try, embarked on another career. "She got an offer from United Parcel, I think, in Seattle," Barney Deary said, "and she took it."

There's still a lady calling plays in the minor leagues, though. Her name is Pamela Postema. She comes from Willard, Ohio. And she's currently working in the Texas League, where—wonder of wonders—she goes about her job with minimal fanfare. "*She*," said Barney Deary, "is an umpire."

Coming from a man, that's quite a compliment.

16

FOLLOW THE
BOUNCING CHECK

Minor league horror stories are a dime a dozen. Not just stories about low salaries, bad playing conditions, crummy hotels, but stories involving minor league operators who don't pay their bills and, in one recent, extreme example, an entire minor league that never should have been allowed to exist.

If there's one thing the minor leagues need above all else, it's responsible ownership and leadership, which is precisely what the Inter-American League lacked.

Chances are, you never heard of the Inter-American League. Don't feel left out. Just consider yourself lucky. A lot of baseball players wish they'd never heard of it.

The Inter-American League was formed in 1979. By a not-so-strange coincidence, that's also when it was disbanded, leaving behind a trail of bouncing checks and disgruntled, short-changed athletes.

It was a six-club league—Miami, Fla., and five Latin American entries. Considering the huge travel expenses involved, you had to wonder why anybody in his right mind would have okayed the idea. But then, who ever said baseball people were all in their right minds?

Surely, it came as no great surprise to some baseball people when the league went belly-up early in the summer of '79. Dallas Green made no bones about his feelings. "It's another example," he said, "of the head people in baseball not listening to the [knowledgeable] baseball people. They railroaded the thing through. It was a big political deal . . . They announced the formation of the league in the office of the OAS [Organization of American States]. We all knew in our hearts this thing wouldn't work. It *couldn't* work. They're flying 15, 18, 20 guys across the seas. You know what air fares are. It was absurd."

And, as usual, it was the athletes who suffered. Players got stiffed out of hundreds, even thousands of dollars when the league folded. Inter-American Leaguers included several ex-big leaguers—Dave Wallace, Mike Wallace, Hal Breeden, Bob Reynolds, Cesar Tovar, Dave May, Bobby Tolan, Pat Dobson, Tito Fuentes and more. It was a particularly miserable experience for all the kids from the low minors who saw the new "Triple A" league as a way to advance their careers. Instead, what they saw—despite Organized Baseball's seal of approval—was a mirage. The Inter-American League was baseball's version of pro football's World Football League fiasco.

Dave Wallace, who pitched briefly in the big leagues with Philadelphia and Toronto, discovered the awful truth after he arrived in Santo Domingo. "It was a mess," he said. "Oh God, it was a mess. Just trouble, trouble, trouble from the start. I begged for my release, but they wouldn't give it to me."

Dave finally wrote a letter to Johnny Johnson, the head of the National Association of Baseball Leagues, the governing body of minor league baseball, asking for help after the Santo Domingo club had reneged on terms of his contract. No use. He was stuck.

"I had a $700 check from the club," Dave said. "I sent it home. The check bounced."

Eventually the team made good on that money, but the worst was yet to come. In early July, with the league in its death throes, Wallace and his Santo Domingo teammates flew to Caracas, Venezuela, for a scheduled game. Their manager, ex-major league pitcher Mike Kekich, was fired before the plane left Santo Domingo. When the players arrived in Caracas there was no meal money and, for several hours, no hotel.

"Now the league folds," Dave said, "and there we are, in Caracas. We hadn't been paid for the last two weeks. I talked to the Caracas players. They told me they hadn't been paid, either. We're told to go back to Santo Domingo to get our paychecks. To get there we have to fly from Caracas to Miami to Santo Domingo. We arrive, and they say they're not going to pay us.

Dave Wallace was lucky. He had enough money with him to get out of the country. It cost him $200 for a plane ticket. The club owed him an additional $1,586 in back salary, but at least he got home. "Some of those guys, I don't know what happened to them," Wallace said. "They didn't have any money."

What happened was, they got on the phone and began calling for help. "They all called me," Johnny Johnson said. "Twenty or 21 players on the Panama roster called from the American embassy in Panama. Seven players got from Panama to Miami [before getting stranded]. I got quite a few calls from Santo Domingo, too. It's really sad."

How sad? Ask Mike Martin, whose brother, Jerry, a Kansas City outfielder now, played for the Chicago Cubs then. Mike, a highly regarded pitcher in the Phillies farm system until he hurt his arm, was in Caracas when the end came.

"It was really an experience," Mike Martin said after his return. "I've never been through anything like that in my life. It was just lie after lie after lie. Everything was 'tomorrow.' Always 'tomorrow.' Some guys I knew with the San Juan club played six weeks without pay . . ."

The final hours of the Inter-American League were unforgettable. "The league folded late that night. Eleven o'clock, midnight, something like that," Mike Martin recalled. "I didn't know if I'd get out of the country or not."

The poor guy had no airplane reservation. He had a ticket—an open return as far as Miami—but his destination was San Antonio, Texas, and it would take an additional $130 to fly there. Worse yet, he didn't have the "yellow piece of paper"—the official document required to clear customs in Venezuela. To put it mildly, he was sweating it out.

"I went to the airport at four in the morning," he said. "I was just praying I'd get out."

He did—some six and a half hours later. Others were still waiting, and sweating, when he left.

Did all the players trapped in the Inter-American affair eventually get their money? Don't be silly.

"I never got a dime" said Dave Wallace. "Nobody on our team [Santo Domingo] got paid."

The last paycheck was June 15. So the players worked the last two-plus weeks for nothing and had to pay their own way home. Since Wallace, for example, had a contract that called for $2,800 a month, and since the season was scheduled to last through Labor Day, the club actually owed him more than $7,000.

The men who played for the Miami Amigos were lucky. They got paid for the full season. The others had to write it off as a bad debt. Dave Wallace still gets angry when he thinks about it—and he thinks about it often since, in his capacity as pitching coach of the Dodgers' Class A team in Vero Beach, Fla., he makes frequent trips to the Miami ball park, where the Inter-American League club played. The current Miami club is called the Marlins, but there are still signs in the stadium with "Amigos" on them, a constant reminder of those unhappy days.

The Inter-American League clubs, incidentally, were *supposed* to deposit $50,000 each with the league office when they began operation. It was never done. The whole thing was ridiculous, an embarrassment for Organized Baseball, a disaster for the athletes who should have been protected.

Sometimes merchants in minor league towns need protection, too. The folks in Reading, Pa., found that out.

From 1973 through 1976, the Reading Phillies were operated by Donald Labbruzzo, a man with a long background in minor league baseball. Things went along all right until '76 when the Reading club ran up unpaid bills that reached five figures, according to statements made by the Eastern League office and the Philadelphia organization at the time.

In case you wondered, leaving a trail of unpaid bills is not high on the list of how to win friends and influence people in the minor league baseball manual.

Anyhow, the affair became messy, even threatening to disrupt the scheduled operations of the league when, in April of '77, a motel in Quebec City threatened to seize all the baseball uniforms and equipment of the Reading Phillies when the club went to Canada. To prevent that from happening, the Eastern League and the Philadelphia Phillies each sent the motel a check for $1,043.80.

The commissioner ultimately ruled that Labbruzzo was liable for the debts in a decision handed down on Oct. 4, 1977. What makes all this especially noteworthy is that despite the publicity the case received, and despite the fact that the commissioner got involved, Labbruzzo remains active in minor league baseball today.

"He's a vice-president in Louisville," current Reading Phillies' owner Joe Buzas said, adding that there were still merchants in the Reading area who had not received their money. "I can't believe that the commissioner made a ruling that he had to pay and then, even though he doesn't pay, he's allowed back in baseball."

Actually, after spending 26 years in the management end of minor league baseball, Joe probably *can* believe it better than most. He's been around long enough to know that common sense is seldom a consideration.

If the Labbruzzo-Reading caper and the Inter-American mess rate as fine examples of what's wrong with the operation of minor league baseball, then Joe Buzas deserves recognition as an example of what's right.

Buzas laughs at those—and there are many—who say the minor

leagues are a short cut to the poor house, that it's virtually impossible to make money running a minor league baseball team. Joe, in fact, laughs all the way to the bank.

"It's so easy to make money," he said one evening after the Reading Phillies—one of the three clubs he operated in 1982—beat the Holyoke Millers at Reading's Municipal Stadium. "And it's so easy to operate correctly that it's funny they can't do it."

"They" referred to that large group of minor league operators who think they're going to have a great, old time with a baseball team to call their own and wind up splashing around in a sea of red ink, gazing out at crowds numbered in the hundreds, not the thousands.

On the night I spoke to Buzas a "crowd" of 625 had attended the Reading-Holyoke Eastern League game. But, knowing Joe, you can bet it was a paid crowd. Joe Buzas doesn't believe in "papering the house" just to make it look good.

Granted, a turnout of 625 on a lovely Friday night in mid-May is nothing to write home about. But the Reading Phillies, under Buzas, are a profitable operation. Joe, a one-time New York Yankee short-stop, loves baseball, but he is not a philanthropist.

He runs two Eastern League clubs—Reading and Bristol, Conn.—and the Peninsula team in the Class A Carolina League. How, you ask, does a man get off owning two teams in the same league? Damn, I was afraid you were going to pop that question. He put the second team in his daughter's name, that's how. It's a tribute to Joe's reputation that he did it with the blessings—indeed, the urg-ing—of the league.

"All you have to do [to make money] is learn the right way to operate," Buzas was saying that night as he sat behind the big desk in his large, wood-panelled office. "Some of these owners, they come to me, they ask for help. I say, 'Any time you want help, I'll be right there. I'll come up at my expense and help you out. If you're strong, then I'm strong and the whole league is strong.' Eight or 10 people asked me this, but they never followed up."

Which goes to show just how foolish they are. Here's a guy who knows the ropes, and who's willing to provide free advice. And brother, do some of these guys ever need it. When Buzas took over the Peninsula operation, he went down there (Hampton, Va.) to see what was going on. "Everything was cheap," Joe discovered. "Just giveaways. The guy wanted to be the most popular man in town. . . ."

His popularity soared, his bank account dwindled. It happens all the time in the minor leagues when people who don't know left field from first base try to run a ball club.

"I've made money every year I've been in baseball," said Buzas.

"I won't say I made money every year on every team, but if I had three teams I made money—good money. I made a living."

No great secret about it. Just common sense.

"You don't operate like a major league franchise," Buzas said. "You operate like a minor leaguer. First of all, you have to improvise as you go along. On an average night I have one ticketseller, one ticket-taker. A lot of guys panic. They say, 'I have to have three or four ticketsellers, three or four tickettakers every night in case we get a big crowd.' You don't operate that way. If necessary, you get somebody out of the stands. You do it yourself. You do whatever you have to do. Like the baseballs. . ."

Joe reached down and pulled out a box of baseballs—*old* baseballs that with a little serious rubbing might look like new baseballs.

"See these?" he asked. "There might be seven in here, and I might salvage four of those for the game tomorrow. I clean 'em up. I give them [the umpires] two dozen new baseballs every night to rub up. When they come for extra balls, I take them out of this group. I never give them new balls [except for the original two dozen]. A lot of guys, they give 'em three, four dozen new balls every night."

Penny-ante stuff, you say? Hey, this is Reading, not New York City. This is minor league baseball, not the majors.

How does Joe get those used baseballs that he tries to clean up? Easy. He gets a kid to patrol each foul line and pays a quarter for each baseball returned.

Joe Buzas may recycle used baseballs. He may cut down on the number of ticketsellers and concession-stand employees, but there are some things he doesn't approach from strictly a penny-saving point of view. "We don't scrimp on hotels," he said. "We get the best possible bus. We take care of the ball players. That's important."

You might wonder why a man who played in the big leagues would get so wrapped up in minor league baseball. That's easy, too. As an athlete, Joe Buzas was always in the spotlight. He grew accustomed to it. He enjoyed it. Running minor league baseball teams enabled him to stay in the spotlight. Not as bright a spotlight, surely. But a spotlight, just the same. Writers still come to interview him. The public still knows him. That's what the minor leagues have done for him.

"I was on stage all the time as a player," he said. "I played basketball, football, baseball. I boxed. I was always on stage—like an actor."

Then he became a businessman. He had a department store for a while, and later he went into the construction business. "I was going nuts," he said. The money was there, but the spotlight wasn't.

Joe tried to buy the Trenton Giants in 1950. No luck. FInally, in

1956, Tommy Richardson, then the head of the Eastern League, asked Buzas if he would run a team in Allentown. "I told him, 'Certainly,' " said Buzas. "I ran it for the league and we made a lot of money. We kept the league afloat. Next year he gave me a franchise."

And he's been running minor league teams ever since. Recently, they gave Joe a testimonial dinner commemorating his 25th year as a minor league owner and *The Sporting News* saluted him in an editorial. The spotlight was getting brighter.

"As far as I'm concerned, it's my hobby," he said. "I can hardly wait to go to the ball park and I hate to leave. I like the atmosphere. I like being with people and talking to people. They see me working concession stands. They see me working on the field, getting it ready. People relate to that. They say, 'What the hell, he's no big shot,' and they'll try to help."

Even without giving away oodles of freebies, Buzas' Reading ball club drew 117,000 fans in 1981, an all-time record for the city. Of course, the major league strike helped boost the gate. The Reading Phillies got more publicity than they ever got before—or probably ever will again. But Joe was more than holding his own long before the strike, and he's still more than holding his own after. Just seeing him drive to the ball park in his $26,000 Cadillac tells you that. And he also owns a second car—a $22,000 Caddy. Not only has Joe been good for the minor leagues, but the minor leagues have been good for Joe.

To some, minor league baseball may be a dying business. To Joe Buzas, it's a thriving business. "I was offered $300,000 for the Reading franchise last World Series," he said. "In Bristol, some stockbroker's been calling me and calling me. He said, 'How much would you sell the team for—$150,000?' I said, 'I wouldn't sell it. What am I going to do—go home and count my money?' "

Joe Buzas would much rather count baseballs and fill up cups with soda pop and grill hot dogs and take tickets and rake the skin part of the infield and do all the things that the owner of a minor league team must do to stay afloat. Unfortunately, not everybody is Joe Buzas.

"There are so many inconsistent, idiotic people running baseball who don't know what's going on," he said. "They come in the league and they don't know what the hell they're doing. They think it's just open the gates and people are going to come in. Like the other night in Holyoke, John Felske (the Reading manager) got 20 wet towels after the game. John sent them back, made them put 'em in the dryer. They came back four at a time (because that's all the dryer could handle)."

Mention the Labbruzzos and some of the other minor league

management people and Joe Buzas' blood pressure heads skyward. In Reading, he's still doing business with people who were stiffed by the Labbruzzo-run ball club of a few years before. "Pepsi-Cola was the big outstanding debt," Joe said. "He tried to pay 20 cents on the dollar, something like that, but Pepsi wouldn't take it."

There are, in Joe Buzas' eyes, a number of people running minor league baseball teams who shouldn't have been granted franchises. "They allow this stuff to go on and on," he said. "That's my big gripe about the whole thing. It's a sorry situation allowing people into baseball that shouldn't be in baseball."

But just as there are good managers down there, and good coaches, and good trainers, and good players, there are also some good owners. Stand up, Joe, while the spotlight's shining. Take a bow.

17

CLIMBING THE GLASS MOUNTAIN

Fred Allen, the late, great comedian, once wrote a book called *"Treadmill to Oblivion."* It would have been a perfect title for a book on minor league baseball.

To those who make it to the big leagues for a while, then slip back, the minor leagues do indeed represent oblivion. Tug McGraw, in describing his battle to come back from elbow surgery, said it was "like climbing a glass mountain. You climb three steps and you slide two. You climb three more and you slide two." Well, for a former big league baseball player trapped in the minor leagues, struggling mightily to get out, the glass-mountain is just as high, just as slippery.

Mike Proly, a relief pitcher who had known some success with the Chicago White Sox and the Philadelphia Phillies, found himself stuck in the minors—in good, old Sec Taylor Stadium in Des Moines, Iowa, of all places—at the start of the 1982 season. From Veterans Stadium to Sec Taylor Stadium represents a terribly long slide down that slippery mountain.

"The differences are amazing," Proly said after the Chicago Cubs gave him a reprieve and made him a big leaguer again.

On opening day in Des Moines they held a parade for the Triple A players, sticking them in convertibles and riding them through the downtown area. For a kid coming up, it must have been nice. For a man who had just slipped down from the big leagues, it was awful. Mike Proly felt like pulling down the top of the convertible that carried him through the streets and hiding. "It's pride, you know," he said. "I felt like it was almost am embarrassment to be back in the minor leagues."

Is there anything tougher than a big leaguer of two or three or

235

four years' duration being forced to cope with the minor leagues again? Perhaps not . . . but at least he has the satisfaction of knowing that he made it for a time. How about the guy who spends years and years and *years* scrambling up the side of that glass mountain, getting within sight of the top, but never quite reaching it? For him, the minor league experience is really a treadmill to oblivion.

There are men who spend five, six, eight, even 10 years in professional baseball without ever spending a day in the promised land.

Why do they keep trying to get there? Why do they wait until they're in their late 20s or their 30s to give up the baseball dream and look for another way to make a living? In some cases, after seven or eight years in the minors, they really can't afford to quit. The Triple A salary, for those minor league veterans who have demonstrated their ability to do the job on that level, may not be half bad. But above all, there's always the lingering hope that somebody will give you a chance. The way Mike Easler finally got a chance.

Mike Easler is a man who kept climbing that glass mountain, kept looking up, kept reaching, kept striving, kept slipping . . . until one day—miracle of miracles—he made it to the top and stayed there. He's the exception, not the rule. Still, he's living proof that the impossible dream isn't *absolutely* impossible, after all.

You have to hand it to Mike Easler. He started playing professional baseball in 1969 in the Appalachian League. The Houston scout who signed him didn't go out of his way to boost Mike's confidence. "He told me I wouldn't last a week in Rookie League ball," Easler said. "I know now that he was just saying that to sign me for lower money. But I'm glad he told me that. It made me work harder and I've been working ever since."

Nobody put much more energy, or many more years into scaling the mountain than Mike Easler. He spent a decade in the minor leagues with only the briefest of trips to the majors—five games with the Astros in 1975 when Greg Gross broke a finger, 10 games with the Pittsburgh Pirates in 1977.

Mike did all right in that brief stop in Pittsburgh. He batted 18 times, got eight hits. What did that .444 average get him? You guessed it: another year in the minors.

Here was a man who had hit .352 for Tulsa in 1976 to lead the American Association, and still he couldn't make it. Keep sending a guy like that sliding down the mountain and you've got to come up with some reasons. "Bad reasons," Mike Easler said. "They'd say 'defense,' they'd say I was slow releasing the ball, they'd say I couldn't hit the good fast ball, they'd say a lot of things. The more they said, the more I worked."

His last Triple A year—in Columbus in '78—was the hardest to endure. "I had really done all I could do in Triple A," he said. "It was very tough. I started off slow, but I ended up winning the batting title [.330]. I don't know why. I just got some inner strength in me. I believe my faith in the Lord brought me through that. But it was still tough."

He made it extra tough on himself by buying a house in San Antonio, Tex., before the '78 season began. "I did it to put pressure on myself," he said, "so I'd continue to work hard. It was a $60–61,000 house, one of the best investments I ever made. Right now it's worth almost $90,000."

Easler was making $22,000 playing in the International League in '78, but that hardly made up for the early years. Ask Mike Easler what he got for playing baseball during his long minor league career and the numbers come flying off his tongue. "I started off at $500 [a month]," he said, "then $525, $575, $675, $800, $1,100, $1,700 . . ." Easler had those figures memorized. They were burned into his brain. He rattled them off as easily, and as quickly, as somebody reciting his telephone number.

Easler learned the frustration of thinking—*knowing*—he was good enough to play in the major leagues, yet being pegged as a career minor leaguer. A man has to be mentally tough to handle that.

"A lot of guys right now," he said, "they've been there seven, eight years and mentally they're not 'up.' Psychologically, they're just not in there. They feel they're getting cheated. They feel they're getting a raw deal."

And it bothers them so much that they can't perform, and they slip a little farther down the glass mountain. Or maybe they quit.

"That's what happens to a lot of guys," Easler said. "They get to a point where they say, 'Why should I keep trying? Why should I keep working?' I see a lot of these guys. They have some kind of letdown and they give up. I just kept saying to myself, 'I don't want to be one of those guys that does that. I'm going to continue to bust my tail and work hard and keep trying to put statistics on the board . . . I believed a lot in God. I knew He would make a way for me if I kept working hard and kept my nose clean. Twenty-six major league ball clubs, *somebody's* got to want me one day.

And one day somebody did. Easler became a member of the Pirates in 1979. "I only started three games," he said. "I pinch hit most of the time. . . ."

But it was the big leagues. People stopped questioning his ability to play there. In the minors, they'd called him "Easy." Good, old

Easy Easler. In the majors they gave him a new nickname: "Hit Man."

"My career is very funny," he said one night in the summer of 1982 as he sat in front of his locker in the Pirates' clubhouse. "It's a very exciting career—long, drawn out. Just take the three years I've been in the big leagues. First year, '79, I was in the World Series. Second year, I hit .338, 21 home runs. Third year, I'm in the All-Star game. See what I'm saying?"

For some people it pays to keep trying to climb to the top in baseball. "Just think if I would've quit," he said. "That's what I tell any minor league ball player. There's a guy going through that right now—Doe Boyland. We were roommates. He's a good friend of mine. He went to San Francisco, they picked up Reggie Smith, he got sent back down. I tell him, 'Keep working. Keep working.' "

But surely there must have been times when Mike Easler didn't feel like making another charge up that mountain.

"I felt really hurt a lot of times," he said, "but I never felt like quitting. I dunno. I got a push from my father and my mother. They were always behind me. Especially my father. I talked to him quite often in the minor leagues. I was just determined to make it. My family was very important to me. They knew what I was going through. Being married in the minor leagues and having children is very tough," said Easler, a father of three.

He made a go of it financially by playing 10 seasons of winter ball—in Mexico and Venezuela and Panama. "I saw the poverty over there," he said. "God, it's terrible. Go to the ugliest places in the slums anywhere in the United States and you can find worse places over there. Seeing all that helped me get through the minor leagues."

And spending all those years in the minor leagues, Easler said, has helped him get through the rough periods in the big leagues.

"When I struggle now, I just think back in the minor leagues," he said. "I say, 'God, I could be down there. Now let me just cheer up and keep working hard and I'll come out of it.' Nobody knows how it feels to be here. Nobody really knows. That's why I try to keep my cool and be calm. It took me a long time to get here. Deep in my heart I still feel I have something to prove."

Those 10 years in the minors aren't Mike Easler's favorite topic of conversation. He'll talk about it if you push him, but only then. Apparently, some of the old wounds haven't entirely healed.

"One day I'm going to tell the whole story," Easler said. "It's a helluva story, too—things managers said to me, all kinds of stuff. But now I don't say nothin' about it. I try to stay away from controversial things now that I'm here in the big leagues. When I get out of the

game I'm going to write a book: *From Easy to Hit Man.*" He laughed
at the thought. "Look the book up, will you?"

Be glad to, Mike. For a man who refused to stop trying to climb
the mountain—and made it to the top—it's a better title than
"Treadmill to Oblivion." But for all those who didn't make it, Fred
Allen's title still hits home. "Players spend so many years down there
and don't have anything to show for it," mused Mike Easler. "I think
they should do something about that."

Some of the finest men I've met in professional baseball are players who didn't get to the big leagues, not even for a day. Most of
them made it as high as Triple A, and performed well there. But
that's where it ended.

Remarkably, when they talk about their careers as professional
baseball players they display little or no bitterness. A Mike Easler,
who finally made it, doesn't really enjoy thinking about those days,
doesn't even feel comfortable visiting a minor league ball park now
that he's a big leaguer. "I hate to go there to play exhibition games,"
he said. "I can't stand it. I just don't like to be around minor league
ball parks. I feel sorry for the people there."

Yet most of the people who spent a lot of years in the minors and
didn't make that final, giant step to the majors seem only too willing
to talk about it, to think about it, even on occasion to laugh about it.

Quency Hill comes quickly to mind. A personable Texan, Quency was a lefthanded pitcher, and a pretty darn good one all the way
up to the Triple A level. He thought his big chance would come after
the Phillies traded him to the Dodgers. After all, when the trade was
completed the Dodgers' general manager called and assured Hill that
he would be given an opportunity to make the big club in spring
training. Quency was sky high. He couldn't wait to get to Vero
Beach, couldn't wait to start his all-out bid to earn a place on the
pitching staff of the Los Angeles Dodgers. And then he got there, and
in one day—in one brief conversation, really—he came crashing
down to earth.

It was the first meeting with Red Adams, the Dodgers' pitching
coach, that told Quency Hill the Dodgers weren't really all that
serious about him. Quency will always remember Adams' first words
when the pitcher introduced himself on the first day of spring training. "Are you lefthanded or righthanded?" the pitching coach
wanted to know.

You'd think there might be a touch of residual bitterness over
that, or the Chicago White Sox decision to release him after he'd

pitched a few innings of perfect baseball in a minor league exhibition. But no. Quency Hill retained his feeling for the game. Not even a sore shoulder that ultimately closed out his pitching career could erase that.

"Baseball's not going to want to give up the [Mark] Fidrych's," he said, "but the Quency Hills they can afford to give up."

Baseball had such a strong hold on Quency, however, that he left a good business in Dallas in the spring of '82 to take a job as pitching coach for the Chicago Cubs' Class A Quad City team.

"I had very, very few regrets [about playing in the minors]," he said, "because most of my first six years were happy. I thoroughly enjoyed them. My family thoroughly enjoyed them. Susy [his wife] and I got to go places. I always felt I was getting to do things at 19, 20, 21, 22 that a lot of people have to wait their whole life—until they're retired—to do. To me, it was all fun. I tried to make the most out of wherever I was, whatever I was doing. The only time I ever had any regrets, at all, was when I first did get out of it. I guess I'm an eternal optimist, but I kept hoping the shoulder would get right and I wasn't prepared for things to come to an end. Once I got out it was really a humbling experience, I guess you'd say. I didn't know what I was going to do, what I was going to turn to."

Why would a man who had been through the minor leagues as a player want to return to the low minors as a coach? Maybe this will explain, in part.

"The thing I found out just going through the minors was that my happiest years were in the lowest minors," he said. "You were young. You usually still had 25 guys pulling for 25 guys. You keep going up and now you've got bitterness from the guys coming down. It just gets a little more intense, dog eat dog."

So here was a man who didn't make it past Triple A, yet who enjoyed—and even now savors—the minor league experience.

Some of the things that happened then were kind of special because the friends a man made in the minor leagues were special. One of Quency Hill's closest friends in the Phillies' farm system was Jack Bastable, an outstanding football player at the University of Missouri who spent six seasons in baseball's minor leagues as a catcher and utility player.

Bastable and Hill were Oklahoma City teammates when Jack's first child was born. The call came when the 89ers were in Evansville, Ind. Jack wanted desperately to get to Oklahoma City before the baby was born. The cause seemed hopeless, but with his buddy's help he was determined to give it a try.

"The town was rolled up," recalled Quency, who had received

permission to accompany Jack, on the trip to Oklahoma City. "We couldn't even get a cab. The two of us walked six, seven miles to the Evansville Airport. A light drizzle was falling. Imagine how ragged we looked.

This was in the wee hours of the morning. "Once we got to the airport we had to wait another hour for it to open up," Quency said.

It might as well have stayed closed. There were no decent connections to Oklahoma City. The only chance was to rent a car, drive to St. Louis, and catch a plane there.

"Jack was doing about 120 miles an hour between Evansville and St. Louis," said Quency. "But it all paid off. We got to Oklahoma City in time. The baby [Rachel] was born at 2:15. The team didn't get back from Evansville until three, so if we'd gone with them we wouldn't have made it."

Friendships like that help to offset some of the negative aspects of minor league life.

"They don't make friends like that in the big leagues," Jack Bastable said. "It's the friends you make in the minor leagues that matter. That's why Bull [Greg Luzinski] and Bob Boone are so close. They played minor league ball together."

Especially, they played *low* minor league ball together. That's where the closest friendships begin.

"I enjoyed every minute of it, really," Jack Bastable said. "I felt fortunate to be playing. For some reason I felt like I had the wisdom to accept it and enjoy it for what it was, and not let it be spoiled by thinking, 'I should be playing in the big leagues.' It was only my last year where I felt like, 'I'm going Nowheresville.' I kind of had a bad taste in my mouth."

He had been cut at the very end by the big club, and they told him he was going to Triple A as a backup catcher. Bastable was so upset he packed his bags and went home. Later, after a call from Phillies owner Ruly Carpenter, Jack agreed to play again. Rather than sit and watch in Triple A, he returned to Double A, where he helped Reading win the second-half pennant in the Eastern League. Big deal, you say. Well, you had to be there to appreciate the enjoyment Bastable and the other members of that team—managed by Lee Elia—got out of the clincher on a rainy night in a dismal, rundown, nearly empty ball park in Jersey City. "It was exciting," Bastable said. "Old Roosevelt Stadium was falling down around you, but it was still exciting." And even in that dungeon of a clubhouse in Roosevelt Stadium, the champagne tasted good.

Bastable's baseball career ended there. He was tempted to accept an offer from the Inter-American League the following season, but fortunately decided to take a job running Nautilus and fitness centers that Bob Boone owned in the Philadelphia area instead.

"I enjoyed playing baseball," Jack said, "but I was ready to move on. If I wasn't going to be able to work towards the goal of getting to the big leagues, that was it. I wasn't going to play just for the sake of playing."

He was a young man who put a lot into baseball; Jack Bastable puts a lot into whatever he does. "I know things aren't going to come easy," he used to say, "and there's going to be a price I'll have to pay."

He paid that price willingly. "How many years is it that you have a chance to play baseball, to give it your best shot?" he asked during that final minor league season at Reading. "I don't want to look back some day and think, 'Gee, if I'd only put out those nights when I came in off those long bus rides.' I don't want to ever look back and think I didn't give it the best shot I possibly could."

A man who does that has no reason to hang his head just because his best wasn't quite good enough.

"As I look back on it," he said, "the real success I think I had in the [minor league] experience was working toward that goal, even if I didn't achieve it. The thing I really learned is that when you bust your butt to reach toward something you reap the benefits as a result of that effort alone. That's what life is all about, I guess."

And certainly that's what life in baseball's minor leagues is all about for the Jack Bastables and Quency Hills, and all the others who never quite make it to the big leagues. It may be difficult to understand, but most of them look back on those years now with warmth and affection. There's a high school teacher and baseball coach in the Philadelphia area named Eddie Molush, whose promising career as a righthanded relief pitcher was cut short by a sore arm. One night recently he and Jack Bastable got together and spent hours rehashing old stories, remembering old friends. If there was a trace of anger, of bitterness, of lingering frustration, it was well hidden. It was a night filled with good memories.

"You know," said Molush, "my managerial record in the minors is 0–and–1. Harry Lloyd, the manager at Pulaski my first year, let me manage the last game of the season."

Harry was "a down home, tobacco-chewing, tobacco-spitting country boy," according to Eddie, a city boy himself. Maybe Harry thought a little of Molush's big-city polish would dazzle the Covington Astros that day. Anyway, he let Eddie talk him into letting him manage.

"I'd have won that game if Larry Christenson had laid down a damn sacrifice bunt like he was supposed to, the big lug," manager-for-a-day Molush recalled, smiling. "You won't believe this, but I put in five pinch-hitters and every guy got a hit. Then I put a suicide squeeze on. Christenson squared around, blew the bunt and the kid [racing down the line from third] got tagged out. We lost, 4–3. The following year I was on the plane for Rocky Mount and Larry was on the plane for Philadelphia."

Happily for Larry Christenson the Philadelphia organization never held that missed squeeze bunt against him.

Like most of the others, Eddie Molush found life in the low minors more fun than life in the high minors. "There's more of a college atmosphere when you're down lower," he said. "It's more of a fraternity. You suffer together. You struggle together."

Sometimes you even do good deeds together. There was a clubhouse boy in Rocky Mount who was a favorite of the players. "He was a 10-year-old black kid," Eddie Molush said. "He was just a real cute, polite, little kid. He loved hanging around. Everybody called him 'Blue'."

The kid's parents had been killed in an automobile accident. He lived in a very poor section of town. Molush knew because he used to drive him home.

"He hung around Jimmy Morrison and me more than anybody," Molush said. "Every once in a while we'd take him out to our place, let him go swimming out at the apartments. Then somehow we found out his birthday was coming up."

Morrison and Molush took up a collection in the clubhouse. "If you'd seen the sneakers the kid had," Eddie said. "I think he had about three T-shirts and he wore the same jeans every day. . . ."

The money collected, Molush told "Blue" to be at the ball park the following morning. "I remember it was real gray and cold. He had no idea where he was going. He had no idea why I was picking him up. I took him over to K-Mart and I got him a new pair of jeans and a new pair of corduroys for school. He wanted a Dallas Cowboys' ski hat, so I got him that, and a pair of red sneakers and work boots for school and a flannel shirt or two. We used up all the money, about 70 bucks. His eyes just popped out of his head. He didn't know why we were doing it. I had to keep telling him it was his birthday. I'm telling you, he was overwhelmed. When he got to the ball park he was beaming from ear to ear. He couldn't wait to show everybody how fast he could run in those red sneakers.

"One thing I always hoped I could do someday was take him to a big league ball game. I knew the kid had never seen one. He'd never been out of Rocky Mount. I told him, 'If I get to the big leagues, I'll fly you to a game.' I remember that off-season I got a letter from him. I wrote back and I told him that I might not be back to Rocky Mount, but if I made it to Philadelphia I was going to make sure he came to a game. I really wish I'd gotten that kid to a big league ball game. That would have been the greatest thing in his life."

Eddie Molush's sore arm prevented him—and his young friend—from making it. But it was a beautiful thought, just the same. Next time you hear somebody say that professional baseball players are a selfish, spoiled lot, you might tell the story of Jim Morrison, Eddie Molush, the Rocky Mount baseball team and a 10-year-old orphan called "Blue."

18

A LOOK BACK...
AND A LOOK AHEAD

Okay then, what is this thing we call the minor leagues? Well, it's many things—from embarrassingly bad stadiums to big, beautiful ones, from playing baseball on July 4 in Denver in front of 50,000 people who are waiting for the fireworks show to playing in front of a few hundred fans in West Haven or Shelby or Davenport.

Want to know what the minor leagues are?

They're a cold spring night in Williamsport, Pa., in 1967 with a 40-year-old Hall-of-Famer-to-be, Robin Roberts, pitching for Reading in an Eastern League game with 391 spectators sprinkled around the wooden, Bowman Field stands.

They're a warm summer's evening in Daytona Beach, Fla., with more than 4,700 fans overflowing the 4,500 seats to see J.R. Richard start his first professional game since suffering a stroke in Houston, a year and 11 months before.

They're a lovely summer's night in Pawtucket, R.I., with two former American League rookies of the year, Mark (The Bird) Fidrych and Dave Righetti, facing each other in an International League game with one man (Fidrych) trying to battle back from a sore arm and the other (Righetti) trying to battle back from a sore owner.

To a Dave Righetti, 23, shipped out by George Steinbrenner in the middle of the 1982 season, the minor leagues represented punishment of the worst kind. "To go back down and walk on those minor league fields that I worked for five years to get away from will be hard," he said.

To a Steve Braun, released by Kansas City at age 32, the minor

245

leagues represented a new start, a place to relax, to have fun playing the game again. "I'll tell you what," the St. Louis Cardinal pinch-hitter said, "I had such a good time playing in the minor leagues again that I didn't want to go back [to the majors]."

That's the fascinating thing about the minor leagues. They're so many things to so many people.

To me, the minor leagues are men like Hub Kittle, who spend most of their lives there without fanfare, without very much money, without complaint. Hub Kittle, 66 now and the pitching coach of the St. Louis Cardinals, is what the minor leagues are all about—or, at least, should be all about.

Can there be anybody anywhere who knows more about life in the minor leagues than Hub Kittle, this cigar-smoking, tobacco-chewing prince of a man whose enthusiasm for the game never diminished through his 38—yes, 38!—summers in the minor leagues?

He's a truly remarkable man, blessed with a memory so sharp that he can relate events that occurred in the '30s and the '40s when he was trying to make it to the big leagues as a pitcher. Hub didn't make it—World War II interrupted his baseball career at the worst possible time—but he made the minor leagues into a marvelous, fun-filled adventure. And an adventure it was.

"He was the trainer, the bus driver, the manager, the pitching coach," recalled Bill Robinson, who played for Hub in Yakima, Wash., in 1964. "He was everything."

Pete Cera, the Phillies assistant clubhouse man who has been in the game nearly as long as Kittle, was Hub's trainer in Terre Haute, Ind., 28 years ago. Does Cera remember Hub Kittle, minor league manager? Hey, does the sun set in the west? *Nobody* forgets Hub Kittle.

"He'd show guys how to slide in hotel lobbies," Pete said.

As Bill Robinson said, Hub Kittle did it all. And loved practically every minute of it. He'd pitch batting practice day after day. So what if the temperature hit 100 in Austin, Tex., and the humidity was brutal and the sweat was pouring down his face? Hub kept going out there, kept throwing.

Dozens of his "kids" made it to the big leagues. Dusty Baker played for Kittle. And J.R. Richard. And Cesar Cedeno. And Jim Owens. And Harry (The Horse) Anderson. And Ralph Garr. And Carl Morton. The list goes on and on.

"It's just good to see him here [in the big leagues] now making a little bit of money," Bill Robinson said. And that's what Hub made through most of those minor league seasons: a little bit of money.

He got $50 a month his first year, $90 his second. Then came a $5 raise that put Hub almost—but not quite—to the triple-figure plateau. The year he won 20 games in Yakima he was making $125 a month. Kittle thought that was worth a big raise—maybe even a $25 raise. "I wanted $150 but they wouldn't give it to me," he said. "So opening day the manager told me, 'The old man isn't going to give you $150, Hub.' He says, 'He'll give you $135 and you better sign.' So I signed."

Hub made a few extra bucks driving the team bus in Bremerton [Wash.], in the mid-'40s. "I was the third base coach," he said. "I pitched. I drove the bus. I did a lot of things and by doing it they gave me 50 bucks a month extra. Then they put a deal in the league [the Western-International] that because of the economy no player could get any extra money for doing something extra. So even though I had a pretty good year—won 16 games—they wanted to cut me 50 bucks."

That was life in the minors in Hub Kittle's day. You liked it or you lumped it. Hub loved it.

"You had to be very frugal," he said. "You made it if you watched your P's and Q's."

It also helped if you kept your eyes on the white line in the middle of the road—especially those mountain roads in Oregon. "I didn't get in any accidents," he said. "Came pretty close at times, though. I had the lights go out one night going down a big grade. Oh my Lord, that scared me. You pull on the brakes and you think, 'The cliff's over there—300 or 400 feet down,' so you pull it to the right and you know you're going to hit the wall, and you skid and skid and skid and all of a sudden it comes to a stop. *That's* scary, baby. We lit 'candles' [flares, really] and put them on the fenders and got one guy on one fender, another guy on the other fender to hold them up so we saw the white line and we just kept going down, going down until we got off the grade."

Spend an hour or so with Hub Kittle and he'll regale you with a non-stop recitation of stories like that complete with dates, names, places. Hub saw it all and his energy, to this day, hasn't waned. One year—in Yakima, Wash.—his team finished 27 games out of seventh place. Then the next two years he won pennants. "You have to learn to lose; you have to learn to win," he said.

Hub Kittle learned, all right, and along the way he ran into some of the darndest characters to ever walk into a minor league clubhouse. One day this summer Hub wracked that fertile brain of his and jotted down some of the players he'd come across who had the craziest nicknames. He filled up two sheets of paper with such dillies as Madame ZaZa Volpi, Cock Eye Molitor, Buckshot Boyd, Bee-Bee Eyes Barisoff, Tin Ear Medegini, Buffalo Head Perry and the inimitable, the unforgettable Any Face DeHaney.

Any Face DeHaney? C'mon, Hub, be serious.

"Got him out of Walla Walla prison," Kittle said. "He was in for fraud."

Hub managed to get him out, had him "pardoned to the ball club." In return for that rather large favor, Any Face—the ingrate—cashed a check at the 24-hour chili parlor that Kittle owned in Yakima. "Great chili," boasted Hub. Special recipe. I called it the world's only fartless chili." Anyhow, Hub had warned the hired hands not to cash any checks for Any face, but one of the girls goofed. "The check bounced," growled Hub. "He still owes me 25 bucks."

To a man who spent all those years living on minor league salaries, getting stiffed out of $25 was no joke. But it could have been much worse. Hub Kittle might have taken a job in the Inter-American League.

Let's be thankful he didn't. It's the Hub Kittles of the world who made the minor league something special. You meet so many people who spend their waking hours complaining about all the bad things. Hub's a guy who only wants to talk about the good things. Even if he didn't make it to the majors as a player—he got as high as the Pacific Coast League, playing for Lefty O'Doul in San Francisco—Hub did what he wanted to do: play and coach and manage and live the life of a baseball man. "I wanted to be a ball player when I was eight years old," he said, "and I was lucky enough to be able to be a part of it. That's something."

That's the beauty of the minor leagues, men like Hub Kittle. there are quite a few of them there, if you look hard enough.

They're bus drivers—guys like Phil Johnson in Reading, Pa., who can't find enough to do for the players of "his ball club." In the afternoon, when they're ready to eat, or late at night when the game is over, Phil is always available to drive them to the nearest decent restaurant or diner.

They're broadcasters—guys like Bus Saidt, who did play-by-play in the old Interstate League in the late '40s and early '50s. Saidt, now a sports columnist for the *Trenton Times*, broadcast the Trenton Giants home games and, when the Giants were on the road, free-lanced in such places as York, Pa., and Lancaster, Pa., and Harrisburg, Pa. Bus did it for the love of doing, not for the money he made. His first year as the voice of the Trenton Giants, he did the games for nothing. At no time in his Interstate League broadcasting career did he get more than $10 a game. Yet he'd work at his 9–to–5 job, then jump in his car and rush out to do a baseball game. "There was no Pennsylvania Turnpike then," he said, "and it was about 125 miles one way to York. I'd drive out, broadcast the game, then drive back."

But that's outrageous, expecting a man to do that for $10 a game.

"Yes," Saidt said, "It was outrageous, but it was beautiful. I loved it. I wish I were going to do it again tomorrow."

That's what the minor leagues are all about. It's the Hub Kittles, the Steve Brauns, the Jack Bastables, the Eddie Molushes, the Quency Hills, the Phil Johnsons, the Mike Easlers, and hundreds of others. It's players and coaches and managers and bus drivers and club owners and little kids in little towns who think it's exciting to see and meet a real, live ball player, even if he is playing in an "A" league.

It's a young man named Glenn (Goose) Gregson, whose career as a professional pitcher started with the Appleton (Wisc.) Foxes, a team so bad that it lost 18 games in a row the year Goose was there. "A day never went by that there wouldn't be people coming by the ball park asking for a tryout," said Gregson. "They figured we were so bad all they had to do was put on a uniform and turn things around." Instead of souring on baseball because of that experience, Gregson—a college graduate—became more determined to give it an all-out try. Today he's coaching in the Chicago Cubs' farm system.

There are a lot of good people involved in minor league baseball. And some bad ones, too. There are some great things about this slice of Americana we call minor league baseball, and there are some rotten ones. There are players who loved it and players who loathed it. Playing in the minors is like going to college, in a way. Go in with a positive attitude and, chances are you'll like it. Go in with a negative attitude, you'll hate it. There's good and there's bad. Whichever you look for, you'll probably find.

So where are the minor leagues headed? Will rising costs and the rapid growth of cable TV, filling homes with sports around the clock, kill the minors once and for all? Or will they survive?

You'll find disagreement on that score among the men who run major league baseball teams.

"Running player development is costing us about $3 million a year," Eddie Einhorn, the president of the Chicago White Sox, was saying recently. "We have over a $400,000 budget to sign draft choices. The rule of thumb is that 2 percent of all those drafted make it to the major leagues. So why are we doing it? Things are changing. I don't think the winning teams in the future will have their own players."

Einhorn went to Japan in 1981 and saw the way they do it. No vast minor league system there. Each major league team has one minor league outfit that plays its games in the same city. The minor leaguers play in the afternoon, the major leaguers at night. Einhorn thought it was great. "You'd save a lot of money," he said, "and you'd be developing, I think, higher quality players. Also, I think we should do more of what basketball and football do. They use the colleges as their training ground. Why don't we?

"I think the myth of the minor leagues of baseball are gone," Einhorn said. "It used to be America's pastime. You had to play in every city, every nook and cranny in the country. But that really isn't true any more.

"Do you realize that most minor league teams, with the advent of television and cable, lose money? Every day is like a promotion, a giveaway day. People really don't care. If Appleton and Glens Falls [N.Y.] didn't have our teams [does anyone think] that the towns would go down? It's not like it was. I think we're preserving the myth that started years ago when we had all these hundreds and hundreds of teams."

That's one man's opinion, but it's not the majority opinion. "Every time a new guy comes into the game he says that," said John McHale, the president of the Montreal Expos. "I've heard that for 25, 30 years. Everybody has a new way of developing ball players."

McHale's way—the way of most of the men who run major league organizations—is still the farm system way. "This is the kind of a game where I think the difficulty of throwing a ball accurately and hitting a baseball—probably one of the most difficult things in all sports—takes a certain number of games and years and at-bats and innings," McHale said. "You're not going to get it done when you're not doing it under real severe competitive situations, which the minor leagues give you. College is not enough. If you want to continue having the best players available, the distillation process has got to be done with lots of players. I think you're going to have some mediocrity if you change it. Those who want to change it, they really don't examine the history of the game. They come in, they've got an immediate, simplistic solution without having paid any attention to the history, the tradition of the game. I don't think you're going to see us have any less than the 100 or so clubs we've got now."

Actually, the 1982 season began with 160 minor league clubs, eight more than in 1981. According to figures released by the National Association of Professional Baseball Leagues, a total of 16,559,704 attended minor league games in 1981—the first time in 25 years that attendance topped the 16-million mark. And 25 years ago there were 28 leagues instead of 17, 217 clubs instead of 160.

Three minor league clubs topped half a million at the gate in '81—
Denver, Nashville and Columbus, Ohio. Granted, it's unlikely that
16 million people *paid* to see minor league baseball in '81. Those attendance figures—like the attendance figures for many college sports
events—are greatly inflated by giveaways and plain, old-fashioned
imagination. But, as a Joe Buzas will tell you, there's still a market
for minor league baseball, still money to be made out there.

Beyond that, there still seems to be a genuine need for a minor
league system. The facilities in many places need upgrading, the
salaries, the treatment of ball players need upgrading, but for all its
shortcomings minor league baseball—in so many ways a throwback
to a bygone era—isn't dead yet. And that's as it should be. Every
young ball player, after all, should have a place to dream.

19

EPILOGUE

Okay then, for somebody who doesn't play baseball for a living, for a person who simply enjoys watching the game and writing about it, what's so compelling about the minor leagues? Why does a sports columnist for a big newspaper in a major league city spend vacation time each summer traveling to minor league towns to watch baseball? (Don't tell me I'm nuts; I bruise easily.)

The fact is, *if you know the people involved*, the minor leagues offer an inordinate amount of drama. I'm talking about genuine, gut-wrenching, personal drama, the kind of thing that doesn't seem to happen all that often in the big-money, antiseptic, AstroTurf, electronic-scoreboard, TV-dominated world of big league baseball. The real struggle in baseball is getting to the big leagues. In the course of waging that struggle you find the real people, the real drama, the real excitement that makes professional baseball such an important part of our society. To me, the most gripping bit of news in the sports section of the morning paper might be a line of agate type on the results page under the heading *Transactions*—a line announcing, for example, that Derek Botelho had been called up to the big leagues by the Kansas City Royals after spending half a season pitching in the minor leagues. That news might not have seemed very exciting to you when it appeared in July of '82, but for somebody who knew Botelho and the battle he'd waged and the years he'd spent trying to make it, that agate line was a cause for celebration.

I've seen a lot of memorable games and performances on major league fields. It would be hard to top that 1978 Yankee-Red Sox playoff game in Fenway Park, or the last two games of the 1980 Phillies-Astros championship series at the Astrodome, or Reggie

Jackson's home-run explosion in the 1977 Yankee-Dodger World Series, or that fantastic sixth game of the 1975 Reds-Red Sox World Series, or the Allie Reynolds no-hitter against the Red Sox at Yankee Stadium in 1951 when he had to get Ted Williams twice on foul pops with two out in the ninth inning (Yogi Berra caught the second one), or Chris Chambliss' pennant-winning homer for the Yankees in '76, or Johnny Bench's game-tying, opposite-fieldhomer against the Pirates in the final inning of the final playoff game of '72 at Riverfront Stadium, or Pete Rose's electrifying, 12th-inning homer that silenced a rowdy Shea Stadium crowd and won the fourth game of the '73 playoffs for the Reds, keeping them alive one more day.

But as vivid as those—and other—memories are, I don't think any of them can surpass the drama of watching 40-year-old Robin Roberts, the winner of 286 big league baseball games, attempting a comeback in the Eastern League. Fifteen years have passed since then, but I can still remember the feeling of watching this future Hall of Famer, this consummate professional who used to rise to the occasion against the Newcombes and the Spahns, hanging his clothes on a nail pounded into the wall of the visiting clubhouse in Williamsport, Pa., then going out and losing, 1–0, to the Williamsport Mets. He was back in the minors, he said, "as a last resort" because big league teams were no longer interested in that aging right arm. Was it sad that night watching Robbie pitch against kids who knew him only as a legend, striving to prolong a career that had reached the point of no return? Or was there something noble and grand about this man's willingness to go back to the bushes, to rekindle the spark of youth, to cling just a little longer to the job he loved more than any other: being a professional baseball player? I remember going out with him after the game. Never once did he complain about the playing conditions, about the cold weather, about the clubhouse, about the nearly 5,700 empty seats in the 6,000 seat ball park. Robin Roberts wasn't looking for sympathy in Williamsport. And he wasn't looking for special treatment. He was a man doing what he wanted to do, and if others chose not to understand . . . well, that was their problem.

For sheer drama, of course, the return of a former big league star to the minors is hard to beat. Robin Roberts might be the classic example, but many others have made it to the big leagues—and made it big—only to suddenly find themselves back in the minors again. Remember Steve Blass, the Pittsburgh righthander who won two games against the Orioles in the 1971 World Series? Once blessed with fine control, he lost the ability to throw strikes and went back to the minors in a futile attempt to recapture his old form. Then there are the Joe Charboneaus, the one-year wonders who rocket to big league fame and then, almost as quickly, plummet to minor league obscurity. And, above all, there are all the sore-armed pitchers, the guys with the scars on their elbows and shoulders, who go back to the minors in an effort to fight their way up to the majors again.

Was there anything more dramatic in baseball in 1982 than the sight of J. R. Richard, the once-overpowering righthander of the Houston Astros, walking out to the mound in City Island Park in Daytona Beach, [Fla.], where an overflow crowd of 4,719 turned out to watch him start a professional baseball game for the first time since he suffered a stroke nearly two years before? Here was a man who had struck out 1,493 big league batters in 1,608 innings facing the St. Petersburg Cardinals of the Class A Florida State League, and giving up three first-inning runs. But it was a start—"a giant step," Astros president Al Rosen called it.

Also in 1982, there was that midsummer night's dream of a pitching matchup in Pawtucket, [R.I.], where Mark Fidrych, the American League's 1976 Rookie of the Year, started for the Pawtucket Red Sox and Dave Righetti, the American League's 1981 Rookie of the Year, started for the Columbus Clippers. Not surprisingly, a sellout crowd of 9,389 showed up at McCoy Stadium, watching Righetti strike out the first five batters he faced and ultimately cheering Fidrych to a 7–5 victory. So many out-of-town sportswriters and broadcasters were on hand for the International League's game of the year that Righetti said, "This is more exposure than when I pitched in the World Series."

To be sure, the return of J. R. and the Righetti-Fidrych duel in Pawtucket weren't your average, run-of-the-mill, minor league occurrences. Even so, it's possible to find plenty of high drama in the minors just about any week of the summer. In search of it, I took a trip to Louisville, Ky., in July of '82 to watch an American Association series between the Omaha Royals, Kansas City's top farm club, and the Louisville Redbirds, St. Louis' Triple A affiliate. Talk about high drama, and low comedy, this series had it all.

The cast of characters was promising, to say the least. The Louisville pitching staff included two "newcomers," John Fulgham, just up from the Class A Florida State League, and Mark Littell, just down from the big leagues. Fulgham was bucking the odds, trying to become the first pitcher to make it all the way back after undergoing rotator cuff surgery. Others—Wayne Garland, for example—had tried, and even won a few games, but nobody had been successful over a period of time. Fulgham, a 10-game winner for the St. Louis Cardinals in 1979, appeared to have a glowing future in baseball until his shoulder started coming apart. Now, after a stay in St. Petersburg, here he was, ready to test himself against Triple A competition.

Littell's problem was in his elbow, not his shoulder. As a hard-throwing relief pitcher with the Kansas City Royals, Mark—his friends call him "Country"—achieved big league stardom. But two elbow operations, the most recent in June of '80, left him with a major rehabilitation program. Through it all, Littell never lost his delightful sense of humor, his rare ability to laugh at himself.

Mark had known some exceptionally good times in the big leagues . . . and some bad ones. He was one of the game's premier relievers in 1976, when he won eight games and saved 16 for the Kansas City Royals. But that outstanding season came crashing down when Chris Chambliss of the Yankees hit a ninth-inning homer off him in the fifth game of the championship series. Littell handled that the way he handles just about everything else: with the composure of a man who does his best and understands that on some days his best isn't going to be quite good enough. On most days, though, it was plenty good, as Whitey Herzog, who managed Littell in Kansas City and later in St. Louis, was quick to point out. "All they remembered Mark for was that home run," Herzog said after the Cardinals gave him the option of taking his outright release or reporting to Louisville midway in the '82 season. "But he was the guy I wanted out there with the pennant on the line. I told him, 'Hey, buddy, we wouldn't have been here if not for you.' He could make that ball whistle in '76."

It stopped whistling after his second elbow operation, though, so here he was, back in Triple A with the Gene Roofs, the David Greens, the John Martins and the other former major leaguers dotting the Louisville roster.

On Littell's first day in Louisville, the owner of the club, A. Ray Smith, was taking a few youngsters on a conducted tour of the home team's clubhouse.

"This is Gene Roof," he said, nodding in the direction of the outfielder, who also happened to be sharing an apartment with Littell.

Roof, a pleasant, young man, greeted the kids cheerfully and walked over to shake their hands.

"And this is Mark Littell," the owner said.

Just in case the name didn't register, Roof decided to fill in a few details, to let these young people know that the man about to shake their hands had left his mark on the national pastime.

"Chris Chambliss hit a home run off him in the playoffs," Roof announced in a loud voice. The kids seemed suitably impressed. Littell? He just laughed and said, "Nice roomie I got."

"Any time," Roof assured him.

The Omaha Royals were also an interesting bunch. Among the pitchers were Jim Wright, the one-time super prospect of the Phillies who broke his arm throwing a fast ball in a spring training game, and Derek Botelho, another top Phillies pitching prospect of a few years past whose baseball career nearly ended when his shoulder went bad. Released by the Chicago Cubs, who had obtained him in a deal for Manny Trillo, Botelho got in contact with a specialist in East Lansing, Mich., flew there at his own expense and paid for the surgery that, he hoped, would revive his pitching career.

If some of the young men on these two Triple A ball clubs were of exceptional interest, so was the city . . . and the stadium . . . in which this series was being played. Louisville had gone nearly a decade without a professional baseball team, and now that it had one again the people were turning out at a record-breaking clip. The four week night games with Omaha drew a total of 45,270 fans. It didn't seem to matter that the weather was uncomfortably hot and muggy or that the Redbirds were in a slump. The people kept buying tickets and making noise. Cardinal Stadium, with its AstroTurf carpet gleaming under the lights and its grandstand well filled with partisan rooters, had the look, the feel, the sounds of a big league ball park. "If you have to play in the minor leagues," said Gene Roof, "this is the place to be."

On this particular week the look, the feel, the sounds of Cardinal Stadium weren't the only things you noticed. There was also a distinctive aroma in the air. The National Appaloosa Horse Show happened to be in progress at the Kentucky Fair and Exposition Center, where the ball park is located. The stables were just outside the clubhouse doors. Horses were everywhere, and so was horse manure. Jim Wright even found some in his shoes one night, placed there by a teammate whose sense of humor smelled.

If you didn't mind putting up with the horse shit, the clubhouses were fine. The lockers, in fact, were bigger than most big league lockers. A. Ray Smith was obviously going first class. He even boosted his players' meal money to $20 a day—five more than the going rate in the league last season. Since clubhouse dues, generally $5 a day, came out of that, A. Ray's players weren't going to be dining in the swankiest places in town every night, but at least they were getting close to half of what their big league brothers received.

Joe Sparks, the Omaha manager, was 44 years old. Twenty-six of those years had been spent in pro baseball, and 25 of them in the minor leagues. Joe wasn't looking to break Hub Kittle's record. His ambition, understandably, was to be a big league manager. When the Kansas City Royals fired Jim Frey in 1981, though, they bypassed their Triple A manager and picked ex-Yankee manager Dick Howser instead. So Sparks was here, still waiting.

A light rain was falling. The infield was covered with tarpaulin. Sparks sat in the spacious manager's office in the visiting clubhouse and said a small prayer of thanks for the inclement weather. The rain meant there would be no batting practice that night. No batting practice meant he wouldn't have to throw. After what had happened to Joe the night before, that was no small item. Twice line drives had rifled over the protective screen and nailed him—once high in the right side, once low. "See," Sparks said, "and he pulled up his undershirt to display one ugly, purple welt, then lowered his long johns to reveal the other. "After I got hit the first time I kept going," he said. "The second time knocked the shit out of me. I staggered over to the dugout."

Sparks smiled engagingly. "If you can manage here," he said, "if you can go through all this, it should be a cakewalk up there."

Down here, Joe Sparks did it all himself. If you wondered why he didn't have one of his coaches pitch batting practice, the answer was simple: he had no coaches.

"They called me when they fired Frey and hired Howser," Joe was saying. "They knew the kind of job I was doing. They said they wanted to let me know first what they were going to do. They didn't want me to get down in the dumps. I said, 'The only thing is, I'm ready. I'm ready and I can do it.' They said, 'We feel that you can, but we had a chance to get Howser. He won 100-some games with the Yankees. We feel he's the guy we need right now.' I said, 'Well, I am disappointed, but I have a job to do and I'm going to do my job. I appreciate the call.' "

So here he was, managing the Omaha Royals instead of the Kansas City Royals, and working as hard at it as he knew how. When the season ended, he'd switch over to his other job—selling cars. "Same dealership for the last 16 years," he said. "And my wife has her own business. It works out good."

But the big leagues would work out infinitely better. And the more he talked, the more Joe Sparks seemed certain that the day would come.

"It's not so much you're paying your dues here," he said. "I don't are going to notice. Somewhere down the road they're going to feel like to use that expression. It's a job. If you do your job well people that you're the right guy for their ball club. Not being a big name major league player, sometimes I think that hurts a lot. I think that if I had been an established major league player for eight or 10 years with the record I've had managing in the minor leagues I'd have been managing in the major leagues four or five years ago."

Still, there has been a parade of long-time minor leaguers who have made it as big league managers, and made it big. Walter Alston made it. Earl Weaver made it. Tommy Lasorda made it. Sparky Anderson made it. Maybe one of these days it will be Joe Sparks' turn.

"I just hope," he said, "that when I get a major league job as a manager I'm fortunate enough to have a club that's a decent ball club."

The second game of the series was special: a matchup between Derek Botelho of Omaha, the young man who spent $2,500 in late April 1980 for the operation that enabled him to resume his pitching career, and John Fulgham, whose career was interrupted by the most feared words a pitcher can hear—rotator cuff.

"I've been through a helluva lot," Botelho said. "It's a different feeling pitching with your shoulder not sore. Now I know I can throw. If I get beat, I get beat. If I get it all together maybe I can get to the big leagues."

On this night, Derek Botelho got it all together. Through seven innings he allowed only one Louisville runner to reach second base. And then, perhaps most impressive of all, when David Green slammed a three-run homer in the eighth to trim Omaha's lead to 5–3, Bothelo retired the last five batters without allowing a ball to leave the infield. Twelve days later he started for the Kansas City Royals at Fenway Park, shutting out the Red Sox for seven innings and gaining his first big league victory.

John Fulgham was another story. He had made the 16-hour drive from St. Petersburg, Fla., the day before, arriving at Cardinal Stadium just in time to be handed the pitching chart and told that he would be the next night's starter. In Class A, he had displayed solid signs of recovery, pitching a shutout his last time out. But Triple A was a big jump from A ball—especially for a guy coming off rotator cuff surgery.

In the first inning, the Omaha Royals tagged him for two hits, but had a runner gunned down at the plate. In the second, three straight singles loaded the bases. Then there was a two-run double off the left field wall by Greg Keatley, a walk, another hit. It took a line-drive double play to enable Fulgham to hold the damage to three runs. Two innings later, the Royals scored twice more and John left the mound. He had given up five runs and 10 hits in three and two-thirds innings. But more important, he was pitching against good competition again; barely 16 months after the operation he was facing Triple A hitters.

"Somebody said to me, 'You got to be a little depressed by the way things went,' " Fulgham said. "I'm not at all depressed because people told me it would take two full years to even pitch in an organized baseball game. For me to be in Triple A at this point and be competitive is great. I have no pain. That's probably what my biggest battle is at this point—the pain, being able to throw without pain and with decent stuff. That's what it's all about for this year. Next year I'll worry about who I'm getting out and why I'm not getting them out."

To Fulgham, simply being able to stand on that mound and pitch again was a significant achievement. "Look at everybody that's had these operations," he said in the Louisville clubhouse after the game. "They're all at home watching games and I get the opportunity to pitch. I just heard [Wayne] Garland got released by Nashville. . . . What can you say?"

He had come a long way in the last 16 months, and he still had a long way to go. "I've got a chance," he said. "It's just a matter of how I progress from today until who knows when."

The young man who beat him on this night understood only too well. "Sure, you feel for him," Derek Botelho told a Louisville writer. "You remember how he used to throw the ball, and then you see him like that, and it makes you want to say, 'Just don't quit, John. Just don't give up. Keep on battling and coming back, man, as much as you can.'

"The reporter said to me, 'There hasn't been a pitcher that's come back from [rotator cuff] surgery,' " Botelho said. "I told him, 'That doesn't mean he can't be the first.' "

John Fulgham . . . Derek Botelho . . . Jim Wright, names on a minor league scorecard in Louisville, each with a story to tell, a comeback to achieve. As much as anybody, they're what minor league baseball is all about—a struggle to get out of the Louisvilles, out of the Omahas and back to the St. Louises and the Kansas Citys. To know them, to know what they've been through and how much they're putting into their comeback efforts is to appreciate the drama that is professional baseball in the minor leagues. In each case, people told them they wouldn't be able to pitch again—and in each case they are doing their damndest to prove those people wrong.

"I feel fortunate," Jim Wright said. "I know I've hurt my arm and I've hurt it bad, but I've never hurt it in a way that I couldn't come back. That's why I'm lucky."

How do you not root for young men like that? How do you not feel a sense of excitement and satisfaction when somebody who has struggled for years in the minor leagues finally gets the opportunity to pitch in the big leagues?

That's the attraction of minor league baseball. That's why, when you spend a considerable amount of time around it, it becomes difficult to tear yourself away. Minor league baseball is the Fulghams, the Botelhos, the Wrights. It's high drama, and it's low comedy. Yes, Max Patkins was in Louisville, too.

"I hope you bring us luck," said Joe Frazier, the Louisville manager. "We haven't won a game in a week."

"You won the last time I was here," Max told him.

The clown was in the Louisville dugout for a pre-game visit. He hadn't put on his uniform yet, but the funny face was in place. As Max is only too quick to tell you, with him the funny face is always in place.

The game was a couple of hours away. Max was "on," though. When there's an audience—especially a baseball audience—he's always "on," always trying to get a laugh. Following Max Patkin through his pre-game adventures is worth the price of admission. The stories, new and old, the gags, good and bad, come non-stop.

"Friday night in Macon, Georgia, I was on the coaching lines for one hour—one full hour," Max was telling Joe Frazier and anybody else within earshot. "They got 12 runs while I was coaching, 12 Goddamned runs. I kept chasing runs in. I fainted on the coaching lines on purpose. I laid there, like I was out cold, and I kept hollering, 'Seltzer . . . seltzer.' The guy said, 'Why do you want seltzer? Why don't you holler, 'Water . . . water.'? I said, 'I'm Jewish.' "

Joe Frazier's team had lost six straight home games, including three straight to Omaha. It didn't matter. Max had him laughing in no time.

"You know what I do now?" the Clown Prince of Baseball asked. "If I get a bad crowd I go into the audience. We've got an hour and a half delay in Chattanooga because of the rain. I go in the stands. I start telling comical, corny jokes. I say stuff like, 'You see that guy over there—the general manager? He got me a hotel room that's so small even the mice are hunchbacked.' "

It must have required an enormous effort on Joe Frazier's part, but the Louisville manager managed to hold back the laughter. Undaunted, Patkin went on.

"I called the desk clerk up," he said. "I told him, 'I got a dead bed bug in my room.' He said, 'There's nothing so bad about one dead bed bug.' I said, 'Yeah, but you should see the funeral his friends are giving.' "

A hint of a smile crossed Joe Frazier's face. A man sitting a few feet away actually laughed. There was no stopping Max now.

"Then I told them the best one yet," he said. "I call up the desk clerk and I say, 'I gotta leak in my sink,' and the desk clerk said, 'Go ahead.' "

On and on, he went, regaling his select audience in the Louisville dugout with those Henny Youngman rejects. Somehow, with Max mugging between punchlines, they came out funny. He was in his element here, around people he knew, surrounded by the trappings of the sport he loved. There isn't a city he visits that doesn't remind Max Patkin of a baseball story.

"Ted Kazanski, the old Phillies infielder, he played here," Max was saying. "I was coaching third. Kazanski hits a ball. It goes out of the ball park, hits a car back of the God-darned fence and comes back in. The guy fields it. He throws the guy out at second base. Would you believe it? The guy's trotting around for a home run. He calls him out. Unbelievable. Two umpires, and they both said the ball was off the fence.

"And did I tell you about the time what's his name—Bob Uecker—almost killed me on the first base side. He struck out—he isn't lying when he said he was a horse shit hitter. Anyway, he struck out and I'm sitting on the bench, ready to go on. He came over, took his helmet and let it fly. It went right by me, just missed me. Think if it'd hit me in the face. I'd have been a funny-looking guy."

Max wriggled that marvelously elastic face into something only a Jewish mother could love and waited for his laugh. Then he checked the time, jumped up and marched into the Louisville clubhouse. "I need the starting nine," he bellowed. "I gotta hold a meeting."

Just what Joe Frazier needed, right? Six straight losses at home and now Max Patkin was getting ready to hold a team meeting.

First, Max decided to get everybody loose. He opened up a manila envelope and pulled out a couple of glossy publicity shots of the famed Patkin face, nose and all. "You wouldn't believe it," he told them, "but that won third prize one year for the ugliest sports picture."

They smiled indulgently, grateful that Max hadn't brought the pictures that finished one-two.

"Okay," said Max, "where's my starting pitcher?"

Orlando Sanchez, a backup catcher recently sent down by the St. Louis Cardinals, snapped to attention. "Right here," he lied.

Max gave him a long look. "You're pitching tonight?" he said.

"Yeah," Sanchez assured him. "I throw the tortilla ball."

Max nodded. "I had a Latin pitcher that pitched to me the other night in Chattanooga," he said. "This guy throws 95 miles an hour. He don't know where the plate is. You know the way I come up to bat at the end of my act? This son of a bitch, he's walked everybody in the park. I put a helmet on the first time in 37 years. I was scared to death. He's supposed to throw me the third pitch easy; I'm supposed to hit it. He's throwing 85 miles an hour on his changeup. I'm trying to hit the ball and get the hell out of there so they can play the ball game. I swing through four balls. then I threw the bat at the pitcher and I ran to third. I had eight people left in the stands by the time I finished my act. They had a two-hour rain delay in a double header. I go on, it's 11 o'clock. Anyway, where's my starting nine?"

They were standing there, at least most of them, listening to Max's monologue with bemused expressions. Most of them knew Patkin's act almost as well as he did. There may be players who spend years in the minor leagues without learning the strike zone or how to run the bases or how to hit to the opposite field, but it's darn near impossible to go through a minor league career of any substantial duration without getting to know Max Patkin's act.

"I know you know this shit," he was saying, "but I got to tell you, anyway. You can help me out a little bit. . . ."

Briefly, he went through the routine. They nodded.

"One thing," cautioned Max, looking at "pitcher" Sanchez, "if you're losing the ball game, if things are going against you, you're not going to be as happy as you are sitting in here now."

Sanchez grinned up at Max. "I'm always happy," he said.

Max gave him another long look, then dashed out of the clubhouse. Time was growing short. He still had to explain a few things to the visiting team—especially first baseman Ron Johnson, who would be the foil in Patkin's mimicking routine. And he had to check out a few details with the public address announcer, which meant running all the way up to the pressbox.

Somehow, Max got it all accomplished. The big crowd—better than 16,000—seemed to enjoy him, especially after the home team broke out of its slump with a four-run rally in the fifth. Orlando Sanchez got in the spirit of things, too. Perhaps to show Max that he really cared, Orlando filled a bucket with water and dumped it on Patkin as the clown took his final bow.

It could have been worse, though. In Omaha, Royals' pitcher Frank Wills threw a bucket of *ice* water at Max. "You should have seen his face when that hit him," Wills said, the memory brightening his day.

Sanchez, on the other hand, settled for tap water. He's all heart, that lad. Besides, he couldn't find any ice.

After an evening with Max Patkin, what do you do for an encore? A suggestion: if it's more laughs you're looking for, spend a week or two with a bad minor league ball club. With that in mind, I took a road trip with the Oklahoma City 89ers.

The 89ers, it seems safe to say, were the worst Triple A baseball team in the business in 1982. They started the season by going 3-and-24. When I caught up to them for a mid-July series in Indianapolis they were 26-and-58. "You won't believe how bad we are," a player told me when I arrived. "Oh, you can't be that bad," I replied. Shows what I know.

Tony Taylor recently had been made manager of the floundering Phillies' farm club and George Culver had been named pitching coach. It was a heartless thing to do to two fine men.

The Indianapolis series opened with a double header, the first game of which told you all you needed to know about the Oklahoma City 89ers. Going into the final inning, they trailed the Indians, 7-6. Then came a stirring rally. Eleven men batted. Seven men scored. The 89ers led, 13-7. It was an advantage that stood up until the home team batted in the bottom of the inning, scored seven runs of their own and won, 14-13. Poor Tony Taylor. Two decades in the big leagues and now he had to watch this.

By way of added punishment, the next stop on the road trip was Sec Taylor Stadium in Des Moines. Fifty-two years before, on May 2, 1930, this city had been the site of what was hailed as the first night baseball game played under adequate lights. As the late Sec Taylor, then sports editor of the *Des Moines Register*, wrote: "A total 146 projectors diffusing 53 million candlepower of mellow lights and the amazing batting of the Des Moines Demons' nocturnal-eyed players made the opening game of the local season a complete success."

The Demons, a member of the Class A Western League, saw the ball so well they scored 11 runs in the first inning and beat the Wichita Aviators, 13-6, before an overflow crowd of about 12,000 at old Holcomb Avenue Park. Among the spectators on that historic night were Judge Kenesaw Mountain Landis, the commissioner of baseball in an era when the title meant something, and Branch Rickey, then the business manager of the St. Louis Cardinals. According to newspaper accounts, not all of the fans were confident that the new-fangled lights would, in fact, be adequate. Some skeptics showed up for the game with flashlights. Come to think of it, that wouldn't be a bad idea for fans attending games in some of to-day's minor league ball parks.

Sec Taylor Stadium, circa 1982, was just as I had remembered it, except that the crowds were larger—a group of local businessmen had taken over the team—and the tiny visiting clubhouse, that horror of years past, had been spruced up a bit. There was a soft drink machine near the door and a 10-inch, black-and-white TV set. The place had been painted and there was wood panelling on the walls. The low-hanging beam, into which countless players had banged their heads over the years, was now padded. Guys still hit their heads against it, but at least it didn't hurt as much. Before, they got concussions. Now, only headaches. Such is progress.

The clubhouse, of course, remained woefully undersized. Players still had to take showers in shifts. And the playing surface—at least the infield—was a mess, lumpy and bumpy and generally substandard. Also, on one of the four days the 89ers were in town there was an awful smell. No, it wasn't the 89ers. The wind was blowing from the southeast, a native explained, thereby assailing the nostrils of customers and players alike with the aromas from the meat-packing plant and the rendering works across town.

In defense of the stadium, let it be said that it was a chummy place. The entrance to the visiting clubhouse, clearly marked "Visitors," was a short distance from a refreshment stand. Players, unable to find room to sit down in the clubhouse, often walked outside to kill time and mingle with the fans and check out which way the wind was blowing. Occasionally, though, the mingling got out of hand, as when a lady pushed open the door of the 89ers' clubhouse some 35 minutes before the game, saw the players sitting around in their underwear, recoiled and squealed, "Oh, I'm looking for the bathroom." Pitcher Larry Bradford looked up, smiled cordially and said, "There's a bathroom in here."

The first game of the series was held up twice by rain before it became official. The crack Sec Taylor ground crew, which worked so diligently to get the infield covered during the first two downpours, slowed down noticeably, however, when a seventh-inning deluge halted play with the home team on top, 6–3. There was no longer any need to hurry; by washing out the rest of the game an Iowa Cubs' victory would be assured.

Tony Taylor was furious. He stood out in that pouring rain and gave the umpires a piece of his mind. In return, they gave him the rest of the night off. For Tony, the ejection was the start of something big. The following night he got tossed out again, this time for arguing over a call at first base. And the night after that he got chased for throwing a towel out of the dugout after disputing a two-out, two-strike balk called against Mark Davis that enabled Iowa to break a scoreless tie. Throughout all his years as a big leaguer Tony Taylor, one of the nicest guys you'd ever want to meet, had been thrown out of only two ball games. Three nights in Sec Taylor Stadium and he was thrown out three times—baseball's version of the hat trick. Just goes to show you what minor league baseball can do to a person.

The series in Des Moines ended on a Tuesday night. The next series, in Louisville, began on Thursday night. So how did the Oklahoma City 89ers spend their "day off"? Playing an exhibition game in Tulsa, Okla., against the Texas League All-Stars, that's how. (And all this time I'll bet you didn't know that the shortest route from Des Moines to Louisville was by way of Tulsa.) Anyhow, pitching coach George Culver was slated to see some action. "I'm going to go as far as I can," he said, "and the bullpen's going to go the other 8⅔."

To nobody's great surprise, the all-stars from the Double A league beat the travel-weary also-rans from the Triple A league, 10–4.

Drive three hours east of Des Moines and you come to the home of the Quad City Cubs of the Class A Midwest League. There, on the west bank of the Mississippi River, in Davenport, Iowa, sits John O'Donnell Stadium. The setting is lovely. The ball park is attractive. The league, with three four-team divisions, is the biggest in the minors.

"You should see a game in Madison [Wisc.]," advised Quency Hill, the Quad City pitching coach. "The fans there are unbelievable. They just have themselves a good time. A guy [on the visiting team] makes an error and they stand and they point and they chant, 'Sieve . . . Sieve . . . Sieve.' It's all done in good humor. . . ."

Joe Buzas would have approved of the setup in Davenport, where a man wearing a dark blue shirt with "Quad City Cubs Roadrunner" embroidered on it was in charge of outhustling the fans for foul balls. This man—he was no kid—was a whiz. One moment he'd be sitting in a box seat munching on pop corn. Next moment he'd be charging through an exit in hot pursuit of a baseball that had been fouled over the stands. He seldom returned emptyhanded. Any fan who went to a game at John O'Connell Stadium in the hope of getting a foul ball had his work cut out for him.

Unfortunately, I picked the wrong night to visit the ball park. It was invaded by insects—May flies, the natives called them, or fish flies. They had long tails and short life spans, living no more than 24 hours, and on this night they were obviously having the time of their lives. There must have been millions of them flying in crazy, zig-zag circles near the light towers when darkness descended. And, as the night progressed, they came down to visit with the folks in the stands, and with the players, too. Mike Harris, the shortstop for the visiting Springfield [Ill.] Cardinals, swatted three hits that night and God-knows-how-many-flies. The highlight of the game was watching him trying to keep the invaders out of his face between pitches. To play shortstop in this ball park on a mid-July night—at least on this mid-July night—a man needed a pair of good hands, a glove and a bottle of Flit.

In baseball, a man also needs a good sense of timing. As pointed out earlier, it helps to be in the right place at the right time. But it's also helpful, if you're in the wrong place, to know when it's time to get out. With that in mind, let's give a low bow in the direction of a pitcher named Mark Lee, a one-time big leaguer whose sense of timing was truly exceptional.

Lee, a pitcher for the Portland [Ore.] Beavers of the Pacific Coast League, was informed late in the 1982 season that he was about to be released. As if that wasn't bad enough, he was asked to stick around for an extra day in the event he was needed in relief that night against Vancouver.

Lee agreed to stay and, sure enough, was called in from the bullpen in the ninth inning to protect a Portland lead. He retired the first man he faced on a pop fly. He threw a third strike past the second man . . . and then, instead of going to work on the third out, he called his manager, Tom Trebelhorn, to the mound. "Nothing against you," he told the manager, "but I'd rather go out this way." And with that Mark Lee walked off the mound, stopping long enough to toss the ball back to the infield, throw off his cap and remove his uniform shirt. He had decided to go out his way, not their way. As he explained later in a newspaper interview, "It was my way of saying, 'You guys can control some of the things, but you can't control all of the things in my life.' " Spend a few years traveling around the minor leagues—particularly the high minor leagues—get to know the young men who play there and what they go through and maybe you'll understand what could prompt a Mark Lee to do what he did.

But for all the sad tales you'll come across in the minor leagues, for all the disappointments you'll find, there's a happy side, a fun side that keeps turning up—if only you know where to look. In 1982, the place to look was Louisville.

If Louisville had been outstanding the first time around, it was downright sensational the second time. Only eight clubs in the history of the minor leagues had topped the half-million mark in attendance for a full season until Louisville's return to Triple A in 1982.* The Redbirds passed the 500,000 mark in the second week of July on their way to establishing a minor league record of 868,418, nearly 200,000 more than any minor league team had ever drawn before.

It didn't matter to the Louisville fans that the team with the worst record in the American Association was coming to town for three nights. On the first night, a Thursday, 15,836 turned out to watch the Redbirds romp, 11–1. A Friday night double header drew 18,831—nearly a thousand more than the Cincinnati Reds and the Chicago Cubs attracted to Riverfront Stadium, about an hour and 40-minute drive away. Then, on Saturday night, 19,885-seat Cardinal Stadium wasn't big enough to handle the crowd that showed up. An estimated 5,000 were turned away as the Redbirds completed their sweep of the four-game series before 20,401.

Louisville had been gripped by baseball fever and civic pride. In contrast to some other Triple A parks, Cardinal Stadium was a fun place to go. There was a Dixieland band, good lights, a good playing surface, a nice scoreboard. It was family entertainment at a price a family could afford. This was minor league baseball at its very best. There were big league parks in 1982 that didn't have the atmosphere of Cardinal Stadium.

"You look up in the stands and you don't see seats," said Oklahoma City pitcher Mark Davis. "You see people, like when (Steve) Carlton's pitching in the Vet."

It's *not* the big leagues, though, and if Tony Taylor needed any reminder of that fact he got it in his very first game there. Tony had inadvertently left relief pitcher Mike Willis' name off the lineup card

---

*Until Louisville broke all records in 1982, the only minor league teams to draw 500,000 or more were: San Francisco (PCL), 1946, 670,563; Oakland (PCL), 1946, 634,311; Baltimore (IL), 1946, 620,726; Los Angeles (PCL), 1948, 576,372; Nashville (Southern League, Double A), 1980, 575,676; Denver (AA), 1980, 565,214; Columbus, Ohio (IL), 1980, 546,074; Hollywood (PCL), 1946, 513,056. It should be noted that all the Pacific Coast League teams listed played 190-game schedules in the post-World War II years.

he presented at home plate before the game began, and this was a night he would need all the relief pitchers he had. After three innings his troops were lagging behind, 11–0.

It was just a formality now. Tony brought in Larry Bradford to pitch the fifth and sixth, then made the call for Willis to finish things out. Bradford headed for the clubhouse, removed his uniform, iced his arm. Willis took his warm-up tosses and prepared to pitch. Whoops. Hold everything. Umpire Tim McClelland checked the official lineup card. No Mike Willis.

Taylor wasn't trying to run in a ringer. Willis had been with the 89ers all season. Everybody knew that. It was just a simple oversight. But McClelland said he couldn't pitch.

There followed a lengthy debate that had the big Louisville crowd confused and ultimately annoyed. Joe Frazier, the Louisville manager, asked the umpires to let Willis pitch. "I told them, 'Get it over with,' " Frazier said. "They wouldn't consider it."

Taylor had nobody else to pitch. McClelland suggested that he bring in Warren Brusstar, whose name did appear on the lineup card. Brusstar had an injured finger on his pitching hand and couldn't come in, but what really enraged Taylor was the colossal nerve of an umpire telling a manager who he should bring in from the bullpen.

Since Willis was being declared a non-member of the 89ers on this night on a technicality, the Oklahoma City manager decided he had no choice but to forfeit the game. Heck, his team was so far behind that a 9–0 forfeit score would be an improvement. Umpire McClelland quickly put an end to that idea. "He told me, 'If you do that it will cost you $1,000,' " Tony Taylor said.

It was a ridiculous situation. Here was a big crowd thirsting for action. Here was a one-sided ball game in the seventh inning. Here were two managers in full agreement that Mike Willis should be allowed to pitch. And here was an umpiring crew adamantly refusing to let him pitch.

"He [McClelland] asked me, 'What if you come back and score 12 runs and he [Frazier] protests?' " Taylor said.

No problem. Joe Frazier, a sensible man, made it clear that he would not protest the use of Mike Willis in that ball game, even if Oklahoma City scored 100 runs. It didn't matter. Willis was banished to the clubhouse. In desperation, Tony Taylor got Larry Bradford to remove the ice pack—"I had to re-thaw my arm out," the pitcher said—put on his uniform and return to the mound. By the time the game resumed some 30 minutes had been wasted. It was all so unnecessary, all so lacking in plain, old-fashioned common sense.

The next day Tony Taylor, still fuming, placed a long-distance call to the league president, Joe Ryan, in Wichita. "I talk to his secretary," the 89ers' manager said. "She say he out to lunch. I call back later. Nobody answers. I call back again. They say he not back yet."

It brought back memories of the time, 10 years before, when Jim Bunning placed an urgent call to the president of the Eastern League in mid-season and was informed that he was on vacation. "The president of a baseball league can't go on vacation in July," Bunning protested.

Of course he can. In the minor leagues just about anything is possible. A manager can get thrown out of three straight games. A league president can take off in the middle of the summer. A pitcher who has been with a club all season can be declared ineligible to pitch because the manager forgets to put his name on a lineup card. A team trailing by a run can score seven times in the last inning and still lose. A relief pitcher can be so fed up with the way he's being treated by the front office that he walks off the mound with one out to go in the ninth inning and starts taking off his uniform. All part of life in the bushes. Minor league baseball. There's nothing like it.

INDEX

Aaron, Hank, 9, 25, 111
Aaron, Tommie, 111
Adams, Red, 239
Aiea Barracks (Army Service team), 85
Albuquerque Dukes (Pacific Coast League), 129
Alexander, Gary, 169
Allen, Fred, 235
Allentown PA minor league club, 233
All-Sports Stadium (Oklahoma City), 73
Alston, Walter, 39, 258
Amaro, Ruben, 47
American Association, 54, 75, 99, 130, 187, 209, 236, 252, 254, 267
American League, 57
Anderson, Harry (The Horse), 246
Anderson, Sparky, 258
Anthony, Ray, 86
Appalachian League, 236
Appleton Foxes (Midwest League), 115, 249
Arkansas Travelers (Texas League), 139
Atlanta Braves, 9, 43, 66, 190
Atlanta Stadium, 43
Auburn Astros (New York-Pennsylvania League), 223

Baker, Dusty, 246
Bakersfield Bears, 11–12, 18
Baltimore minor league club (International League), 267
Baltimore Orioles, 110, 200, 253
Bannister, Alan, 7, 46, 53, 65–66, 68–72
Barber, Red, 1
Barisoff, Bee-Bee Eyes, 248
Bastable, Jack, 29, 74, 40–42, 249
Bastable, Rachel, 241
Baumer, Jim, 207
Bayless, Jeff, 18, 20
Bayless, Joan, 9–11, 18–21, 25
Bayless, Lowell, 9, 12, 18, 22
Bayless, Pat, 9–25, 159, 191
Bedell, Howie, 47, 77–78, 135
Bench, Johnny, 253
Berardino, Johnny, 90
Berra, Yogi, 253
Bevens, Bill, 1
Bisbee minor league club, 155–56
Blass, Steve, 253
Bockman, Eddie, 10, 22, 25
Boitano, Danny, 133, 215–17, 253
Boitano, Susan, 215–60
Bolger, Ray, 86–87
Bolling, Frank, 83
Bonham, Bill, 32
Boone, Bob, 126–27, 133–37, 198, 241–42
Boone, Sue, 126, 134

Borowy, Hank, 90
Bosetti, Rick, 75–77, 82, 99–100, 166–70, 174
Boston Red Sox, 252–53
Botelho, Derek, 164–66, 256, 258–60
Boudreau, Lou, 89
Bouton, Jim, 200–201
Bowa, Larry, 7, 11–14, 20–21, 25, 125, 143–45, 153, 186–87
Bowa, Sheena, 25
Bowman Field (Williamsport PA), 245
Boyd, Buckshot, 248
Boyer, Ken, 76–77
Boyland, Doe, 238
Bradford, Larry, 264, 268
Bradford PA minor league club, 159
Brandon, Darrell (Bucky), 45, 64–65
Braun, Steve, 181, 245, 249
Breeden, Hal, 228
Brett, George, 138
Bristol, Dave, 102, 158–60
Bristol Red Sox (Eastern League), 231
Brock, Walter, 3, 134–36
Bronson, Jimmy, 40, 93
Brooklyn Dodgers, 1. *See also* Los Angeles Dodgers
Brown, Bobby, 214
Brown, Joe E., 86
Brunet, George, 49–50
Brusstar, Warren, 4–5, 82, 268
Buffalo minor league club (International League), 37, 95
Bunning, Jim, 36–83, 93–94, 101, 145, 166, 168–69, 174–75, 211, 269
Bunning, Mary, 45, 80–81
Buskey, Mike, 79
Butkus, Dick, 23
Buzas, Joe, 230–34, 251, 265

California Angels, 126, 184
California League, 10
Callison, Johnny, 117
Campbell, Nolan, 15, 136, 223–24

Candelaria, John, 182
Cannizzo, Tony, 157
Caracas winter league club, 179–80
Cardenal, Jose, 188
Cardinal Stadium (Louisville), 267
Cardinal Stadium (St. Louis), 256, 258
Carlton, Steve, 62, 267
Carolina League, 7, 99, 104, 106, 124, 135, 219
Carpenter, Bob, 38
Carpenter, Ruly, 59, 64, 68, 205, 212, 241
Carroll, Joe, 158
Cartwright, Bob, 21
Carty, Rico, 111, 171
Cash, Dave, 60
Cedar Rapids IA minor league club, 110
Cedeno, Cesar, 246
Cera, Pete, 193, 245
Cerone, Rick, 208
Cey, Ron, 129
Chambliss, Chris, 249, 253, 255–56
Charboneau, Joe, 5, 254
Charleston minor league club (American Association), 37
Charleston WV Charlies (International League), 5
Chicago Bears, 23
Chicago Cubs, 164, 235, 249, 256, 267
Chicago White Sox, 133–34, 145, 203, 235, 239, 249
Christenson, Larry, 48–49, 54, 57, 60, 243
Cincinnati Reds, 77, 146, 190, 208, 253, 267
City Island Park (Dayton Beach), 254
Clark, Alan, 106, 181–82, 218–19
Clark, Herb, 106
Clark, Ron, 54–55, 60, 65, 177–78
Cleveland Indians, 5, 89, 105, 189
Clinton IA Giants (Midwest League), 115
Cobb, Ty, 89
Colavito, Rocky, 83

Columbus OH Clippers (International League), 214, 237, 254, 267
Combe, Geoff, 211
Connie Mack Stadium, 40, 59
Covington Astros, 242
Coward, Sterling, 224
Cox, Larry, 127
Crosetti, Frank, 89–90, 93
Cruz, Pablo, 182–83
Cullen, Blake, 219–20
Culver, George, 33, 59–62, 64–65, 69, 263, 265
Cunningham, Billy, 21

Dancy, Bill, 72
Darcy, Pat, 169–70
Davenport IA minor league club (3–I League), 37
Davis, Mark, 4, 25, 31, 265
Davis, Ron, 208
DeArmas, Rollie, 177–78
Deary, Barney, 222–26
DeHaney, Any Face, 248
Demeter, Steve, 181
Denver Bears (American Association), 95, 215–17, 252, 267
Des Moines Cubs (American Association), 264
Des Moines Demons (Western League), 263
Detroit Tigers, 38, 189
Diaz, Bo, 180–81
Dilone, Miguel, 182
DiMaggio, Joe, 86, 89, 214
Dobson, Pat, 228
Dodger Stadium (Los Angeles), 132, 150, 184
Dolson, Frank, 212
Dooley, James, 23
Downs, Dave, 8, 43–44, 190–91
Downs, Kelly, 43, 177–78
Doyle, Denny, 12, 143–44
Dressen, Charlie, 38
Dublin GA minor league club, 110
Durham Bulls (Carolina League), 3, 135–36
Dykes, Jimmy, 38
Dwyer, Jim, 82, 133, 142

Easler, Mike, 140, 236–39, 249
Eastern League, 7, 13, 29–30, 39, 43, 56, 124, 128, 165, 230–31, 233, 253, 269
Edmead, Alfredo, 182–83
Edmonton Trappers (Pacific Coast League), 204
Einhorn, Eddie, 249–50
Elia, Lee, 33–34, 39, 46–50, 55, 58–62, 68, 121, 241
Elizabethton TN Twins (Appalachian League), 159
Escogido winter league club, 165–67, 169, 173–74
Essian, Jim, 43, 56–57
Eugene Emeralds (Northwest League), 224–25
Eugene Emeralds (Pacific Coast League w/Phillies; now with Northwest League w/Reds), 6, 14–18, 36, 44–53, 94, 96, 127, 143, 153, 184

Fain, Ferris, 86, 89
Fanning, Jim, 110
Farmer, Barbara, 189
Farmer, Ed, 7, 33, 63, 130, 189–90, 202
Feller, Bob, 90
Felske, John, 5, 27–28, 233
Fenway Park (Boston), 132, 184, 252
Ferrer, Sergio, 174–75
Fidrych, Mark (The Bird), 245, 254
Fields, Steve, 219–21
Flavin, John, 161
Florida State League, 112, 254
Forsch, Bob, 96, 133, 142
Fox, Charley, 161
Franklin, Tony, 101
Frazier, George, 170–71, 199–200
Frazier, Joe, 147, 260–61, 268
Freed, Roger, 188
Fremuth, Mike, 126, 197
Fresno Giants (California League), 142
Frey, Jim, 257
Froemming, Bruce, 220
Fuentes, Tito, 228
Fulgham, John, 254–55, 258–60

Gaedel, Eddie, 90
Gamble, Oscar, 127–28
Gantner, Jim, 27
Garagiola, Joe, 64
Garcia, Dave, 105
Garland, Wayne, 254, 259
Garr, Ralph, 246
Garvey, Steve, 84, 152
Garber, Gene, 61
Gemignani, Gerald, 24
Geneva Cubs (New York-Pennsylvania League), 223
Georgia-Florida League, 221
Gera, Bernice, 222–25
Gibson, Bob, 53, 102–6, 110, 113
Gordon, Joe, 86
Gottlieb, Eddie, 90–91
Green, Dallas, 37–38, 59, 78–80, 83, 127, 188, 193, 198–99, 227
Green, David, 255, 258
Greenville minor league club, 144
Gregg, Eric, 112, 172–73, 219
Gregson, Glenn (Goose), 115–16, 249
Grieve, Tom, 188
Gross, Greg, 236
Gura, Larry, 55

Halas, George, 23
Harmon, Terry, 211
Harper, Sue, 66–67
Harris, Bucky, 38
Harris, Mike, 266
Harris, Scotty, 96
Harrisburg PA Senators (International League), 87, 89
Hartford CT minor league club (Eastern League), 88
Hartmayer, Doug, 224
Harvey, Doug, 225
Havana Sugar Kings, 91
Helms, Tommy, 158
Herman, Billy, 184
Hernaiz, Jesus, 77
Hernandez, Keith, 138–40
Hernandez, Willie, 75
Herzog, Whitey, 199, 255
Hill, Quency, 69, 168–70, 239–42, 249, 265
Hill, Susy, 170, 240

Hodges, Russ, 1
Holcomb Avenue Park (Des Moines), 263
Hollywood minor league club (Pacific Coast League), 267
Holyoke MA Millers (Eastern League), 231
Honolulu Islanders (Pacific Coast League), 153
Honolulu Stadium, 129
Hornell NY minor league club (New York-Pennsylvania League), 159–60
Horner, Bob, 125
Hornsby, Rogers, 90
Hough, Charlie, 129
Horton, Willie, 166
Houk, Ralph, 162–63
Houston Astros, 236, 252, 259
Houston Astrodome, 252
Howsam, Bob, 95
Howser, Dick, 257
Hutchinson, Freddie, 38
Hutto, Jim, 73

Indianapolis Indians (American Association), 32, 263
Inter-American League, 227–30, 241, 248
International League, 54, 56, 209, 219, 245, 254
Interstate League, 248
Iorg, Dane, 7, 43, 64, 74–75, 99–100, 130–33, 142
Irvin, Monte, 104

Jack Russell Stadium (Clearwater FL), 187–88
Jackson, Reggie, 252–53
Jay, Joey, 135
John O'Donnell Stadium (Davenport IA), 265
Johnson, Deron, 126
Johnson, Johnny, 228–29
Johnson, Phil, 30, 248–49
Johnson, Rod, 262
Johnson, Walter, 36
Johnstone, Jay, 57–59
Joshua, Von, 129

Kaat, Jim, 145–46
Kahn, Lou, 60
Kansas City A's, 162
Kansas City Royals, 164, 189, 198, 255, 257
Kazanski, Ted, 261
Keatley, Greg. 259
Kekich, Mike, 228
Kenney, Jerry, 72
Kerrigan, Joe, 4–5, 27–28, 30, 32, 200–201
Kerrigan, Joey, 201
Kiser, Larry, 74, 76–77
Kittle, Hub, 246–49, 257
Klobas, Rusty, 64
Kniffin, Chuck, 72–73, 100
Knight, Bob, 105
Koegel, Pete, 49
Kosc, Greg, 174
Kosco, Andy, 68
Kuenn, Harvey, 81
Kuhn, Bowie, 207

Labbruzzo, Donald, 230, 233
Lampard, Keith, 46
Landis, Judge Kenesaw Mountain, 263
LaRoche, Dave, 214
Lasorda, Tommy, 73, 98, 129, 150–53, 161–63, 172, 258
Lavagetto, Cookie, 1
Mark Lee, 266
Lerch, Randy, 30, 32, 74–75, 82, 122
Lezcano, Sixto, 175
Licey winter league club, 170, 173
Lieberman, 225
Lis, Joe, 127–28, 143, 211
Littel, Mark, 138, 254–56
Little Rock minor league club (American Association), 37. *See also* Arkansas Travelers (Texas League)
Lloyd, Harry, 242
Lombardi, Vince, 62
Lopes, Davy, 129
Lopez, Marcelino, 184
Los Angeles Dodgers, 151, 239, 253
Los Angeles minor league club (Pacific Coast League), 267

Louisville Colonels, 111
Louisville Redbirds (American Association), 97, 254, 267–68
Lucas County Recreation Center (Toledo), 53
Lucchesi, Brian, 157
Lucchesi, Cathy, 154–55, 157–58
Lucchesi, Frank, 13, 39, 143, 153–58, 185–86
Luhr, Terry, 225
Luzinski, Greg, 3, 7, 40, 134–36, 241
Luzinski, Jean, 134

MacArthur Stadium (Syracuse NY), 62
McClelland, Tim, 268
McClure, Bob, 76
McCormack, Don, 192, 197–98, 201
McCovey, Willie, 142
McCoy Stadium (Pawtucket RI), 77, 251
McDonald, Joe, 146–47
McGraw, Hank, 193–94
McGraw, Tug, 56, 182, 191, 193–95
McHale, John, 250
Mack, Connie, 87–88
McMahon, John I. (Jack), 17, 21–24
McNally, Mike, 87–88
Macon Georgians, 157
Maddox, Garry, 102, 140–43, 165
Maduro, Bobby, 91
Major League Players Association, 81, 203–7, 213–14
Manos, Pete, 192
Mantle, Mickey, 1, 45
Maracaibo winter league club, 168, 177, 179
Marsh, Randy, 220–22
Martin, Jerry, 48, 57, 229
Martin, John, 255
Martin, Mike, 48, 229
Martinez, Buck, 138
Martinez, Tippy, 200
Matthews, Gary, 142
Matuszek, Karen, 176, 215

Matuszek, Len, 176, 179–80, 192–93, 214–15, 217
Mauch, Gene, 39, 95
May, Dave, 228
Mays, Willie, 1, 106
Mazza, Patrick, 17–18, 194
Medegini, Tin ear, 248
Medford OR minor league club, 156
Merrill, Durwood, 175
Messerly, Jerry, 210–12
Messersmith, Andy, 206
Metro, Charlie, 155–56
Metropolitan Stadium (Norfolk), 69
Mexican League, 44
Miami Amigos (Inter-American League), 229
Miami Marlins (Florida State League), 229
Midwest League, 219
Mile High Stadium (Denver), 76, 101
Millan, Felix, 174–75
Miller, Marvin, 194, 204–10, 213–14, 266
Milwaukee Braves, 111. *See also* Atlanta Braves
Milwaukee Brewers, 5, 26–27, 116, 171, 203
Minnesota Twins, 207
Moeller, Joe, 52
Molitor, Cock Eye, 248
Molush, Eddie, 29–30, 68, 70, 121–22, 183–84, 242–44, 249
Montague, Eddie, 220
Montague, John, 75–76
Montreal Expos, 160, 250
Moreland, Keith, 137, 198
Moreno, Jose, 173
Moreno, Omar, 267
Morrison, Jim, 74, 82, 99, 131, 133, 142, 168–70, 174, 243–44
Morton, Carl, 246
Mota, Manny, 170
Moultree GA minor league club, 221
Municipal Stadium (Reading PA), 40, 231

Nahorodny, Bill, 68–69, 76, 99
Nashville Sounds (Southern League), 267
National Football League, 122–23
National League, 57
Newark minor league club, 95–96
Newcombe, Don, 118–19, 123, 253
New Orleans minor league club, 133
New York Giants, 1, 104. *See also* San Francisco Giants
New York Mets, 36, 56, 146, 149
New York Yankees, 89, 110, 148, 214, 217, 252–53
Nicosia, Steve, 182
Nixon, Richard, 81
Noles, Dickie, 119–21, 190–91
Nordhagen, Wayne, 75–77
Norman, Bill, 38
Northern League, 161
Northwest League, 224–25

Oakland minor league club (Pacific Coast League), 267
Oden, Gene, 154
Odom, John (Blue Moon), 148
O'Doul, Lefty, 248
Ogden UT minor league club, 151–52
Oiler Park (Tulsa), 76–77
Oklahoma City 89ers (American Association), 32, 37, 73–77, 95, 99, 101, 120, 131, 133, 187, 201, 214–15, 240–41, 263–65, 268
Oliver, Bob, 100–101
Omaha Royals (American Association), 254, 256–58
Owens, Jim, 242
Owens, Paul, 12, 15, 17–18, 26, 37–38, 59, 79, 122, 128, 159, 187–88
Ozark, Danny, 60, 78

Pacific Coast League, 7, 54, 124, 128, 209, 220, 248
Paciorek, Tom, 129
Palatka FL minor league club (Florida State League), 160
Palermo, Steve, 175

Parker, Dave, 181
Parker, Salty, 174
Parks, Dallas, 112
Patkin, Eddie, 92
Patkin, Joy, 92
Patkin, Max, 84–88, 260–62
Paul, Gabe, 160
Pawtucket Red Sox (International League), 54, 63, 245, 254
Peninsula Pilots (Carolina League), 231–32
Perry, Buffalo Head, 248
Peters, Hank, 27, 201
Philadelphia Athletics, 87
Philadelphia Phillies, 4, 9, 15–16, 20–21, 24, 36–37, 46, 56, 62, 65–66, 68, 73, 75, 77–79, 82, 110, 121, 126, 131, 134, 146, 153, 185, 187–88, 198–99, 201, 203, 207, 210, 214–15, 230, 235, 239, 246, 252, 256
Philadelphia 76ers, 21
Philadelphia Warriors, 90
Phillie Phanatic, 97
Phoenix Giants (Pacific Coast League), 104, 142
Pine Bluff AR minor league club, 154, 156
Pioneer League, 124
Pittsburgh Pirates, 20, 182, 236–38, 253
Pocatello ID minor league club, 155–57
Poff, John, 4, 203–204
Poff, Patti, 204
Polo Grounds (New York), 1
Porter, Darrell, 115–19, 122–23
Porter, Dick, 87–88
Portland OR Beavers (Pacific Coast League), 266
Postema, Pamela, 226
Priddy, Gerry, 86
Proly, Mike, 235
Pryor, Greg, 133
Pulaski minor league club, 242
Pulli, Frank, 175–76, 218–19

Quad City City Cubs (Midwest League), 265
Quebec City minor league club (Eastern League), 27

Queen, Mel, 161
Quigley Stadium (West Haven, CT), 30–31, 192

Rau, Doug, 129
Randolph, Willie, 27
Rasmussen, Jim, 177–78
Reading Phillies (Eastern League), 4, 6, 11–15, 17, 29–30, 35–44, 74, 121, 125–26, 130, 143, 192, 194, 230–33, 242, 245
Reed, Jerry, 177–78
Reese, Don, 122
Reid, Scott, 52, 68, 183, 214
Reynolds, Allie, 253
Reynolds, Bob, 228
Richard, J. R., 245–46, 254
Richards, Paul, 95, 216
Richardson, Tommy, 233
Richmond minor league club (Ohio-Indiana League), 37
Rickey, Branch, 263
Riggs, Bobby, 87
Righetti, Dave, 245, 254
Ripplemeyer, Ray, 188
Ripplemeyer, Ray (Cincinnati), 267
Riverfront Stadium (Pittsburgh), 253
Rizzuto, Phil, 89–90
Roberts, Robin, 81, 187, 245, 253
Robinson, Bill, 109–12, 127–28, 246
Robinson, Billy, 112
Robinson, Craig, 127
Robinson, Jackie, 106, 108
Rochester Red Wings (International) League), 5, 54, 63, 200–201
Rocky Mount Phillies, 4, 182–88, 244
Rodgers, Andre, 173–74
Rodgers, Bob (Buck), 170
Rogers, George, 122
Rojas, Larry, 47
Rogodzinski, Jean, 126
Rogodzinski, Mike, 8, 34, 45–46, 55, 61, 126–27
Roof, Gene, 251–52
Rose, Pete, 84, 158, 215, 253
Rosen, Al, 254
Rosenblatt Stadium (Omaha), 76

Roswell TX minor league club, 107
Roosevelt Stadium (Jersey City), 241
Runge, Paul, 219
Ruth, Babe, 89
Ruthven, Dick, 7, 65–67, 69–72, 82
Ryan, Joe, 269
Ryan, Nolan, 144

Saidt, Bus, 106, 197, 248–49
St. Louis Browns, 90, 154
St. Louis Cardinals, 75, 96, 102, 140, 187, 246, 255
St. Petersburg Cardinals (Florida State League), 139, 254
Sakata, Lenny, 27
Salem Pirates (Carolina League), 182
Sally League, 102
Salt Lake City Gulls (Pacific Coast League), 141–42, 155
Sanchez, Orlando, 262–63
San Diego Chicken, 84, 97
San Francisco Giants, 140–42, 238
San Francisco minor league club (Pacific Coast League), 267
Santiago winter league club, 168–69
Sauciers, Kevin, 137
Scarce, Mac, 43, 62
Scheffing, Bob, 39
Schlesinger, Bill, 184–87
Schmidt, Mike, 7, 15–16, 20, 125–28, 266
Schneck, Dave, 69, 72
Scranton minor league club (Eastern League), 88
Searles, Joe, 69
Sec Taylor Stadium (Des Moines), 32–33, 54, 235, 263, 265
Seminick, Andy, 17, 45, 128–29
Senger, Charley, 33, 70–71, 73
Severson, Rich, 46
Shea Stadium (New York), 147, 253
Sherbrooke Stadium (Quebec), 40–41
Sherry, Larry, 185–86
Siegle, Tony, 27

Silicato, Tom, 58
Simpson, Wayne, 8, 65–66, 169, 174, 190
Sinatra, Frank, 150–51
Smith, A. Ray, 255–56
Smith, Lonnie, 75–76, 82, 99–102, 112, 173
Smith, Reggie, 238
Solomon, Buddy, 129
Southern Association, 219
Spahn, Warren, 253
Sparks, Joe, 256–58
Spartanburg minor league club (Western Carolinas League), 190
Spartanburg Phillies (now Traders; South Atlantic League), 4, 143–44
Speaker, Tris, 89
Spence, Bob, 51–52, 94–95, 127
Spokane Indians (Pacific Coast League), 6–7, 51, 153
Springfield Cardinals (Midwest League), 132, 266
Stargell, Willie, 7–8, 107–10, 112
Stearns, Bill, 147
Stearns, John, 7, 55–56, 114, 146, 148–49
Steinbrenner, George, 115, 205, 208, 245
Stewart, Sammy, 200
Stoddard, Tim, 200
Superior, NE minor league club, 145
Sutter, Bruce, 125
Syracuse Chiefs (International League), 72

Tacoma Tigers (Pacific Coast League), 186
Tanner, Chuck, 98
Tate, Lee, 111
Taylor, Billy, 162
Taylor, Sec, 263
Taylor, Tony, 165, 263–65, 267–69
Texas League, 139, 221, 226
Texas Rangers, 153, 215–17
Thetford Mines minor league club (Eastern League), 5, 26–30, 40
Thomason, Erskine, 64

Thomasville GA minor league club, 112, 155
Thomson, Bobby, 1
Thornton, Andy, 127
Thorpe, Jim, 92
Three Rivers minor league club (Eastern League), 40–41
Three Rivers Stadium (Pittsburgh), 109
Tidewater Tides (International League), 54, 69, 95, 146–49
Tiefenauer, Bob, 120–21, 224
Tiger Stadium (Detroit), 53
Tighe, Jack, 38
Tolan, Bobby, 228
Toledo Mud Hens (International League), 32–34, 37, 53–72, 95
Tovar, Cesar, 228
Trebelhorn, Tom, 266
Trenton Giants (Interstate League), 106, 232, 248
Trillo, Manny, 164, 177–78, 181, 256
Tulsa Drillers (Texas League), 138, 236
Uecker, Bob, 261

Valencia winter league club, 180
Valentine, Bobby, 172
Vancouver Canadians (Pacific Coast League), 266
Veeck, Bill, 89–90
Veterans Stadium, 41, 132, 215, 235, 267
Virgil, Ozzie, 162
Volpi, Madame Zaza, 248
Vukovich, George, 137
Vukovich, John, 31, 126–28, 211

Wallace, Dave, 45, 50–53, 58–59, 67, 74, 100, 228
Wallace, Mike, 5, 45, 228
Watson, Tom, 202
Waycross GA minor league club, 110–12

Weaver, Earl, 200–201, 258
Welch, Bob, 119
Welch WV minor league club, 159
Wellman, Bob, 29, 144
Wendelstedt, Harry, 218–22
Werhaas, John, 51
West, Joe, 101
Western Carolinas League, 219
Western-International League, 247
Western League, 105
West Haven minor league club (Eastern League), 30
Weyer, Lee, 220
White, Bill, 104–106, 112–13, 117, 167, 173–74
Wichita Aeros (American Association), 101
Wichita Aviators (Western League), 263
Wilkes-Barre minor league club, 87–89
Wills, Frank, 262–63
Williams, Ted, 1, 92, 184
Williamsport Tigers (Eastern League), 37, 93
Willis, Mike, 267–68
Wills, Maury, 51
Winfield, Dave, 125, 266
Winkles, Bobby, 46
Wissel, Dick, 44, 58, 60, 63
Wren, Christine, 224–25
Wright, Jim, 137, 187–89, 256, 259–60
Wrigley Field (Chicago), 77

Yankee Stadium (New York), 29, 132, 214
Yeager, Steve, 129
Young Cy, 36

Zimmer, Don, 260
Zipeto, Ted, 32, 35, 61–62, 70, 79, 93–94